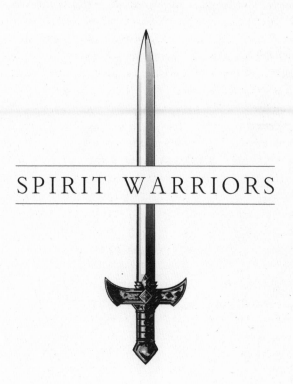

SPIRIT WARRIORS

"Never in our lifetime has a study of spiritual warfare been more relevant. Stu Weber, a seasoned contender for the faith, has produced a masterful briefing of the conflict raging all around us. A spiritual life saving manual, it should be required reading for all believers."

A SOLDIER LOOKS AT SPIRITUAL WARFARE

SPIRIT WARRIORS

STRATEGIES FOR THE BATTLES CHRISTIAN MEN AND WOMEN FACE EVERY DAY

STU WEBER

Multnomah®Publishers *Sisters, Oregon*

SPIRIT WARRIORS
published by Multnomah Publishers, Inc.

©2001 by Stu Weber

International Standard Book Number: 1-59052-150-1

Cover illustration by Martin French

Scripture quotations are from:
New American Standard Bible® © 1960, 1977, 1995
by the Lockman Foundation. Used by permission.

Also quoted:
The Holy Bible, New International Version (NIV)
© 1973, 1984 by International Bible Society,
used by permission of Zondervan Publishing House
Holy Bible, New Living Translation (NLT) © 1996. Used by permission of
Tyndale House Publishers, Inc. All rights reserved.
The New Testament in Modern English, Revised Edition (Phillips)
© 1958, 1960, 1972 by J. B. Phillips
The Holy Bible, New King James Version (NKJV) © 1984 by Thomas Nelson, Inc.
The Amplified Bible (AMP)
© 1965, 1987 by Zondervan Publishing House.
Revised Standard Version Bible (RSV)
© 1946, 1952 by the Division of Christian Education
of the national Council of the Churches of Christ
in the United States of America

Multnomah is a trademark of Multnomah Publishers, Inc.,
and is registered in the U.S. Patent and Trademark Office.
The colophon is a trademark of Multnomah Publishers, Inc.

Printed in the United States of America

For information:
MULTNOMAH PUBLISHERS, INC. • P.O. BOX 1720 • SISTERS, OREGON 97759

Library of Congress Cataloging-in-Publication Data:
Weber, Stu.
    Spirit warriors / by Stu Weber.
        p. cm.
Includes bibliographical references.
    ISBN 1-57673-803-5
1. Spiritual warfare. I. Title.
BV4509.5 .W375 2001
235'.4—dc21

                    2001003322

04 05 06 07 08 09 — 10 9 8 7 6 5 4 3 2

ACKNOWLEDGMENTS

Special thanks to the entire Multnomah team—it's a pleasure to call you guys "Good Shepherd East."

And particular thanks to the preaching team at Good Shepherd Community Church. Alan Hlavka, Barry Arnold, and I have been fellow warriors in many of life's battles. You'll see their fingerprints all over this manual on spiritual warfare. It's an honor for me to call them my friends, my fellow workers, and my fellow soldiers.

CONTENTS

THIS IS NO SUNDAY SCHOOL PICNIC!

P icture the idyllic countryside setting: wide blue skies, open green pastures, puffy white clouds, warm summer temperatures, and people with picnic baskets and lawn blankets just looking for an interesting diversion from the workday world. That's Manassas Junction, Virginia, a little burg about twenty-five miles outside Washington, D.C. Today the site of the Battle of First Bull Run is still a quiet pasture surrounded by trees and an old split-rail fence.

It was quite another ambience that marked the place on July 21, 1861.

In the morning it was indeed idyllic—delightful, with soft summer breezes, wildflowers, and an air of expectation, even celebration. By evening it was a house of horrors—full of screams, pain, and death.

No one had anticipated the horrors of war.

Oh yes, there was to be a battle. Everyone knew that much. In fact, the opposing armies had been gathering for some time. But how bad could it really be? Folks seemed to think this really wasn't that much of a war. The uniforms might have been different colors, but weren't they all American boys? Surely this little dustup wouldn't amount to much. Obviously, the bluecoats would quickly send their Confederate counterparts back to their homes. The rebellion would soon fizzle, and that would be that. Life would return to normal.

So it was that buggies full of festive spectators traveled the few miles from the capital to "watch the fireworks." Parasols opened. Ladies in lacy summer dresses settled themselves on quilts laid out on the ground. Curious onlookers opened picnic baskets and prepared to watch the show.

CHRISTIANS ARE TO KEEP

HEAVENLY PRIORITES ABOVE EARTHLY ONES

Read
2 Tim
2:3
&
2:4A

No one expected what unfolded.

By evening, hundreds of men on both sides lay dead in the pasture. Thousands of wounded moaned or screamed for help. No one had the stomach for a picnic anymore. And for four long years, no one experienced much of a good time.

War is like that. People think it's glorious…until it hurts.

Today *we* are at war. But not so you'd notice. Things are pretty festive on the outside. We expect tomorrow to be like yesterday. Just another day at the office. Life is good. And then…our world explodes around us! Dazed and frightened, we wonder how—right in the middle of our workday world—our dresses got torn, our shirts tattered, our souls ripped to shreds, and our lives filled so full of aching pain.

It's called spiritual warfare. And, my friend, that kind of war is no picnic, either. Know it or not, like it or not, you and I are in a war! And we need to begin living as if we were in a battle for our lives.

Because, in fact, we are.

Jesus understood that reality. So did the disciples—after they finally caught on. And Paul certainly did. To watch their lives is to watch soldiers at war. But sometimes I think we'd rather read the poets than the soldiers. Browning once penned, "God's in His heaven; all's right with the world." It's a nice sentiment, but it doesn't square with real-life experience, does it? Oh, in the ultimate sense of God's overarching sovereignty we know that eventually everything will be just fine.

But right now, today, it's not like that at all. Though we've brought parasols and picnic baskets, our little party has been disrupted by the sounds of screams, pain, and death.

Yes, Jesus won the victory on the Cross. He settled the outcome and established the eternal beachhead that holy D day. But now we are fighting our way through the hedgerows to the destruction of the enemy heartland and the V day to come. The life devoted to God is a soldier's life.

If you are a Christian—male or female—you are a spirit warrior.

Read it for yourself. Paul says that a Christian is to participate "in hardship like a good soldier of Jesus Christ" (2 Timothy 2:3). Christians are to keep heavenly priorities above earthly ones: "No soldier in active service entangles himself in the affairs of everyday life" (2 Timothy 2:4a). Why?

Today we *are at war. But not so you'd notice. Things are pretty festive on the outside.*

Because the boss at work is not the real boss. And your employment is not your primary mission.

Christ is your commander in chief. As a soldier, your life focus is "to please the one who enlisted [you] as a soldier" (2 Timothy 2:4). Paul even came to regard his personal friends not so much as buddies but as soldiers in the same foxhole. They were not fishing buddies, or business partners, or ministry assistants. They were fellow soldiers (Philippians 2:25).

Everywhere the New Testament insists the Christian life is about being a faithful warrior. The Christian life is about fighting the good fight, waging war, and wrestling or struggling with a fierce, implacable enemy.

The life of the Christian man or woman is the life of a spirit warrior. So let's open our eyes to that reality. The stakes are high, the hazards are great, and the hurts and wounds are all too real. Men and women, boys and girls—perhaps even close friends and family members—are taking hits and going down all around us.

In America's Civil War, the generals in their tents must have longed for some way to see the battlefield from above, to get the big picture of fortifications, ambushes, supply lines, and marching armies. But no one even dreamed of EP-3 surveillance planes in those days, let alone spy satellites orbiting the planet with all-seeing eyes. People's lives often hung on the sketchy reports, hunches, or best guesses of scouts or commanders in the field.

But spirit warriors are blessed with intelligence resources beyond compare. God's Word lays bare the enemy's plans and strategies, and it describes our ultimate victory over the forces of darkness.

The Bible is a book about that war.

It is a book about spirit warriors...like you.

PART 1

The NATURE *of the* BATTLE

The art of war is of vital importance.... It is a matter of life and death, a road either to safety or to ruin. Hence, under no circumstances can it be neglected.

SUN TZU, 500 B.C.

Our struggle is not against flesh and blood, but against the rulers, against the powers, against the world forces of this darkness, against the spiritual forces of wickedness in the heavenly places.

PAUL OF TARSUS, A.D. 61

WELCOME TO THE WAR

On a lonely midwinter day, I and a couple hundred other soldiers took a flight across the ocean. Boarding that commercial airliner, we stowed our gear and fastened our seat belts just as we had so many times before. It all seemed so routine. But the next time they opened that door, "routine" vanished like a dream. The sights, sounds, and smells that bombarded our senses were overwhelming. It was a whole new world. It was like nothing we had seen before.

When that door swung open, heat and humidity rolled over us like a tsunami. Every pore in our bodies seeped sweat. And the smell was something else: a strange brew of jet fuel, sewage, rotting vegetation, and smoke. It exploded in our nostrils.

This was Vietnam.

It looked like the depiction of a war zone that you might have seen in the movies. But this was no movie. There were no marching bands. No cigar-chomping John Wayne to welcome us. No swaggering George Patton to fill us with courage. No shouts of "Rangers lead the way!" Just a single, somewhat tired GI pointing to a line of waiting buses, engines running. His message was simple; thousands of GIs had heard one or another of its variations:

"Welcome to the war."

Just like that. Welcome to the war. Somewhere around three million Americans would experience the shock and disorientation of those first few moments in country. Yet it was different for every one of us. From the security of home to the uncertainties of war overnight. One moment we were standing on familiar soil surrounded by parents, wives, children—people who loved us. The next moment we were in a whole new foreign and hostile world, surrounded by people who actually wanted to kill us.

Welcome to the war.

You're in a War Zone Too

It's that way for you too, Christian. One minute you were safe and warm in your mother's womb. A minute later someone was dragging you kicking and hollering into a whole new world. Then, just to show you what this new reality was going to be like, somebody hauled off and slapped you on the backside. And all along the way, growing up, you've wondered why life felt kind of rough…why so many times it felt like a battle.

It's because life—especially the Christian life—*is* a battle.

Every Christian is a walking battlefield. Every believer carries deep within himself a terrible conflict. And most of us will gravitate to anything that will help us win the battle. Call it the battle between the flesh and the spirit. Call it the quest for the victorious Christian life. Call it what you want. But it's a flat-out knock-down-drag-out war. And when it's over, you want to be among those who are still standing.

Every Christian is a walking battlefield. Every believer carries deep within himself a terrible conflict.

The principles of war are taught in military academies all over the world. In most ways, spiritual warfare is no different than physical warfare. Every soldier who expects to not only survive but *win* must understand and employ these principles in his own daily battles "against the powers of this dark world and against the spiritual forces of evil in the heavenly realms" (Ephesians 6:12b, NIV).

That's what this book is about: understanding the principles of war for the career soldier—the true aim of every believer.

Back to Vietnam…

The buses that tired GI pointed us toward weren't exactly Gray Line tour coaches. They were brutish, olive-drab hulks. Their windows were covered with steel mesh to deflect any objects (grenades, for example) that might be thrown in our direction. Our jet-lagged minds began to focus on the unmistakable indicators that we were in a war zone. A multiple-row perimeter of barbed wire, punctuated with sandbagged bunkers and an occasional guard tower, designated the "secure" area. Metal symbols marked off the mine fields. Buildings were surrounded by waist-high walls of sandbags.

And then it happened.

Just as we shuffled off the buses, sirens went off as though on cue. People around us began moving toward the bunkers. Somewhat witless and wondering if this was just some kind of orientation drill, we fell in with the trotting hordes, yellow-orange dust filling our noses. Once in the bunkers we got the scoop from those who knew—we were about to taste our first "incoming."

It turned out to be a couple of 122mm rockets fired harmlessly into the compound by the Vietcong/National Vietnamese Army (VC/NVA). The missiles didn't hit a target of any consequence, and they seemed more intended to disrupt and harass than do any actual damage. But if anyone had doubted that GI's initial greeting, no one did now. This really was a war zone.

Eleven o'clock that night found me sitting in the military air terminal waiting to catch a C-130 (a four-engine behemoth that looked like a military bus with wings) north to Nha Trang to join my unit, the Fifth Special Forces Group. Ten other newbies waited with me.

And then—those cursed sirens again! When they went off this time, we dropped to the floor, slipped our heads under the chairs, and waited. I had to chuckle at the sight of "America's best"—heads on the ground, fannies in the air, waiting for the inevitable.

This time the rockets actually hit something, something not far away: a fully loaded F-4 Phantom fighter jet. The explosion was enormous. Ordnance blew in every direction, raining shrapnel on the roof of the terminal. It wasn't funny anymore.

By three o'clock in the morning, I had completed the flight to Nha Trang, checked in with the duty NCO, dragged my duffel to a temporary "hootch," and flopped onto a cot for at least a couple of hours' sleep. But those sirens followed me! I stumbled from the cot, grabbed my helmet, and fell in line with the stream of people moving toward the perimeter bunkers. I remember thinking, *Less than twenty-four hours in country and three rocket attacks! Three hundred sixty-four days to go!*

This time there was more of a show: "Spooky" was on patrol in the area. That was the nickname for the C-47 gunships armed with what amounted to multibarreled Gatling guns—each capable of firing six thousand rounds a minute, one of which was hosing down the hills west of the perimeter where the incoming was thought to be originating. The night sky was lit up with the arcs of tracers and the eerie, gray glow of slowly descending flares. It was both fearsome and beautiful.

The Christian life is like that, isn't it? Fearsome and beautiful.

Welcome to the war.

Do You Really Believe It?

But wait just a minute. You don't really believe it, do you? You think all this "battle" talk is just some fired-up ex-soldier running off at the word processor.

Like newbie GIs in a foggy, sleep-deprived daze, many Christians trudge half numb through this life, oblivious to the perils all around them.

That just illustrates the danger: The problem for many Christians is that they have no concept that they are actually living in a war zone. Like newbie GIs in a foggy, sleep-deprived daze, many Christians trudge half numb through this life, oblivious to the perils all around them. The war zone indicators are all there, but we act like it couldn't possibly be real.

All too often, Christians become casualties— shot to pieces in a war they didn't take seriously. I can't get out of my mind my former friends that were destroyed—pulled down by the temptations around them. Some of their names and faces flash across my mind even now.

Men I studied with in seminary.

Men I served with here at Good Shepherd Community Church.

Good men who loved God.

Just recently one of the leaders in my church fell to adultery. Satan's artillery shot straight through his heart, and the shrapnel cut through the chests of a lot of others standing nearby: a wife, some wonderful children, several of us fellow pastors, a bunch of friends, and really the whole church family. Like so many others, he became battle fatigued and dropped his guard. And the enemy picked him off. It's happened too many times over the years, right in our own church.

I seldom see many of these good people in formation anymore. They're too wounded to fight, too shamed to care. I suspect that in the night watches they lay in their own shadows, moaning deeply.

Oh, it's a war all right. And we've got to learn, in the apostle's words, to "stand firm" (Ephesians 6:11). That's a very military term, ordering you and me to hold on to the high ground at all costs.

Yes, this is a combat zone. And the enemy has a thousand weapons to aim at you. Sometimes it's just small-arms fire. Sometimes it's heavy artillery. Sometimes it's a deadly booby trap hidden under innocent-looking turf.

The enemy knows how to slip past our perimeters, doesn't he? Somehow the dark side seems to know just where our buttons are—and how to push 'em. It may be something as small as flying off the handle at some guy tailgating us or as profound as falling off the marriage bed into the arms of another. Small or heavy, it's all destructive. And death dealing. In Paul's words, each of us needs to be a "soldier in active service" who constantly refuses to "entangle himself in the affairs of everyday life, so that he may please the one who enlisted him as a soldier" (2 Timothy 2:4). If we're not, we're going to get picked off in this battlefield.

You don't think so? You're still unconvinced?

Have you ever noticed how life often feels like it's just chock-full of battles? You know what I mean; it's both in us and all around us.

Pick a newspaper—almost any newspaper, any city, any day—and read the headlines. The overwhelming majority are negative. And painful. They deal with trouble, pain, death, fear, destruction, loss, disaster, struggle, scandal, and hurt. Whether it's an accident on the freeway, a hurricane in the South, a crime on the street, a dictator in the Balkans, a child drowned in a pool, a dip in the market, or the adulterous affair of a prominent leader, the headlines are largely dark. This is a troubled planet, and people are hurting and dying everywhere.

Let's finally face it, Christian. This is a war zone.

Okay, forget the newspaper. Just look right around you. No need to step out of your own neighborhood. Some time back I did a little battlefield inventory of the comfortable, suburban neighborhood where we lived for twenty years and raised our boys. It's a middle-class neighborhood lined with respectable homes, shaded by mature trees, and occupied by your typical workday families. No ghetto. No gangs. It's actually a very desirable place to live.

My inventory didn't have to go very far before the stories got negative. My mind simply surveyed the pain within a half-dozen homes immediately surrounding ours. I didn't interview anyone; I just took stock of the most obvious wounds that everybody knew about. Next door lived a friend that was dying of cancer. Up the street there had been a teenage suicide. Across the way a little family was aching over a son's sexual orientation. Down the road a home was missing a father because he was in prison. Another home was facing up to incest and sexual abuse charges. And another was dealing with the fallout of attempted murder.

It shocked me. I had known about these things as they happened along the way, but I had never actually tried to add them up. The war was worse than I'd realized.

And then there was me.

Just the other day, I was driving home on Interstate 84 after four wonderful days of vacation. All of a sudden, into my world of peace and comfort came a little red car. He must have been doing over eighty. I was in the passing lane, just moving by the vehicle to my right. That little red bomb roared up to within what seemed like a foot of my rear bumper. And stayed there! It felt like he'd attached his radiator to my tailpipe, as though we were engaged in some kind of midflight refueling exercise. He just parked on my rear bumper, riding my tail and acting like the road was his.

And in that instant, something in me wanted to do battle. Just that quickly, hot anger seared through my veins…and there was a war brewing.

Somehow I managed to choke back the desire to retaliate. I fought off an almost overwhelming urge to do battle. Down the road a ways, after my pulse had slowed a bit, I patted myself on the head for being a good boy.

Oh, but it was close.

Continuing to drive (and steam), I realized there were two battles going on simultaneously—I was fighting a war on two fronts. One was outside, with my external circumstances and the irritation they caused. The other was inside, with my eternal soul and its attitude. For me, it seems the internal battles are usually the larger and the longer.

Sometimes life just feels like it's lived in a war zone. We're *always* going up against something—fighting issues, fighting time, fighting lawlessness, fighting city hall, fighting spouses (unfortunately), fighting ourselves—just plain fighting. And most of the toughest battles are down inside our chests—facing off with one temptation and attitude after another.

As we drove down the road that day, my mind continued to wander through the atlas of spiritual warfare all around us. I thought about Kosovo and the hundreds of thousands of displaced, disoriented people. Children unable to speak and looking lost. Distraught mothers, their faces contorted by pain. Grown men unable to stop weeping. I thought of the Jewish Holocaust, Stalin's purges, the rape of Nanking, two world wars, Korea…and, yeah, Vietnam. And that's just one century. The injustice is staggering.

Then there was my friend's little girl.

Recently a fellow pastor in another city faced a battle, the likes of which I hope I never know. His eleven-year-old daughter, while baby-sitting the neighbor kids two doors down, answered a knock on the door. She did everything right: She kept the door locked and denied the stranger entrance. But the intruder simply forced the door open and brutally raped the little girl.

When I heard of it, something in me screamed to do battle. I wanted to go to my friend, arm the two of us to the teeth, and go after the rapist. To be honest, everything within me at that moment wanted to kill that man, to remove his loathsome presence from this world and send him on to judgment.

This unjust war rages on a thousand fronts. I'm reminded of that Bible-toting president of the United States that wagged his finger at the American people and said, "I did not have sex with that woman." And, when there were no alternatives left and he was trapped like a rat in a corner, he confessed. Then, claiming to have repented, he mounted a vigorous legal defense. Didn't sound like repentance to me. Whatever happened to simple shame and genuine contrition—let alone truth and justice? Whatever happened to truthfulness and authenticity? Seems like they're all casualties in this pervasive spiritual war.

A while back I had coffee with a man who was so deep into pornography that his family was coming apart at the seams. His poor wife was beside herself and sick way down inside. All she'd wanted was to raise a family with a man she could count on. But her whole world had been turned upside down—all because he'd let his appetites get out of control.

And while I'm on the subject of injustice within the church, here's another troublesome battle: A full 40 percent of every Christian congregation, folks who consider themselves good Christians and church members, give *none* of their money—nothing, absolutely zero—to Christ and His kingdom through local church giving. Doesn't seem right, does it?

Battle after battle after battle. You could talk about Littleton, Colorado, and the massacre in the white upper-middle-class school hallways. Add Paducah, Kentucky, to that list, and Springfield, Oregon, and other schoolhouse "incidents." Add the Wedgwood Baptist Church shooting. Don't get me started about the slaughter of more than thirty million innocent children in this country via abortion. And on…and on…and on. Myriads of battles in your life and mine.

Welcome to the war.

THE LONGEST-RUNNING WAR

They say "Old Blood 'n' Guts" George Patton was born in the middle of a battlefield. He was meant to be a soldier.

And so were you.

In fact, we have it on good authority—the Word of God—that every one of us was born in the midst of "the mother of all battles."

Sometime, somewhere in eternity past, a powerful angelic being named Lucifer challenged the rule of almighty God.

The war started long before you were born. It began a long time ago in a century far, far away, at the beginning of time as we know it. About the time when the earth was formless and void and darkness was over the face of the deep. Sometime, somewhere in eternity past, a powerful angelic being named Lucifer challenged the rule of almighty God. Prior to those opening salvos, God's universe had known only peace and harmony. Not so much as a shadow of war.

Before that opening challenge, there was only God and His angels. Together. In perfect peace. There was no division, no separation, no pain, no confusion, no anxiety, and no death. But the head angel, Lucifer himself, decided it was time to make a move. To move on up. To assert himself, so to speak. The fall of Satan (Lucifer's alias, which means "adversary") was sparked by our old nemesis, pride. It was the old "I'll do it my way" lie.

Right in the middle of this cosmic "mother of all battles" between God and Satan, planet earth was birthed: a bright, blue-and-white marble spinning in the black velvet of space. And the capstone of creation on that little planet was humankind, male and female. That's you and me. That's men and women, boys and girls. Born for battle. Weaned for war. Meant to be soldiers.

You see, the earth was created to be a model, a microcosm, a kingdom demonstrating to a watching universe what life under the rule of God was like. It was a kingdom worth defending.

God accepted Satan's challenge and decided to let the battle run its course for a bit. All the earth is a stage, a giant arena for battle, the ultimate fight site. Numberless angels fill the seats awaiting the outcome.

You and I are on the battlefield, right at the point of action.

Every morning you scrimmage at the fifty-yard line. The enemy is running at you, and he has your number.

Within the last year, two of our daughters-in-law each presented our sons with their firstborn. Linda and I became grandparents, twice over. I think often and long about the world those little tykes—who, until just recently, were resting comfortably in their mothers' wombs—will experience. It's a tough world, and it seems to be getting tougher all the time. I pray for those two grandchildren and for any more that may join them in the future. I pray for their protection, their upbringing, their commitment to Christ, and their strength in the battles they will undoubtedly face on this planet.

Welcome to the war, kids.

Sometimes I think those should be the first words we say to every newborn child: "Welcome to the war, little fella, little gal. You were born in a war zone."

Okay, okay, I admit we shouldn't spoil the joy of the delivery room with too many thoughts about the dark side. I wholeheartedly agree that every child should have the magnificent experience of an innocent, protected, joy-filled childhood. But I also believe that the point of every Christian home is to raise that child with a growing, maturing awareness of the very real spiritual war zone in which he or she now lives. You don't play in the street, you don't talk to strangers, and you don't ignore the everyday reality of spiritual warfare.

Like a bewildered GI stepping off the plane in Vietnam, every child is born into a hostile world. One moment that beautiful little baby is in his mother's womb enjoying a world made for him. It's warm and comfortable. It is a protected world, a nourishing world, a perfect world created by God, where life can flourish. The next moment that little one squeezes through a narrow birth canal into a world of harsh sounds and bright lights. Someone swats him on the bottom. And he's got to learn to either breathe on his own or die. Life outside the womb is a significant contrast to the previous months of life inside the womb. And most of life will have more than its share of battles, spiritual and otherwise.

BACK TO THE BASIC QUESTION

What's going on here? What's with all these pain-filled headlines and all these hurtful events in people's lives? Are these just a bunch of isolated, unrelated incidents? At first glance, that's how it seems. But with careful thought you can begin to see them as indicators of one painful, overarching reality—earth is a war zone. All of these incidents are part of the fabric of injustice and inescapable tension in this fallen world.

Every time you or I yield to sin, we give him a little bit of ourselves.

Like tremors after an earthquake, these battles and skirmishes are scattered far and wide, experienced and described differently by a wide variety of people. But they all stem from a singular source deep beneath the surface. The aftershocks reverberate through every single soul, every single day. The epicenter of this global earthquake, far beyond measure on any Richter scale, is what we call *original sin*—Adam's tainted sin nature passed inevitably and without exception to every one of his descendants.

But it's even more complicated than that. There is so much more to it than meets the eye. Some say it is the "invisible war," that there is a whole unseen world out there. It's a world of principalities and powers. A world of incredible influence and overwhelming power. That first earth tremor, Adam's sin, was set off by an outside catalyst. Satan is his title, Lucifer is his name, and he wants your allegiance—not to mention your eternal soul. And every time you or I yield to sin, we give him a little bit of ourselves.

One writer summarized it like this:

> The truth to which all these [elements] point…is the truth that God's good creation has in fact been seized by hostile, evil cosmic forces that are seeking to destroy God's beneficent plan for the cosmos…. The general assumption of both the Old and New Testaments is that the earth is virtually engulfed by cosmic forces of destruction, and that evil and suffering are ultimately

due to this diabolical siege…. God waged war against these forces, however, and through the person of Jesus Christ has now secured the overthrow of this evil cosmic army. The church as the body of Christ has been called to be a decisive means by which this final overthrow is to be carried out.[1]

Individual human beings are often caught out in the open, trapped in the cross fire of a battle that is much larger than they are prone to realize.

Yes, this world is at war.

The earth is a battlefield.

You are living in a war zone.

Its explosive nature is readily visible all around us. Divorce. Child abuse. Epidemic addictions—alcohol, drugs, sex. Violent crime. Incredible dishonesty at the highest levels of government and culture.

Like any battlefield, life is filled with confusion. Loud noises, chaos, the smell of explosives, and shock after shock after shock. It's downright dangerous. Satan wants you, your marriage, your children, your grandchildren, and your future. He's firing away with everything at his disposal, and there is plenty of room for battle fatigue on any of these many fronts.

Much of this spiritual warfare is being played out all around you. And much of it is inside your chest.

There. Aren't you glad you picked up this book?

Uncle Sam may want you to sign up, but Jesus Christ *expects* you to sign up. If you belong to Him, He isn't asking; He's ordering. So how 'bout it? You ready to sign up for the duration as a solider of Christ "fit to fight"? Your assignment follows. Stick with me…and let's have some fun at it.

The LORD is a warrior; The LORD is His name.

EXODUS 15:3

The purpose of war is peace.

AUGUSTINE, A.D. 427

And I saw heaven opened, and behold, a white horse, and He who sat on it is called Faithful and True, and in righteousness He judges and wages war. His eyes are a flame of fire...He is clothed with a robe dipped in blood....And the armies [of] heaven...were following Him on white horses. From His mouth comes a sharp sword, so that with it He may strike down the nations...and He will rule them with a rod of iron...and on His robe and on His thigh He has a name written, KING OF KINGS, AND LORD OF LORDS.

THE BOOK OF THE REVELATION
OF JESUS CHRIST, 19:11–16

THE BATTLEGROUND

fter watching the sun slip behind the snowy Alps, you step off a narrow, cobbled street into a diminutive Swiss café. You sit down at a tiny table and order (what else?) a cup of hot cocoa. As your eyes scan the quaint decor, you're startled by a sight that seems wildly incongruent in that idyllic, postcard setting.

A pyramid of assault rifles, just inside the door.

Following your gaze, the waitress explains that there is a major shooting festival in town, and almost every man will be carrying a rifle.

That's an accurate snapshot of Switzerland. In every home, stored in the closet or leaning in a corner, a military-issue assault rifle and a specified number of rounds of ammunition wait at the ready. Every adult male in the country is provided such a weapon for militia service. Shooting ranges dot the countryside.

Visitors from "politically correct" nations like Great Britain—where guns are banned to all but the police—initially think they've walked in on some kind of revolution. The truth is, they're touring one of the most peaceful nations on earth.

In Switzerland, shooting is the national sport as well as the backbone of its national defense policy. And, by the way, there is virtually no crime in the nation. The *Wall Street Journal* summarizes: "More per-capita firepower exists in Switzerland than in any other place in the world, yet it is one of the safest places to be. [It] has a lower murder and robbery rate than England, where most guns are banned."

Aside from an obvious blow to the theories of gun control advocates, what's the point? Switzerland, armed to the teeth, is a nation of peace lovers, the very bastion of neutrality. How can this be? I'll tell you how: The nation exists in a perpetual state of readiness! The most peaceful nation on earth is the nation most widely prepared for war.

Similarly, Bible-reading, peace-loving Christians must be in a continual state of wartime readiness. Possibly the most consistent observable trend in human history is that this planet is a battlefield. Christians know those battles to be multidimensional—both physical and spiritual. The spiritual warfare is constant, often breaking out into the physical realm.

There is no such thing as neutral territory in spiritual warfare.

The Swiss, though passionately committed to peace, have accepted the reality that this world is a dangerous place. For them, war is a reality, an inevitability, and they have committed an entire population to a strategy of readiness. The Swiss have not allowed themselves to be mesmerized into a nice-and-easy belief that they are immune to the ravages of the enemy.

Would that the church of Jesus Christ could say the same.

Christians would do well to take a lesson from the Swiss—and wake up to the reality of war within the borders of our souls. The Swiss are prepared for a war yet undeclared. Not so the Christian. The war has already been declared, and we've got some catching up to do if we intend to meet the challenges that the powers of darkness have already put forward.

There's one difference between what the Swiss can do and what Christians can do: The Swiss are neutral in all wars. Christians do not enjoy that luxury. There is no such thing as neutral territory in spiritual warfare. Jesus Himself stated it in no uncertain terms: "He who is not with Me is against Me" (Matthew 12:30). You are either a captive of Satan or a soldier of Christ.

Such a "bystander" attitude is nonsense for you as a Christian, though your enemy would love for you to sit by. Hitler loved it when Great Britain sat on the sidelines while he gobbled up real estate on the Continent. It plays into Satan's strategies when you are so foolish as to think you are uninvolved—much less targeted for destruction. Every believer who wants to make a difference for Christ can count on living in the crosshairs of the enemy.

RUMORS OF WARS

Our God is at war. He is the ultimate warrior. And if you are His follower, then you are one fully operational soldier. Paul put it in blunt military terms: "Put up with your share of hardship as a loyal soldier in Christ's army. Remember…that no soldier on active service gets himself entangled in business, or he will not please his commanding officer" (2 Timothy 2:3–4, Phillips). That's Scripture's way of stating the old military maxim: "You're in the army now. Salute and execute."

War is the consummate reality for every believer. War is reality for the God of heaven. The mentality of Scripture is a wartime mentality. It is imperative that Christians begin to grasp this reality. To assume a peacetime posture during a time of war is self-destructive. The church of Jesus Christ—that's you and me, fellow Christian—must begin to understand that ours is a wartime economy.

This warfare theme so pervades Scripture that the first hint of Christ in the Bible (Genesis 3:15) describes Him like a wounded warrior. The last picture of Christ in Scripture (Revelation 19:11) depicts Him as a victorious commander in chief, spattered in blood (His own), astride a great warhorse. First and last, Jesus is a warrior. Between these two soldierly pictures of our Lord, the Bible makes countless references to this ongoing spiritual battle. Life on this planet and beyond is a battle.

The pages of the Bible bristle with the vocabulary of war. Think of it. The Bible refers regularly to such things as wounds, attacks, blood, sacrifice, swords, shields, battles, shameful defeats, and glorious victories.

The New Testament letters continually urge us to engage in the very real battles of spiritual warfare. We are told to fight "the good fight" (2 Timothy 4:7), to "fight the good fight of faith" (1 Timothy 6:12), and to "stand firm" against the enemy's assaults (Ephesians 6:11). Everywhere throughout the Bible, Scripture reminds us that it is the Lord God Himself who "fights" for His people. The warfare theme permeates the pages of Scripture, in both the Old and New Testaments.

Personally, I've never understood the question posed by one popular Bible teacher: "Lord, is it warfare?" The answer is as plain as anything in all of Scripture: You bet it's warfare! No doubt about it whatsoever! It's one of the most basic themes woven throughout the pages of Scripture.

Why do so many believers seem oblivious to this ongoing battle? Wouldn't it be nice if God just sat down and laid it out for us in a formal declaration of war?

Well, He has. Several times, in fact.

GOD'S DECLARATION OF WAR IN SCRIPTURE

Before any just war is engaged, it is to be declared and defined with purposeful objectives. As America learned with sorrow in the jungles of Vietnam, it is impossible to win a war if you cannot articulate your purpose and the specific methods you intend to use to achieve it. You must have clear strategic objectives.

The Lord of hosts has declared this war in no uncertain terms. God's declaration of war appears in different forms in several passages of the Bible. One of the shortest and clearest of such statements has to do with Christ's incarnation: "The Son of God appeared for this purpose, to destroy the works of the devil" (1 John 3:8).

It can't get much clearer than that. Or more militant. It's war, all right, full-out and declared. The objective of the great war of the ages is to destroy the counterfeit kingdom of the devil and glorify God.

The Son of God appeared for this purpose, to destroy the works of the devil.
1 JOHN 3:8

God's clear objective for this war appears in 1 Corinthians 15:24–25. It uses the warfare terminology of kingdoms in conflict. When all is said and done and earthly history is wrapped up, Christ will "hand over the kingdom to the God and Father, when He has abolished all rule and authority and power. For He must reign until He has put all His enemies under His feet."

PSALM 82

One of the most sweeping declarations of war in all Scripture appears in Psalm 82. We'll spend some time here.

The God of the Bible, Yahweh Himself, Jesus Christ our Lord, is a warrior! He is the master strategist. That is the plain teaching of Scripture. That is the primary point of Psalm 82, which is nothing less than Yahweh's declaration of war against what the New Testament calls "the rulers...the powers...the world forces of this darkness, against the spiritual forces of wickedness in the heavenly places" (Ephesians 6:12).

God's message to these dark forces in Psalm 82 is simply this: "You're done. Dead. Finished. Because of who you are and what you do, I will destroy you." Here's the whole psalm:

> God takes His stand in His own congregation;
> He judges in the midst of the rulers.

How long will you judge unjustly
    And show partiality to the wicked? Selah.
Vindicate the weak and fatherless;
    Do justice to the afflicted and destitute.
Rescue the weak and needy;
    Deliver them out of the hand of the wicked.
They do not know nor do they understand;
    They walk about in darkness;
All the foundations of the earth are shaken.
    I said, "You are gods,
And all of you are sons of the Most High.
    "Nevertheless you will die like men
And fall like any one of the princes."
    Arise, O God, judge the earth!
For it is You who possesses all the nations.

This magnificent and foundational psalm may at first glance appear to be more confusing and disjointed than magnificent and foundational. But it is in actuality an ancient, carefully crafted statement of reality, a definition of what is. It is a biblical exposé of the hidden underworld—the invisible realm of spirits, principalities, and powers, of rulers of darkness. And it is Yahweh's declaration of war upon these dark forces.

The psalmist's message flows through five identifiable sections as the psalm unfolds.

Verse 1 sets the scene. The NASB's marginal (alternate) translation could be rendered, "He judges in the midst of the *gods.*"

I believe what we are seeing here is the living Creator, the Ancient of Days, the possessor of heaven and earth stepping right into the midst of the assembly of the underworld rulers. He is the sovereign God to whom no place in all the universe, seen or unseen, is off-limits. These are gods with a small *g*—false gods or spirits. They are the assembled angelic spirits who followed the evil one in his prehistoric rebellion. The true and living God steps powerfully into their assembly and takes the place of authority. He judges. He declares. He pronounces.

Verses 2–4 represent a portion of God's address to them. "How long will you judge unjustly…?" In essence, He threatens them by reminding them there is a time frame to the present order of affairs. How long will you carry on this way? The implication is that there is a terminal point coming! Their unjust exercise of power and their partiality to the wicked is not going to go on forever.

In verses 3 and 4 He reiterates His own principles and the expectations of His kingdom and His ways to "vindicate the weak and fatherless; [to] do justice to the...destitute; [to] rescue the weak; [to] deliver."

Then in verse 5 I believe God describes the scene on battlefield earth, focusing particularly on the human victims of these dark forces of wickedness: "They do not know nor do they understand; They walk about in darkness." God notes that our world is filled with confusion, ignorance, and dark things. He indicates that humans move about on the battlefield like the hapless victims of these false gods or spirits. Not alert to the underworld, humans are ignorant and unaware of what is actually happening to them as they consume themselves. They simply wander about in the grip of darkness. The bottom line is clear—in earth's present condition, the "foundations are shaken." The very footings of meaningful life are cracked. Unrighteousness rules for the moment.

In verses 6 and 7, God then wipes out these false gods with a sweeping statement of judgment. He reminds them that they are His own creatures: "You are gods...sons of the Most High." *Sons* is a very general term, used here, I believe, to denote all God's created beings—both human and angelic.

But while He acknowledges their creation from His hand, He also puts them in their place by pronouncing their ultimate judgment in no uncertain terms: "You will die like men." As a result of their rebellion they will die like the finite creatures they are. They will fall. They will go down. Theirs will be a horrible and destructive end.

Verse 8 is a return to the bottom line of all Scripture: "Arise, O God, judge the earth!" God here asserts the ultimate point of the psalm. In contrast to the fall of these false rulers, the true Ruler will *rise*. He will take the place of ascendance. This is ultimately His world. And He will one day decree that the war is over, that evil is conquered, that the dark side is finished. Darkness will be overcome with light—the full light of His presence. Indeed, "the earth will be filled with the knowledge of the glory of the LORD, as the waters cover the sea" (Habakkuk 2:14).

We must envision ourselves on a rather vicious, cosmic battlefield.

This great psalm forces us to see our lives as part of something that is much, much larger than ourselves. We must envision ourselves on a rather vicious, cosmic battlefield. Our lives are not about ourselves. This life, the "three score and ten" we live here on earth, is not about our desires and dreams, our personal fulfillment, or our happiness. Our lives are part of a much larger reality—victory over darkness both in and around us. Your life is about nothing less than the ultimate glory of God.

So then, Christian, every time you or I pursue our own ends, we smudge the glory of God. Every time you take a bullet and go down—every time you fall to one of Satan's fiery darts—you contribute to the cause of Satan. Your sin is not just some simple little weakness or mistake. It's a blow to Christ and His kingdom. So armor up, soldier!

BATTLEFIELD EARTH

Earth is a battlefield, quite literally the designated fight site between God and Satan, good and evil, right and wrong, life and death, heaven and hell. Battlefield earth roils with the smoke, pain, shock, and disorientation of warfare. Ask any soldier who has experienced combat. If he can put words to it, he'll describe a scene of chaos, confusion, pain, and shock.

I heard one World War II navy vet describe the experience of sleeping one night at his battle station, just below the five-inch guns on the forward deck of a destroyer. Sometime just before dawn, those guns opened up and began firing at Japanese aircraft. The sleeping sailor awoke in an explosion of earsplitting noise, fiery flashes of light, and acrid, choking smoke. The concussion from those blasts literally blew his pants legs up to his hips. Talk about a rude awakening! That was one swabbie who didn't need a cup of coffee to get his eyes open!

Violence! Disorientation! That is the history of our planet in every century—and most particularly our own. Contrary to improving or evolving in our ability to govern ourselves, we have demonstrated most graphically in the twentieth century—by far the single most bloody and pain-filled century in history—that we are hopelessly trapped in the disorientation of battlefield earth. This battlefield is crisscrossed by wandering, stumbling human beings who are deeply wounded, shell-shocked, and confused. Their only hope for recovery is the battle plan of God Himself.

The point of the discussion on these pages and the pages of Scripture is that history is being played out on at least two levels. One is highly visible and in-your-face—life on planet earth. The other is largely unseen—the underworld of principalities and powers. One is very human, very daily, very earthy. The other is supernatural and involves the devil and his angels. But both are engaged in the same great, cosmic war. And although the end of the Book guarantees the outcome of that war, your life and mine and our contribution to it as soldiers of Christ hang very much in the balance.

See that contrast in the following Scriptures:

- Satan is "the god of this world" (2 Corinthians 4:4)—note the small *g*.
- "The whole world lies in the power of the evil one…" (1 John 5:19).
- Satan is "the prince and power of air…the spirit that is now working in the sons of disobedience" (Ephesians 2:2).
- Satan asserts that he owns "the kingdoms of the world and their glory" (Matthew 4:8).
- "Our struggle is not against flesh and blood, but against the rulers, against the powers, against the world forces of this darkness, against the spiritual forces of wickedness in the heavenly places" (Ephesians 6:12).

Contrast that with the situation on a day yet future:

- "Judgment [will come]…upon this world;… The ruler of this world will be cast out" (John 12:31).
- "Then [the King] will also say… 'Depart from me, accursed ones, into the eternal fire which has been prepared for the devil and his angels'" (Matthew 25:41).
- "And the devil who deceived them was thrown into the lake of fire and brimstone…. Then I saw a great white throne and Him who sat upon it, from whose presence earth and heaven fled away…. Then death and Hades were thrown into the lake of fire…. And if anyone's name was not found written in the book of life, he was thrown into the lake of fire" (Revelation 20:14–15).

Dr. Donald Barnhouse captures a summarizing theme for the state of affairs on this earth:

> War has been declared. The great, governing cherub has become the malignant enemy. Our God was neither surprised nor astonished, for—of course—He knew before it happened that it would happen, and He had His perfect plan ready to be put into effect. Although the Lord had the power to destroy Satan with a breath, He did not do so. It was as though an edict had been proclaimed in heaven: "We shall give this rebellion a thorough trial. We shall permit it to run its full course. The universe shall see what a [mere] creature, though he be the highest creature ever to spring from God's Word, can do apart from Him. We shall watch this experiment

and permit the universe of creatures to watch it, during
this brief interlude between eternity past and eternity
future called time. In it the spirit of independence shall
be allowed to expand to [its full extent]. And the wreck
and ruin which shall result will demonstrate to the universe, and forever, that there is no life, no joy, no peace
apart from a complete dependence upon the Most High
God, possessor of heaven and earth."[1]

That is the story of human history: war, rumors of war, pain, confusion, desperation, and destruction. We cry "peace" but there is no peace.
We seek security but there is no security.

There is *nothing* of lasting value on this earth apart from Christ. We
seek wealth and it dribbles through our fingers like sand in a desert—completely unsatisfying and swallowed up in death.

And that is the story of your life, too…when you follow your own will
and wander from God's. If you do not follow God's marching orders, you
will experience the dissatisfaction and pain that is the inevitable fruit of
soldierly disobedience. The self-assertion of any will but God's always
results ultimately in pain, sorrow, adversity, sadness, and death. Yes, you'd
better believe it's warfare! And if you involve yourself in ungodly activity,
you can expect to pay the price.

Bottom line: If you intend to survive this war, let alone make a contribution to victory, then you'd better read your orders very carefully. You
must gain an understanding of your personal mission and operational
orders as a Christian soldier, male or female, in this spiritual war that spans
the ages.

Our God is a warrior. And He expects His kids, like good soldiers, to
follow orders, to live like spiritual warriors. The battle is still raging. And
you're in it! Let's strengthen your warrior's soul.

HOW WILL IT ALL END?

Of course, the centerpiece of this spiritual warfare is our Lord and Savior
Jesus Christ. His first coming to earth was to fulfill the role of the Lamb
of God, the wounded warrior whose blood was to be spilled to cover the
sins of the earth. In his first coming, the Lord of life has secured the victory over the evil intentions of the lord of death.

But the last shot has not been fired. That already-secured victory will not be realized to its full extent until the second coming of our Christ. Then He will fulfill the role of the Lion of Judah, the designated warrior-champion, King of kings and Lord of lords, ruler over the earth.

When King Jesus rules here one day, planet earth will have realized the purpose for which it was created. Satan's dark reign will be over. The battlefield will be cleansed, the scars of battle healed, the debris of war removed. Earth itself will be rebuilt, restored to the beauty of her original paradise. And the lion will lie down with the lamb.

On that future day, the dream of which the prophets so often spoke will be realized. Back to Psalm 82: "Arise, O God, judge the earth! For it is You who possesses all the nations" (v. 8).

In Isaiah 6:3, the mighty seraphim cry out: "The fullness of the whole earth is His glory" (author's translation).

But it may be Habakkuk who summarizes it best:

> For the earth will be filled
>   With the knowledge of the glory of the LORD,
> As the waters cover the sea.
>
> HABAKKUK 2:14

What a magnificent picture. I can't wait to see it! As the waters cover the sea, the earth will be covered with the radiant glory of our Lord. On that day, absolutely everywhere you look on this earth you will see the glory of God. There will not be a single negative, hurtful headline in any newspaper on the globe. Jesus will reign supreme! And earth will reflect His glory!

Think of it this way: The war's outcome is secure. Final victory is guaranteed. The decisive battle has already been fought...and won. Christ's victory was won, not on San Juan Hill or Pork Chop Hill or Hamburger Hill or some other piece of famous high ground, but on a hill called Calvary, the most decisive battlefield in all of history.

But that does *not* mean the bullets have stopped flying. D day is one thing. V day is another.

No one in my father's generation will ever forget June 6, 1944. D day. Omaha Beach. The World War II invasion of the European continent at Normandy. It was the turning point of the entire war. By the end of that "longest day," the outcome of World War II was determined. Victory was certain. The Third Reich's defenses had been penetrated with a lethal offensive, and Hitler was doomed. After D day it was just a matter of time.

But the battles continued. The war, even with victory guaranteed, was just as real and deadly as it had been before. Hitler threw thousands of teenage boys—raw recruits—onto the front lines of the hopeless conflict. The bullets were still real. The blood was still red. Soldiers still perished in agony. Though the outcome had been rendered certain, the battles continued to rage.

So it is today. Calvary, two thousand years ago, secured the ultimate victory. The Cross is the turning point of the war—of all history. Through the Cross, Christ reconciled man to God (Colossians 1:20), destroyed the power of death (Romans 8:38), and guaranteed eternal life for His followers.

The Cross is the turning point of the war—of all history.

Yet the war drags on.

But God has given us a peek at the future headlines: He wins! And in Jesus, so do we.

I have no misgivings about...the cause in which I am engaged, and my courage does not...falter.... I am willing...to lay down all my joys in this life.... If I do not [return]...never forget how much I love you, and when my last breath escapes me on the battlefield, it will whisper your name.... Do not mourn me dead...for we shall meet again.

MAJOR SULLIVAN BALLOU,
JULY 1861

Christ shall even now, as always, be exalted in my body whether by life or by death. For to me, to live is Christ, and to die is gain.

PAUL THE APOSTLE,
CIRCA A.D. 62

WHAT ARE WE
FIGHTING FOR?

B ack in the 1950s, the Army had a weekly television program
called *The Big Picture*. Fresh from World War II and Korea
and filled with images of the modern army, it was an attempt
to help the American people gain a better perspective of our
armed forces in a dangerous world.

Perspective is an easy thing to lose when the bullets are flying.

War is ugly and painful. Battlefield soldiers face death every day. The
guys in the trenches know it up close. But up close doesn't always yield
the most accurate perspective.

In fact, it seldom does. Usually, perspective requires a climb to the
high ground.

I'll never forget one night some years back when I had to per-
form a wedding on a Saturday evening just before I was scheduled
to leave for a much-anticipated hunting trip. By the time the wedding was over and I'd managed to leave the church, it was already nine
o'clock in the evening. We were clearly going to get a late-night departure.

We loaded the horses in the trailer and drove through the long
night, arriving at the trailhead at about four in the morning. We got
about an hour of sleep on the ground and then were up with first light,
saddling the horses and packing the mules. It was a hot morning and an
uphill climb all the way. I was riding at the back of the mule train to
make sure the packs were balanced and riding nicely. Needless to say, I
ate a lot of dust in that hot, uphill climb.

But then the whole world changed in a moment. Right when the trail seemed hottest, the switchbacks seemed steepest, and the sand and dirt seemed deepest, we broke over the crest of Sand Pass. It took my breath away. Walt Disney could never have created a scene like the one we beheld. Breaking away below us in ridgeline after ridgeline was the magnificent Eagle Cap Wilderness.

From our vantage point, we surveyed an endless array of short-needled alpine trees. We saw the crashing, pure streams sparkling in the sun. Three deer grazed peacefully about three hundred yards below us. Across the swale in the high meadow, a few elk were enjoying the beautiful Indian-summer day.

And the point is this: One moment I was all caught up in being hot, sweaty, dirty, thirsty, and exhausted. The next moment, because of a simple change in perspective, I was thinking, "I must be somewhere near heaven." Perspective matters.

If you want to know what the war is about and how it's really going, eventually you've got to go higher. The most accurate perspective is not what is happening six inches in front of the GI's nose. You've got to step back, climb a high mountain, get a good 360-degree sweep, and look over the whole theater of war, so to speak.

It's no different in spiritual warfare. If you spend all your time in the trenches, your perspective is usually doomed to distortion. Even Christian warriors suffer loss of perspective. Yes, even pastors.

At one season in the growth of our church, we experienced significant pressure from multiple directions at the same time. The building program was stalled by no fewer than seven layers of government bureaucracy. Of course, that meant that giving to the building fund was near zero for lack of a clear and reachable goal. Several of us in the leadership team were experiencing personal health issues. And then there was the moral failure of one of our ministerial colleagues. It really took the stuffing out of us.

Never in my life, nor probably in several of the other guys' lives, had we been so discouraged. Mood swings plagued more than one of us. Relational tensions between the rest of us tended to rise and fall on good or bad days.

But then we found ourselves together at a baptismal service. We had rented out the aquatic center of the Mt. Hood Community College. Just walking into that swimming pool area somehow changed everything. Hearing the buzz of the people in the stands and seeing the many smiling, eager baptismal candidates was magnificent. I thought, *Hey, time out. Look at*

*this. Catch a little perspective here. Isn't this what it's
all about?*

We need to get a new perspective.

During the Vietnam War, I remember seeing a
hippie antiwar protester bearing a sign written in
hand-lettered script: "There's nothing worth dying
for." I recall thinking that the misguided young man
just couldn't get beyond himself. Every time he
looked up, all he could see was himself. And his limited perspective played with his mind. Why get
stressed out with bullets overhead when you could
stay cool, even blissful, with a few good hallucina-
tions?

*Too many of us live
with the hallucination
that this life here on
earth is what it's
all about.*

Too many of us live with the hallucination that this life here on earth is
what it's all about. Nothing could be further from the truth. This life is nothing more than the doorway to the *real* world, which is still to come.

I'm sorry to have to disappoint our hippie friend, but we're all going to die
anyway. You might dodge the draft, but you won't dodge death; it's an even
more consistent constant than war. So we need to spend more time reflecting
and a lot less time deceiving ourselves with self-indulgent delusion.

What about his sign? *Is* there anything that might be worth dying for?
Not to mention living for? Not to mention *fighting* for? Those are the questions at the heart of life's big picture! After death, then what?

THE NEXT STEP

People throughout history have always been curious about what lies beyond
death. And people of the twenty-first century are no different. Men and
women who have walked right up to death's door and turned back seem to
return with some significant experiences tucked away in their memories.
Whole books, both sacred and secular, are written on the subject. One of
them, *Life, Death, and Beyond,* by Kerby Anderson, tells the story of a
seventy-year-old accountant who knocked on death's door. Here's an excerpt:

> Next thing I remember was going through a dark pas-
> sage. I didn't touch any of the walls. I emerged out into
> an open field and was walking toward a big white wall
> which was very long. It had three steps leading up to a
> doorway in the wall. On a landing above the stairs sat a

man clothed in a robe that was dazzling white and glowing. His face had a glowing radiance also. He was looking down into a big book, studying.

As I approached him, I felt a great reverence and I asked him, "Are you Jesus?" He said, "No, you will find Jesus and your loved ones beyond the door." After he looked in his book he said, "You may go through." And then I walked through the door, and saw on the other side this beautiful, brilliantly lit city, reflecting what seemed to be the sun's rays. It was all made of gold or some shiny metal with domes and steeples in beautiful array, and the streets were shining.

There were many people dressed in glowing white robes with radiant faces.... I saw two figures walking toward me and I immediately recognized them—they were my mother and father; both had died years ago. They were beautiful!... I suddenly felt this tremendous surge of electricity through my body as if someone had hit me in the chest.

They were defibrillating my heart. I had been restored to my former life![1]

Near-death experiences. We've all heard of them. For whatever reason, such close encounters with the hereafter seem to be increasingly common. (Perhaps people have always had them, but never thought of marketing them before!) There always seems to be an audience for these accounts—probably because the overwhelming majority of people believe they are going to heaven—and will have some similar positive experience.

Interestingly, 70 percent of the American people believe in hell, but only about 20 percent think they know someone who might be going there—you know, terrorists, mass murderers and the like.

What we don't usually hear are the many near-death stories that are not nearly so positive. Kerby captures one such horrific account in the man's own words. Thomas Welch was an engineer's assistant employed by a lumber company. He hit his head and then fell thirty feet into a pond:

The next thing I knew I was standing near a shoreline of a great ocean of fire. This is the most awesome sight one could ever see. I remember more clearly than any other thing that has ever happened to me in my lifetime every detail of every moment, from what I saw and what happened during that hour I was gone from this world.

I was standing some distance from this burning, turbulent, rolling mass of blue fire. As far as my eyes could see it was just the same. A lake of fire and brimstone. There is no way to describe it except to say we were eyewitnesses now to the final judgment. There is no way to escape, no way out. This is the prison out of which no one can escape except by divine intervention. I said to myself in an audible voice, "If I had known about this I would have done anything that was required of me to escape coming to a place like this." But I had not known. Soon I was back entering into my body again. It was like coming in through the door of a house. I could *hear* the people I was staying with, praying, minutes before I could open my eyes or say anything. Then suddenly life came into my body and I opened my eyes and spoke to them.[2]

Just what *does* happen after death? And if the Bible gives us answers to that question, what should we do about it? How should "that tomorrow" change "this today"? Can you have a hand in planning your personal eternal future?

You'd better believe it!

How often have I sat at the deathbed of some of our dear Christian saints whose lives are very short now and who are about to move into the presence of our Lord. How often have I seen their hearts comforted and their faces break into smiles, all the while their eyes never open, but their hearts are touched by the presence of God.

A while back at Good Shepherd we lost one of our dear saints—Evelyn Hofeld. Evelyn was a gracious, sweet, praying lady. Evelyn grew in Christ enormously during her years here at Good Shepherd. She would say the last two years were the best. And do you know what was the most exciting thing in her life during those last two years? Attending Good Shepherd's Seminary! Her comment to one of our pastors was, "Oh my, what a God! So much more than I had known or even imagined!"

Not long ago, Evelyn died what most would call a horrible, painful death, riddled by cancer. But Evelyn didn't regard it as a horrible, painful death. I suppose you could say her final week was characterized by an over-riding anticipation. She wore a smile both in her heart and on her face, with an acute awareness of the presence of heaven in her room.

At one point the visiting pastor, Alan Hlavka, related to Evelyn the home-going experience of another of our saints, Agnes Thoren. He told her that Agnes had experienced the tangible presence of the next world in her room before she died. Alan said, "Agnes was 'there' before she left."

"Yes, I know," Evelyn responded. "I've been 'there' a couple times myself today."

Death is life's most inevitable experience. It's incredibly common—in fact, it's 100 percent. At the same time, death is probably life's most univer-sally feared experience. It is certainly life's most mysterious event. Someone has said that the greatest question that can cross our minds is this: *What will happen to me when I die?*

The Bible answers that question. Clearly. It tells us that every Christian soldier will stand before the Commander in Chief for evaluation. The bot-tom line, folks, is that life is too short and eternity too long to do something stupid or throw your life away.

Most Christians, I believe, tend to breeze through life thinking, *Well, the only important thing is that we make it to heaven. And, hey, Christ has provided totally for that! So, no big deal. We're heaven bound.* And then our thinking jumps to the assumption that everyone in heaven will experience it to the same degree.

It's not that simple. Eternity is magnificent, to be sure. And heaven will be glorious. But it is not impersonal. People will retain their particular iden-tities. It's not as though the individual ceases to exist and somehow blends indiscriminately into some mushy sort of groupishness. Quite the opposite: Eternity is intensely personal.

The Scriptures indicate that we will find that eternity is intensely personal.

We tend to imagine that this life is *really* life, and after it's all over we'll just slip into the crowd up there in the great, misty beyond. You know, sort of blend in with the scenery and remain pretty much anonymous in heaven's enormous numbers. But the Bible doesn't leave us with that impression.

On the contrary, the Scriptures indicate that we will find that eternity—by God's direct intention and design—is intensely personal. In fact, the Bible gives clear direction on how you can actually plan your eternal estate, so to speak. Think of it—every Christian soldier will have a unique, personal, eternal future.

How does a soldier plan his career and retirement? Through choices along the way.

The Bible clearly states that the choices you and I make through the course of our lives—spirit-warrior career choices—directly effect our eternal "retirement" program. What kinds of choices are we talking about? Let's look at one man who made many such choices, most of them very good decisions.

THE MAN WHO CHOSE WELL

Moses was one of the great spirit warriors. Somewhere along the line, he learned some significant things, which resulted in significant decisions. By virtue of those decisions, Moses quite deliberately planned his eternity.

God gives you and me the same information, and the same opportunity for similar kinds of choices. As good soldiers, we must make them in light of our desire to please the One who enlisted us.

When Paul urges Timothy to be a good soldier and work hard to please his Commander (2 Timothy 2:3–15), he does so in the specific context of rewards. The apostle insists that our everyday choices will directly effect our eternal rewards or "share of the crops." Our eternity, he tells us, is not only about our salvation, but also about "eternal glory" (v. 10).

In the same way, Moses' choices and behaviors served to tailor his personal eternity. It's the same for us. Our eternities will be as personally tailored for us as Moses' was for him. Let's look at it in Hebrews 11:24–26:

> By faith Moses, when he had grown up, refused to be
> called the son of Pharaoh's daughter, choosing rather to
> endure ill-treatment with the people of God than to
> enjoy the passing pleasures of sin, considering the
> reproach of Christ greater riches than the treasures of
> Egypt; for he was looking to the reward.

That is a phenomenal passage! Very straightforward. The Bible says Moses made his choices in this life in order to gain a greater reward in the life to come. Read the passage again. Circle several keywords. Meditate on them. Turn them over in your mind. Begin to apply them to your own life.

Moses took a good long look at life. He climbed a mountain and gazed into the misty depths of eternity. And then he did some choosing. He made some decisions that involved refusing to seek his own pleasures here and now, but he endured hardship as a good soldier of the living God. Like all the great saints of the faith, he made choices based upon what he had learned from God about eternity. Take a minute or so with me to ponder some phenomenally potent words from this passage.

GROWN UP

What a key term in all our lives! It is why we are alive—to grow up. It's encouraging to know that Moses was making these choices as an adult (after his share of mistakes in the early decades of his life), as part of his ongoing spiritual maturing process.

One of the most telling indications of developing maturity is delayed gratification. It is the child who cannot wait. The mature adult can wait. It is the maturing Christian who chooses not to seek his fulfillment here, but invests his life in the delayed gratification of heaven.

CHOOSING

This is a word that unlocks spiritual growth and sets you on the way to planning your future in heaven. Your eternity involves decision making. Your personal eternal future in God's presence will be directly linked to the thoughtful choices you make every minute of your life on earth.

Decisions to avoid sin.

Decisions to shun certain thought patterns.

Decisions to sacrifice for the kingdom.

Decisions to spend yourself in ministry.

Decisions to deny yourself and take up His Cross.

Decisions to put the Lord first in your life.

Decisions to consider the needs of others before your own.

The Bible assures us that those decisions pay off big time in the life to come.[3]

REFUSED

This is a word that helps to govern our decision making. It actually means that, like Moses, we must turn from one identity to another. Here Moses refused to be called Pharaoh's grandson and forsook the pleasures of sin that would've come with that title.

He not only rejected a wild, sinful lifestyle, Moses also deliberately refused to miss God's calling on his life. He steadfastly refused to spend his life on himself. He wasn't just hanging out and being a pretty nice guy. No, Moses was much more deliberate than that. With farsighted calculation, Moses purposely chose to follow God's plans, God's intentions, God's will, and God's Word.

In other words, Moses' focus was to live for God. He fleshed out what Jesus later commanded in the Sermon on the Mount: "Seek first the kingdom of God" (Matthew 6:33, NKJV). Moses' sin here would have been doing his own thing as opposed to pursuing Christ and His kingdom. Christian, if you just try to be a "pretty good person," staying out of big trouble, and avoiding major sin, you're falling short of the point here.

This is going all out. This is getting active. This is deliberately presenting your body as a "living and holy sacrifice" (Romans 12:1).

If you do not live intentionally for Christ and His kingdom, you are guilty of the sin which Moses refused. Moses believed, as all growing Christians must, that his life was not about himself, but rather about God and His glory.

My heart aches for some of my friends who have not gotten hold of this truth. Let me tell you about someone that I believe probably ended up missing his life's calling. He's always been a good man. Still is. In college, he fell in love with Christ. He became a very active believer: highly committed, effective on the campus, seeing people come to Christ. After college, he went into full-time Christian ministry.

But along the way, he got distracted. He needed a little more money. Then he needed a lot more money. So he started a business on the side. It grew; the ministry didn't. So he left the one for the other.

Was he successful? Yes, sort of. But think about it: What will he take with him through death's door? Certainly none of the power that the business has afforded him. Certainly none of the prestige that the business has given him in the local community.

Ralph Waldo Emerson got hold of some of this truth:

> How do you measure success?
>   To laugh often and much;
> To win the respect of intelligent people
>   And the affection of children;
> To earn the appreciation of honest critics
>   And to endure the betrayals of false friends;
> To appreciate beauty;
>   To find the best in others;

> To leave the world a bit better
>> Whether by a healthy child,
> A redeemed social condition,
>> Or a job well done;
> To know even one other life has breathed
>> Because you lived—
> This is to have succeeded.[4]

Pretty sound thinking overall, wouldn't you say? No mention there of money. Or status. Or notoriety. Certainly no mention of power. Or possessions. Nothing about size, or rank, or prestige. Just a consistent reference to a mature-minded serving of people and principle. The Bible is like that. It doesn't say much about success, but it does refer often to the heart, to relationships, and to the sacrificial serving of others. After all, life consists of relationships—connecting with and serving others. As a matter of fact, in God's economy, true rewardable success is actually defined in terms of servant-hearted personal relationships. Jesus made the point powerfully when He said, "Whoever in the name of [being] a disciple gives to one of these little ones even a cup of cold water to drink, truly I say to you he shall not lose his reward" (Matthew 10:42).

ENDURE

Here's another key word that suggests the Christian life is more about soldiering than picnicking. Moses recognized, as must we, that when you make good choices life takes on a quality of endurance. You make the tough choices and then you have to hang in there.

The spirit warrior's life is not about personal fulfillment. In the same way, your life isn't about you. My life isn't about me. My life isn't about my personal contentment or fulfillment or happiness. Soldiers don't live that way. There is a certain amount of enduring that comes with living a godly life in this sinful world.

Moses changed the bottom line of his life! He passed over the treasures of Egypt.

Moses made his choices for the people of God, identifying with God's kingdom program. He recognized that such an identification would bring with it a certain amount of harassment, ill-treatment, and hardship. But looming even larger than that was a simple delay of gratification. Think of it—Moses chose to exchange everything for the King and His kingdom. He traded in his identity, his associations, his connections, his future, his lifestyle, his wealth, his security, and his net worth. Basically Moses changed the bottom line of his life! Did you see it? He passed over the treasures of Egypt.

That was no pittance! Moses was in line for the top spot in the most powerful company in the world. This was a bigger deal than Bill Gates. The treasures of the Egyptian pharaohs were enormous. Today, thousands of years later, people still stand in long lines just to see a small portion of those fabulous riches. The wealth of the ancient Pharaohs, even the minor ones, is still stupefying today! And Moses walked away from it all.

Now why in the world did he do that? Because he was just naturally some kind of superspiritual guy? Because he was wired that way? Because he couldn't help himself? No, look at the text.

He did it for a reason. He did it for the reward. For the eternal reward.

And the Bible's point is that this is normal Christian living. Every soldier, every Christian, is to do exactly the same thing. If you do, the rewards are out of this world!

REWARD

Moses literally looked away from the treasures of Egypt and deliberately turned his gaze to the true riches in Christ, "for he was looking to the reward."

Moses did what he did for the eternal reward.

There are Christians today who try to piously deny that working for reward is a spiritual necessity. It's too selfish, they say. Too mercenary. The Bible, however, doesn't treat it that way at all. Rewards are one of the most basic motivators God uses to enlist His people to good soldiering.

God gives you and me the same information He gave Moses. In fact, He gives us more: We have the whole Bible, something Moses never saw. And God gives you and me the same kinds of opportunity for choices. Our personal eternities will be as individually tailored for us as Moses' was for him.

Paul, that great spirit warrior of the New Testament, felt the same way: "Do you not know," he wrote, "that those who run in a race all run...and everyone who competes in the games exercises self-control in all things. They then do it to receive a perishable wreath, but we an imperishable. Therefore...run in such a way, as not without aim.... I discipline my body and make it my slave" (1 Corinthians 9:24–27).

I run to win! To win the imperishable, eternal prize! That's precisely what Moses was doing. Not unlike Jesus, who "for the joy set before Him" endured the pain of the Cross.

Christian, run to win...but to win in the eternal, not in the short haul.

Christian, look way out there. See into the distance. Avoid driving only to the limit of your fog lights. Don't live life right up in front of your own face. Get the big picture. Visualize eternity. We must learn, as the apostle Paul insisted, to "look not at the things which are seen, but at the things which are not seen; for the things which are seen are temporal, but the things which are not seen are eternal" (2 Corinthians 4:18).

Don't waste your life driving with only the fog lights on, living just a few seconds ahead, thoroughly shortsighted. Don't spend yourself on a good time here for a few short decades. Invest in eternity. Put the high-beam lights of eternity on your road and drive!

Moses did what he did because he was wise enough to plan his own personal eternal future according to God's instructions. Moses focused upon, and saw, the unseen.

Sometime when you want a really mind-blowing Bible study, study the whole context of Hebrews 11. In verses 8–10, you'll read that even Abraham didn't experience the fulfillment of God's promise here on earth. Verses 13–16 tell us that all the great heroes of the faith died "without receiving the promises." They got a glimpse of them "from a distance" and took God at His word for their fulfillment in another, "better country, that is, a heavenly one."

Do you realize what this means? One, it means that most of the promises of God are not for this world at all. Two, it means that if you want to experience those promises in the world to come, you must live like a simple pilgrim down here.

Don't put your roots down here.

Don't settle in here.

Don't build your kingdom here.

Don't put your desires here.

Don't stack up your investments here.

This world is merely a shadowland, a vestibule, an entryway to the real world and real life to come.

This world is not the real world. This world is merely a shadowland, a vestibule, an entryway to the real world and real life to come.

Soldier, here's the message of the Bible in a nutshell: Life after death will last forever. Forever is, at the least, a very, very long time. Our average lifespan is a mere seventy years—absolutely nothing compared to eternity. (If you could travel a million miles an hour for a billion years you wouldn't be any closer to the end of eternity than when you started.) All of human history—before Columbus, before Caesar, before the pharaohs of Egypt, before Noah, all the way back to Adam and Eve—is nothing, not a pinprick, not a feather stroke, on the surface of eternity.

Life is way too short and eternity is way too long to throw away your investments for some foolish fling of the flesh. Jesus' work for you, His death on the cross, allows you into heaven. Your work for Him gains you reward in heaven.

God's work for man involved sending His Son to die in our place. Man's work for God involves obedient service for His sake. God's work provides salvation. Man's work earns reward. You get in based on who you know—Jesus as Savior. You gain reward based on what you did—as a servant. That's another way of saying your salvation is based on what you believe and your reward is based on how you behave. To put it yet another way: Salvation is a free gift based solely on faith; your reward is earned based on good works.

The Bible insists that your life *after* death is determined by your life *before* death. Eternity is not populated by millions of nameless, numberless masses. It's not a get-lost-in-the-crowd kind of thing. There is no human herd in eternity. Eternity is, by God's decreed intention, intensely personal. All of eternity for you personally (and for me) is determined by what we believe and how we behave *before* we enter eternity through the doorway of physical death. Your death is the final buzzer. No time-outs. No king's X. No "do overs." No extensions. Period. Your eternal account is frozen at your death. The final exam is over. There will be no extra credit, no repeating of a grade.

C. T. Studd, the great missionary, said it well: "Only one life / 'Twill soon be past / Only what's done / For Christ will last." Randy Alcorn said it even more succinctly when he said, "Thirty seconds after we die, we'll know how we should have lived." Randy goes on to say:

> Because this life is so brief, we might easily conclude it
> is also inconsequential.... Our brief stay here may
> indeed seem unimportant, but nothing could be further
> from the truth. For the Bible tells us that while men
> may not remember or care what our lives have been,
> God remembers perfectly and cares very much. So
> much that the door of eternity swings on the hinges of
> our present life on earth.... Eternity will hold for us
> what this life has invested in it.[5]

Dan Wooding, a journalist, captures the same spirit in his description of seminar giant Peter Lowe:

Peter Lowe…is the founding president and CEO of a twenty-five-million-dollar organization that is responsible for the largest seminars in the world. Peter Lowe's Success Seminars attract sell-out crowds from coast to coast in the U.S., with more than a half-million people attending each year. The unique combination of celebrity superstars, business trainers, music, special effects, patriotic spirit, and inspirational messages has made Peter Lowe's Success Seminars an American phenomenon.…

I met up with Peter at the Forum in Los Angeles where he was again hosting a massive seminar and asked him how he defined success.

"First of all you have got to look at the long term…I like to share with business people, 'If I could show you how to be a millionaire in 30 days would you like that?' They say, 'I'd love that.' 'Okay you'll be a millionaire in thirty days, but only for one day, then you'll be bankrupt for the rest of your life.' Then it doesn't sound so good."

When you look at the timeline of eternity, what does thirty, or fifty, or seventy years of so-called success mean, if you don't have eternal life? True success is preparing for eternity. Whatever happens in this life is really incidental.[6]

Soldier, prepare for eternity! Please the One who enlisted you. It's more than just getting saved. It's being saved to serve. It's more than escaping hell. It's relishing the presence of Christ and enjoying His rewards in heaven. To use the apostle Peter's words, "If you do these things, you will…receive a *rich* welcome into the eternal kingdom of our Lord and Savior Jesus Christ" (2 Peter 1:10–11, NIV, emphasis mine).

So how will you answer that basic question, "What will happen to me when I die?"

Dr. Bruce Wilkinson of Walk Thru the Bible Ministries developed a seminar some years ago on the subject of eternal rewards. Bruce identified in Scripture seven distinct elements or stages in our eternal future. Here is what he said:

The Scripture is full and overflowing with concrete and direct revelation that, although the stages of eternity will be the same for everyone in that we'll all go through them, what will occur at the various points of eternity strictly depends upon what you and I individually have done with our lives on the earth. The justice of God will once again be apparent to everyone. Right now many of us feel the wicked go unpunished for their sins. In fact, many rich and famous people we may know about are the most sinful! And that doesn't seem fair, because the godly often seem to go unrewarded in this life. But God will even out the score for everyone—the godly and the wicked…. God's primary "payday" is yet in the future.[7]

Over the centuries, numerous great spirit warriors have encouraged our careful thinking in this critical area of planning our own very personal eternal lives.

Martin Luther was a great spirit warrior of the sixteenth century. He governed his life in terms of eternity. In fact, he insisted that there were only two days on his personal calendar: "Today" and "That Day" (the Day of judgment).

How about you? What does your calendar reflect? Will you seek to live Today in light of That Day?

Donald Grey Barnhouse, a great spirit warrior of the twentith century, said it this way: "Let us live, then, in the light of eternity. If we do not, we are weighting the scales against our eternal welfare…. We may be sure that the consequences of our character will survive the grave, and that we shall face those consequences at the Judgment Seat of Christ."[8]

Jesus Christ, the ultimate spirit warrior and the commander in chief of the hosts of heaven, said this in the last book of the Bible: "I am He who searches the minds and hearts, and I will give to each one of you according to your deeds" (Revelation 2:23).

Soldier, live in light of eternity. Salute and execute here and now. Live every moment in light of Randy Alcorn's pithy statement: "Thirty seconds after we die we will know how we should have lived. But it will be too late then."

The most precious commodity with which the Army deals is the individual soldier who is the heart and soul of our combat forces.

GENERAL J. LAWTON COLLINS

*Life brings sorrows and joys alike.
It is what a man does with them—
not what they do to him—
that is the test of his mettle.*

TEDDY ROOSEVELT

[He is my] fellow soldier.... Hold men like him in high regard, because he came close to death...risking his life...in your service to me.

PHILIPPIANS 2:24-30

THE SOUL OF THE WARRIOR

Do you have what it takes to be a warrior?

I remember asking myself that question many years ago. I was in college during the midsixties. The Vietnam War was building up big time. In 1965 an ROTC instructor on campus approached me. He said Congress had just passed the ROTC Revitalization Act and college scholarships were available. He said he'd even fill out the application for me if I'd just take the physical examination.

It sounded good to me. Like most college students, I didn't have much money for school. So I filled out the scholarship application and took the physical. Then I forgot all about it.

The end of the term came, and I went home for a summer of work. Then in late July the telephone rang. It was the ROTC instructor. He said that I'd won a scholarship and now I had a decision to make. He wasn't kidding.

Did I want to take the scholarship and find myself in the Army? Did I want to be a soldier? I'd never particularly thought of myself as a warrior. No one in my family had been anything close to being a career soldier. I was just a kid from the sticks; did I have what it took to be a warrior? Would I have the "right stuff" when it was put to the test? How would I react under fire? Those kinds of questions rattled around in the back of my mind all through my senior year—as the television accounts of Vietnam heated up.

Just what does it take to be a warrior? I guess it depends on your definition of *warrior.*

If you're talking about passing muster with some guy sitting behind the desk at a military recruiting office, then the standards will be fairly narrow. The right age. The right papers. The right health clearance. The right body type. The right IQ.

How about a bright, seventy-year-old grandmother?

How about a kind, faithful young man with Down's syndrome?

How about a courageous young mother in a wheelchair?

How about a lively twelve-year-old?

How about a wise and godly farmworker without a green card?

How about an overweight, middle-aged man with a bad track record and a limp?

Not one of these people would get by the military recruiter. Not one of them would pass the battery of required tests. Every one of them would be turned away. Yet each of these individuals has magnificent potential to be a mighty spirit warrior—a soldier of Christ able to stand against fearsome foes and ancient enemies.

Somehow we have come to mistakenly associate spiritual warfare with tossing demons around in front of TV cameras.

Somehow we have come to mistakenly associate spiritual warfare with tossing demons around. We think it's whuppin' up on evil spirits in front of TV cameras. We think it's charismatic personalities strutting across brightly lit platforms raising their voices at the unseen world.

But spiritual warfare is so much more than that. And a spirit warrior is so much more than a show. The strength of a biblical warrior is in his soul. His character. Who he is when the cameras are off, when the crowds have gone home, when he's alone in the dark where nobody sees.

Sometimes what you see with your eyes isn't the whole story. Not every person of steel looks like one. Not every knight is dressed in armor. Not every soldier wears battle fatigues and packs an M16. Combatants aren't always immediately recognizable. This is especially true when it comes to spiritual warfare.

What does a spirit warrior look like?

Could you look out over the folks who fill the pews in your church this Sunday and spot the true warriors in the crowd? How close would your picks be to the Lord's picks? Would you even pick yourself? Scripture cautions us about making snap evaluations. Remember the prophet Samuel's experience?

> When they came, [Samuel] looked at Eli'ab and
> thought, "Surely the LORD's anointed is before Him."
> But the LORD said to Samuel, "Do not look on his
> appearance or on the height of his stature, because I
> have rejected him; for the LORD sees not as man sees;
> man looks on the outward appearance, but the LORD
> looks on the heart."
>
> 1 SAMUEL 16:7, RSV

Years later, the Holy Spirit said this through the psalmist:

> The strength of a horse does not impress him;
>   how puny in his sight is the strength of a man.
> Rather, the Lord's delight is in those who honor him,
>   those who put their hope in his unfailing love.
>
> PSALM 147:10–11, NLT

When it comes down to being a warrior, it's what's inside the man that makes all the difference in the world. External strength and power, macho or not, is of little value on the modern battlefield. What does matter is what's inside: the strength of character. What does matter is the heart and the sum total of the choices that man makes in his inner soul.

THE WARRIOR SOUL

Mighty warrior. What comes to your mind when you hear those words? Broad shoulders? Bulging muscles? A hard, lean, anvil-shaped body? Probably. But as far as that goes, you might as well be describing a gorilla at the zoo. A dumb beast with a hairy chest and an attitude.

So just toss in a brain, right? After all, didn't Mel Gibson's William Wallace in *Braveheart* repeatedly point to the head as the soldier's most potent weapon? Yes. But as much an improvement as brains may add to our image of the ideal warrior, the picture still falls short. Some of the smartest people in the world are dismal failures at all kinds of things, particularly character issues.

So where does that lead us? Pound for pound, inch for inch, the warrior's greatest asset is his soul. It is the warrior's soul that gives direction to his mind and strength to his body. It is character that determines whether a man or woman measures up as a spirit warrior. Beating up on demons and rebuking spirits on the religious channel has very little to do with it.

General George Patton, the consensus choice for America's greatest World War II battlefield general, once reflected: "The secret of victory lies not wholly in knowledge. It lurks invisible in that vitalizing spark, intangible, yet evident as lightning—the warrior soul."

Do you have that spark? The truth is that warrior souls may remain invisible—blended into the background—until the moment of crisis falls, until the first shots are fired. We may not even recognize that spirit in ourselves.

I can't help but think of a young man by the name of George Tullidge, a twenty-year-old Buck Sergeant in the 82d Airborne Division. George gave his life in the invasion of France on June 7, 1944, the day after what history has called D day. The youngster was awarded the Bronze Star with "V" device for heroic conduct under fire on the main road into St. Mere Eglise, France. George, virtually single-handedly, successfully held the road junction, which was vital to his entire division's mission. Here is a portion of the Bronze Star citation:

> "Our troops were subjected to heavy attack by the enemy, which threatened the entire position. Sergeant Tullidge set up a light machine gun and held off the enemy, [eliminating] many of the enemy and causing others to withdraw. Although wounded in the engagement, he refused to withdraw until the enemy had been completely routed from the area."

George Tullidge died the next day of his wounds. The verse his parents recorded below their son's name reads simply and eloquently, "Greater love has no man than this, that a man lay down his life for his friends" (John 15:13, RSV).

Young George Tullidge had the right stuff. The warrior spirit showed up strong in battle. But it had been there all the time, deep down in his soul.

Even more revealing than his conduct in battle is the expression of his soul in his last letter home before his death. The letter, written from "somewhere in England" just prior to the D day invasion, is addressed to Tommy, his younger brother, and refers to Arch, the youngest brother still at home. The letter reveals where George got that "right stuff" in his chest.

> Mother writes and tells me how big a boy you are getting to be. It seems like a mighty long time since I have seen you boys, and I guess it will be just a while longer;

probably I will have a hard time even recognizing you. I just know and pray that you will turn out to be the kind of boys that Mother and Dad are teaching you to be. Just please take a word of advice from somebody who has had a small look around anyway. Maybe I am not so old, but this two years in the army has shown and taught me lots of things about life that I never dreamed of before. I won't go into a long discussion but just remember when you are out with the boys and girls what is wrong and what is right. Please don't let them get you and Arch off on the wrong foot because they will if you are not careful. There are lots of things in life bigger and finer than some immediate pleasures; and some few seemingly small things at present can break up the finer ones for you later. You know what I am talking about, drinking and loose women. I see men every day who are ruining themselves through dissipation, both sexual and alcoholic. They don't think so, and seem to be perfectly happy at this time. They even seem happier than others, but sooner or later it will get them; some sooner, and others later.

Another thing that has helped me a lot is my firm belief in the Lord. Often times when I feel depressed and blue it does me an awful lot of good to read my Bible…. A good belief in Christianity (very broad term) gives a fellow something to grasp when the going gets tough, and it does at times. A lot of boys have a hard time because they do not have it there to take hold of. Of course, it is there for all to have if they want, but due to wrong living and poor home life, they haven't been made to realize that it is there. On this coming invasion, the thing called "luck" will play a big part as to whether a fellow gets back or not. This luck is God's protection, I think so anyway. Good soldiering will certainly play its part, but the Lord looking over you will be the big factor, and fellows then will really need plenty of mental help….

As long as I seem to be preaching a sermon, I want

to ask a big favor of you. You know this mess will "bust" inside open one of these days, and I imagine I will have a firsthand look at what is going on. Of course, Mother knows this, too, so I want you to be a comfort to her. There will probably be a long time, maybe a couple of months, that she won't hear from me. I know it will be a big strain on her, so I want you boys to help her as much as possible. Dad will be worried, too, but won't show it perhaps as much, so just be as good and helpful as you can. Thanks!

Best wishes and may God bless you always.

Your best pal,

George[1]

Thanks, George, for having "that vitalizing spark, intangible yet evident as lightning." We stand on your shoulders today. We appreciate your sacrifice in our behalf. And we look forward to a conversation one day in that ultimate "old soldier's home," the heaven our Lord has prepared for His spirit warriors.

Gideon was hunkered down in a winepress, secretly threshing wheat, hidden away from the prying eyes of the Midianites, when the Lord appeared to him. Do you remember the greeting of heaven?

> "The LORD is with you, mighty warrior…. Go in the
> strength you have and save Israel out of Midian's hand.
> Am I not sending you?"
>
> JUDGES 6:12, 14, NIV

Him, a mighty warrior? Hiding in a winepress? He was supposed to go save Israel? The strange visitor had Gideon's attention all right, but the wary Israelite wasn't quite ready to sign on the dotted line.

> [Gideon] said to Him, "O Lord, how shall I deliver
> Israel? Behold, my family is the least in Manasseh, and I
> am the youngest in my father's house."
>
> JUDGES 6:15

The Lord wasn't buying Gideon's excuses: "Surely I will be with you, and you shall defeat Midian as one man" (v. 16, NIV). And that's exactly what happened. Though the invading army was "too numerous to count" (v. 5, NLT),

Gideon and a small company of handpicked troops wiped out a vast army from Israel's borders.

God didn't choose the warrior Israel might have expected. He didn't even choose the warrior that Gideon expected. But He knows a warrior's heart when He sees one, and He delights in demonstrating His power through humble, obedient men and women.

The Lord is with you, spirit warrior!

An American battlefield general from another war understood the warrior spirit well. William Tecumseh Sherman said it eloquently: "There is a soul to an army as well as to the individual man, and no general can accomplish the full work of his army unless he commands the souls of his men, as well as their bodies and legs."

How do you develop that kind of character? What, exactly, does a spiritual warrior look like? How do you know if and when you're qualified? Are spiritual warriors born or made? Is it a spiritual gift?

All of us, men and women, boys and girls, young and old, must become spiritual warriors. We're all under attack. We're all commanded to stand firm against the enemy's assaults. The only question asked of every man and woman is, "Do you have the makings of a spiritual warrior?" Let's take a few pages to consider what those raw materials might include.

A CAUSE BIGGER THAN ME

Last fall my dad and I stood at the graveside of Doug Munro. My father's pushing eighty now. He and Doug were schoolmates in our little hometown of Cle Elum, nestled in the foothills of central Washington's Cascade mountain range. Dad's claim to fame when he and Doug were high schoolers was beating him in the fifty-yard freestyle at the town's Fourth of July picnic. It was a big deal, considering Doug was the community swimming pool lifeguard. Dad got the two-dollar first prize!

Then came World War II. Doug, a year or two older than Dad, shipped out first. In fact, he even asked Dad to escort his girl to the prom for him while he was away in the military. As it turned out, Doug Munro would never marry or have a family. He died on September 27, 1942, on a faraway Pacific island called Guadalcanal.

So last September, as part of our determination not to forget, Dad and I drove up above the coal mining town to the little hillside cemetery that holds more than one of our heroes. Not far from Doug's grave rest the bodies of the Prokopovich brothers. Mike died on June 6, 1944, at a place called Omaha

Beach in Normandy. His brother Steve died within a couple months with the Sixth Ranger Battalion in the Pacific theater. Mr. and Mrs. Prokopovich, within the brief span of a just a few weeks, gave their entire family for our freedom. And there are many such heroes in that humble little cemetery. Like they say, if you're enjoying your freedom, thank a veteran.

But Doug's gravestone stands out. It bears the unmistakable emblem of the Congressional Medal of Honor, our nation's highest award for valor. Doug Munro is still the only member of the U.S. Coast Guard to ever win the CMOH.

On that September day in 1942, Doug had commandeered five Higgins boats—wooden, flat-bottomed landing craft—to rescue a battalion of five hundred U.S. Marines pinned down on the beach by numerically superior Japanese forces. The enemy's strafing fire from advantaged positions had our Marines helplessly immobilized for slaughter.

Directing four of his boats directly to the Marines, Doug positioned his own boat in such a way that it acted as a shield between the Japanese guns and the Marines and their rescuers. Maneuvering his boat back and forth to draw the enemy's fire and rattling his own twin bow guns to suppress what Japanese fire he could, Doug managed to protect the operation long enough to complete the rescue.

But the odds to which he'd exposed himself caught up with him, and Doug took several Japanese bullets through his body. His last words to his mates were about the mission: "Did we get 'em all off?" Informed that indeed they had got them all off, Doug simply smiled and died.

Now here's the question to you. *Why?* Why would a young twenty-something man, not all that long out of high school, throw his life away like that? Why, with an entire lifetime to look forward to—love, marriage, family, career—would anyone expose himself to such certain death?

I'll tell you why. He fought for a cause bigger than himself. Bigger than his own life.

This is the common theme in all of the storied legends of warfare. Most of those stories include long marches…

He fought for a cause bigger than himself. Bigger than his own life.

- on short notice,
- over impossible terrain,
- without food or sleep,
- to fight overwhelming odds.

In these legends, it is the warrior soul, a deeply settled conviction in the rightness of his cause—willpower more than firepower—that propels him on the march and ultimately carries the day.

The warrior's soul makes all the difference against long odds. Contrary to the common way of thinking, more than a few students of warfare have recognized the reality that "right makes might." Halfhearted wars are seldom won. Men fight hardest and longest for a cause that flows out of a just and righteous warrior soul.

I had long wondered about the convictions that motivated Doug Munro. Was he a thinking man? Was he a righteous warrior? Or was he just another GI who lived a well-known moment? So that September day at his graveside, I asked Dad about him. Was he really a man of character? Or did he just get caught up and swept away in a witless moment?

Dad's answer was quiet and thoughtful. "No," he said, "Doug was a solid Christian kid. He knew what life was about. That was like Doug." Though hardly out of his teens, this young man from Cle Elum had developed a warrior's heart. A self-sacrificial soul. A chest filled with character. An acute awareness that his life was not his own, that he was part of something much bigger than himself.

The heart of a warrior is a muscular soul, a center of conviction, that beats for a large and noble cause. A transcendent cause. We're talking about the kind of guy who knows he's one small part of something much bigger and is willing to invest himself in it, even to the point of death.

In Stephen Pressfield's book *Gates of Fire,* the Spartan warrior Dienekes tells a younger soldier:

> "Never forget, Alexandros, that this flesh, this body, does not belong to us. Thank God it doesn't. If I thought this stuff was mine, I could not advance a pace into the face of the enemy. But it is not ours, my friend. It belongs to the gods and to our children, our fathers and mothers and those of [our community] a hundred, a thousand years yet unborn. It belongs to the city which gives us all we have and demands no less in requital."[2]

Similarly, only with fuller accuracy, the Christian belongs entirely to Christ and His kingdom, to the Christian community and to the eternal city. Such a King and kingdom is surely worthy of our all.

In 480 B.C., another Spartan stood at the gates of that ancient Grecian mountain pass, Thermopylae. He gathered with three hundred Spartan soldiers facing what amounted to a suicide mission. Their goal was to hold off the invading thousands of mighty Persian military hordes. Day after deadly day, they withstood the onslaught. Their king, Leonidas, gave voice to that same warrior's spirit when he stood before his soldiers and those mountain walls. Here's Pressfield's idea of what he may have said:

> Nothing good in life comes but at a price. Sweetest of
> all is liberty. This we have chosen and this we pay for.
> We have embraced the laws of Lykurgus, and they are
> stern laws. They have schooled us to scorn the life of
> leisure, which this rich land of ours would bestow upon
> us if we wished, and instead to enroll ourselves in the
> academy of discipline and sacrifice. Guided by these
> laws, our fathers for twenty generations have breathed
> the blessed air of freedom and have paid the bill in full
> when it was presented. We, their sons, can do no less.[3]

Such a spirit, so essential to the effective warrior, springs directly from his character—character that takes shape in "the academy of discipline and sacrifice."

The mission statement of the United States Military Academy nails the concept. Does it focus on physical strength? No. It doesn't even mention it—although, of course, West Point is well known for its rigorous physical training. Does West Point's mission statement center on the development of the mind? No—though no one disputes the superior quality of the Corps's academic program.

The mission statement of the USMA, short and to the point, reads simply: "It is the purpose of the United States Military Academy to provide the nation with leaders of character." A warrior without character is merely a brute.

It was a transcendent cause that placed a young teenager named David squarely in front of Goliath, the nine-foot-tall champion of the Philistines. The honor of the God of Israel was at stake. Yahweh's reputation among the nations was in jeopardy. David—young as he was—seemed insignificant in his own eyes compared to that cause. Hot with indignation, he asked the terrified Israelite soldiers: "Who is this uncircumcised Philistine, that he should taunt the armies of the living God?" (1 Samuel 17:26).

Inspired by a cause larger than himself, David took it upon himself to give all he had to oppose this towering brute:

> Then David said to the Philistine, "You come to me
> with a sword, a spear, and a javelin, but I come to you in
> the name of the LORD of hosts, the God of the armies
> of Israel, whom you have taunted. This day the LORD
> will deliver you up into my hands, and I will strike you
> down and remove your head from you…that all the
> earth may know that there is a God in Israel, and that all
> this assembly may know that the LORD does not deliver
> by sword or by spear; for the battle is the LORD's and
> He will give you into our hands."
>
> 1 SAMUEL 17:45–47

David had a bigger picture of the fight than just his own victory, his own reputation, or even his own life. It was this vision that gave him the strength and stamina to persevere through the long years of running and hiding that would follow.

A millennium later, when the elders at Ephesus begged Paul to sidestep the dangers at Jerusalem, the old apostle was incensed. He said in effect, "What's the game plan here, fellas? If it's saving my own hide, I'm in the wrong business. If it's waltzing down the easy road on the sunny side of the street, I've been wasting my time. Hey, this missionary stuff isn't about me. It is not about *my* comfort, *my* desires, *my* safety."

> "And now, behold, bound in spirit, I am on my way to
> Jerusalem, not knowing what will happen to me there….
> But I do not consider my life of any account as dear to
> myself, so that I may finish my course and the ministry
> which I received from the Lord Jesus, to testify solemnly
> of the gospel of the grace of God."
>
> ACTS 20:22, 24

Paul's purpose was bigger than himself. Bigger than his hopes and plans and dreams. Bigger than his fear of injury or death. Bigger than the value of his own life. Finishing the course meant everything to the apostle, even if it cost him everything.

And from that little hillside cemetery outside Cle Elum, Washington, I think I can hear a silent amen.

IRON MEN AND AN IRON HORSE

Scripture's favorite description of the warrior is captured in the oft-repeated phrase "mighty men of valor." Valor is a matter of character. Webster defines valor as "strength of mind and spirit." It is this soulish strength, this personal bravery, which "enables a man to encounter danger with firmness." It is the warrior's heart and soul which is the fountainhead of courage, sacrifice, and unselfishness.

What comes to your mind when you picture an iron man? Certainly conditioning. Clearly, a strong person. Maybe you've watched the Iron Man Triathlon in Hawaii. It's a brutal competition in which athletes swim 2.4 miles, then bike 112 miles, then run a marathon of 26.2 miles, all with no rest between events.

But any truly great athletic competitor is more than a body. It takes some kind of inner heart to be an iron man. While we're talking about the strength of a warrior's heart, think for a minute about the man known as baseball's "Iron Horse." His name was Henry.

Henry was born in New York City on July 19, 1903. He was the only one of four children to survive to adulthood in his poor immigrant home.

Henry didn't start playing baseball until he entered school. It didn't really come naturally to him, but he worked hard at it and excelled. He played at Colombia University and later for Hartford, a minor league team in the 1924 season. A .329 batting average caught the attention of Yankee scouts, and the following season Henry stood on first base for New York. Henry hit .295 his first season in the majors. Turns out it was his worst. The next season began a string of thirteen consecutive years in which Henry never swung the bat at less than .300.

Then the seemingly inexplicable happened. Just eight games into the 1939 season, Henry pulled himself out of the lineup. Disappointed with his performance, he felt like he was letting his teammates down. He wasn't coming through in clutch situations. His body felt stiff and weak. It ended up being more than an ordinary batter's slump.

In what has become a well-known speech world over, Henry Lou Gehrig addressed a hushed crowd at Yankee Stadium on July 4, 1939:

Fans, for the past two weeks you have been reading about
a bad break I got. Yet today, I consider myself the luckiest
man on the face of the earth. I have been in ballparks for
seventeen years and I have never received anything but
kindness and encouragement from you fans.

No one had heard much about Amyotrophic Lateral Sclerosis. But everyone today knows about Lou Gehrig's disease. As the disease progressed, baseball's "Iron Horse" began to have difficulty with the most simple tasks, like breathing and swallowing. He died in 1941, but he remains immortalized as one of the mightiest athletes of the twentieth century. Why? Because Lou Gehrig's strength consisted of more than muscle. In fact, the real Lou Gehrig grew stronger even as his body deteriorated around him. He had developed strength of character.

God is more interested in what you can become than in what you are.

Here is a key principle every spirit warrior learns in God's basic training program: God is more interested in what you can become than in what you are. My friend Crawford Lorritz says it this way: "God is much more concerned with your character than your comfort."

God tells us His plans for us are for good and not for evil (Jeremiah 29:11). But to get there you have to come to a point where you realize that the sum of your talents, your lineage, your appearance, and your personality can never add up to success. Your strength as a spiritual warrior lies not in your external assets, but in your *internal* assets. In a word, character.

God will use whatever it takes to bring you to the end of yourself. Remember what David said when he felt like he was going down for the third time?

Hear my cry, O God;
    Give heed to my prayer.
From the end of the earth I call to You
    when my heart is faint;
Lead me to the rock that is higher than I.

PSALM 61:1-2

At the end of yourself, you find more than yourself. You find a Rock to stand on. On such a foundation, warrior souls take shape.

PHYSICAL PREPARATION FOR BATTLE

Let's take a look at another magnificent Old Testament passage. First Chronicles 5 lists some of history's greatest spiritual warriors. At first glance it appears to be just another battle in the annals of Israel. But there's more. It is a chapter about warfare, swords, and shields—and it's also about spiritual warfare. The warriors in this passage knew very well they were fighting a two-fronted war, one physical, one spiritual.

> The sons of Reuben and the Gadites and the half-tribe of
> Manasseh, consisting of valiant men, men who bore shield
> and sword and shot with bow and were skillful in battle,
> were 44,760, who went to war.
>
> 1 CHRONICLES 5:18

Let's look at what this passage teaches us about the physical components of what makes a spirit warrior.

GOD'S WARRIOR'S ARE IN SHAPE

One of the first things we might note here is the simple fact that God's warriors are physically fit. They're able-bodied men and women. As long as you're alive, your body and your spirit will either complement or inhibit each other. You can't separate the way you care for your physical body—the way you feed it, exercise it, doctor it, and nourish it—from your spiritual vitality. As Dr. Joe Aldrich used to say, "The body and the spirit are so close together they catch each other's diseases."

Now, obviously, we don't all have the same bodies or the same natural abilities. Some people can leap forty-four inches vertically and some of us are glad to jump only four. We're not all the same, but we all share the same responsibility to steward the body God has provided.

I'll never forget the toughest training I ever experienced in the military: the U.S. Army Ranger School. Two hundred eighty-seven of us stood in that first formation. Every day afterward, some fell by the wayside. Some dropped out; some were declared unfit; some were physically hurt; and some were mentally incapable of enduring. By the time the nine weeks were over, there were only 110 men still standing. Of that 110, only 80 got to wear the coveted Ranger tab. Most of those who dropped out did so in the first couple of weeks. It became painfully evident that they simply didn't show up in shape.

God's warriors are in shape. Ouch. That pinches a bit, doesn't it? God's warriors benefit from the energy, alertness, and stamina of healthy, physically fit bodies.

God's Warriors Are Properly Equipped

The warriors described in 1 Chronicles 5:18 had all the shields, swords, and bows they needed. What do *you* need to serve God effectively? Think in real, practical terms. Think carefully about what's ahead of you and choose the tools and the assets that will be most useful.

Most likely you can't afford everything you need right away, so be wise. Should you invest in a biblical reference library? Maybe, maybe not. Get advice. Plan. If you're going to need a twelve-hundred-dollar computer a year from now, think how you might save for it. If you cut back on pizza, soft drinks, and fast food between now and then, the computer might come easier. What equipment do you *need* to be effective? Gear up.

By the way, remember that too much stuff can weigh you down and decrease your effectiveness. More is not better. So don't collect stuff just to have it. You can only take so much into battle. Get rid of encumbrances. Put on assets.

The Oregon Trail was littered with the "throwaways" that family after family had determined to bring with them out West. Some things proved not only unnecessary but great burdens and were discarded.

God's Warriors Are Well Trained

If you're young, don't detour education. Lay a broad foundation even if you don't see how it's going to benefit you. Once you're out of school, keep reading, keep honing your knowledge and skills. Take a class at the local community college—just to sharpen your mind. Deepen your knowledge of the Scriptures through Bible school, seminary, or a good correspondence course. Involve yourself in a solid church program where you're exposed to good teaching. Take advantage of all the resources you can lay your hands on.

God's Warriors Are Appropriately Aggressive

Appropriate is the operative word. Brawn is good; brutishness is not. Brave is good; brawling is not. But the point is basic: If a soldier never contends on the battlefield, he's only a disengaged coward. Effective soldiers, kingdom impact players, are active on the battlefield. It's well known that on the battlefield, a fairly high percentage of soldiers seldom if ever pull the triggers on their weapons. Soldiers must engage.

I recall something that happened to my son when he was in high school. After a football practice, he and a friend were talking. My son was drinking a Coke to replenish some of his body's fluids. Some upperclassman approached and demanded that my son give him his Coke. My son refused. Things heated up and there was a bit of a melee: my son against two or three upperclassmen. My son's friend did not get involved.

Later, when this boy's father heard the story, he gave his son very clear instructions: "When one of your friends is being unjustly attacked and faces potential harm, it's a no-brainer: You dive in and be counted."

That's the spirit we're talking about. Dive in and be counted, spirit warrior.

SPIRITUAL PREPARATION FOR BATTLE

Physical preparation is important. But for the Christian, it isn't the whole ball game. As important as it may be for facing warfare and hostile forces, *spiritual* preparation for conflict is every bit as important.

You say, "Wait a minute. Isn't spiritual preparation an automatic if I'm contending for God and engaging in spiritual warfare?" Not at all. The Bible is filled with the flaming wreckage of people who tried to do God's work in their own way and in their own power.

Let's look at the next verses from 1 Chronicles 5:

> [The Israelites] made war against the Hagrites, Jetur,
> Naphish and Nodab. They were helped against them,
> and the Hagrites and all who were with them were
> given into their hand; for they cried out to God in the
> battle, and He answered their prayers because they
> trusted in Him.
>
> 1 CHRONICLES 5:19–20

Here are some thoughts related to spiritual preparation.

GOD'S WARRIORS UNDERSTAND THEIR LIMITATIONS

Verse 20 says, "They were helped." Of course they were helped. Lone Rangers only win in the movies. You and I have to know our limitations. We have to look at life with clear-eyed realism and understand what it will take to bring us victory. Modesty is an essential quality in God's warriors.

GOD'S WARRIORS ARE QUICK TO CALL IN OUTSIDE HELP

This passage depicts nearly forty-five thousand well-trained, well-equipped soldiers in the heat of battle. And what are they doing? They're praying! Calling in divine artillery. If the soldiers of God's army needed to pray, how much more do you and I need to?

I recall the spring of 1970, when our Special Forces A camp in Vietnam was surrounded by enemy troops. The siege was made particularly difficult because the weather was such that there was no air support available to the soldiers holding the camp. Portions of the camp were overrun for lack of sufficient backup. But then the weather broke, and the fast fliers joined the battle. It was over almost immediately. Soldiers on the ground, heavily engaged, need all the outside help they can get.

The immature conscript thinks he can prevail without the Lord. Rambo is his idol. Those kind end up in body bags. Even worse, they often put other people at greater risk. The mature person knows it's foolish to trust in anyone but God.

THE BATTLE IS THE LORD'S

Look at verse 19 again. Who started the war? "The tribes of Israel waged war," it says. They started it. But who *owned* the war? If you were to look at verses 21 and 22 you'd see that Israel "took away their cattle: their 50,000 camels, 250,000 sheep, 2,000 donkeys; and 100,000 men. For many fell slain, because the war was of God."

Okay, who owned that war? It was never Israel's battle. In the same way, your spiritual battles aren't really yours. The battle was God's…and it still is. The warriors of Israel did everything they could do and they believed God would do everything He could do. That's an unbeatable combination.

Spiritual warfare is inevitable. Therefore, just like the tribes of Israel we must:

- prepare responsibly,
- engage strategically,
- pray constantly,
- trust wholeheartedly,
- and God will win decisively.

There's one more step you need to take. Take a look at the last sentence of 1 Chronicles 5:22 in the NIV: "And they occupied the land until the exile."

Never relinquish territory God has entrusted to you, fellow soldier. Occupy humbly. Never pull back. Backsliding will kill a once-good soldier.

Let's wrap this chapter up by reading a familiar New Testament passage in an unfamiliar way. This is what the heart of a true spiritual warrior looks like. We call 1 Corinthians 13 the love chapter. Maybe it ought to be the chapter that defines the soul of the spirit warrior.

> A spiritual warrior is patient, a spiritual warrior is kind.
> He does not envy, does not boast, is not proud.
> Spiritual warriors are not rude, they're not self-seeking,
> not easily angered, and they keep no record of wrongs.
> A spiritual warrior does not delight in evil but rejoices
> with the truth. They always protect, always trust, always
> hope, always persevere. A spiritual warrior never fails.
>
> 1 CORINTHIANS 13:4–8, MY PARAPHRASE

Faithfulness. And quiet loyalty. And sacrifice. And love. These define the soul of the spirit warrior.

I don't see a lot of flash and dash in those words. I don't see much glitz and glamour. I don't see the red lights of TV cameras or hear the applause of a studio audience. I do see faithfulness. And quiet loyalty. And sacrifice. And love.

I see Doug Munro. I see the Lord Jesus. And by His enabling power and in His grace, I see you and me.

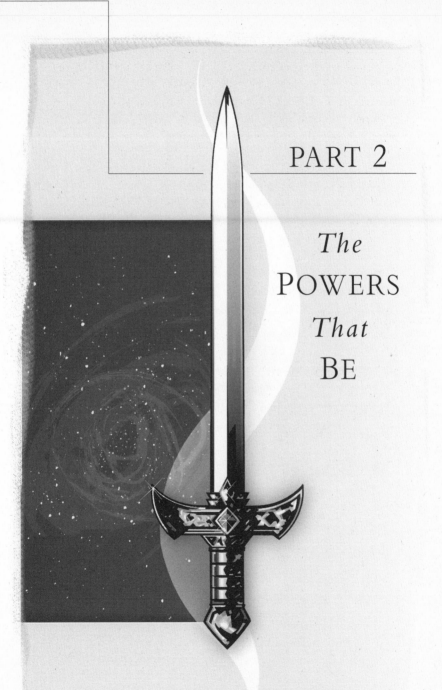

PART 2

The
POWERS
That
BE

The word of God is living and active and sharper than any two-edged sword, and piercing as far as the division of soul and spirit, of both joints and marrow, and able to judge the thoughts and intentions of the heart.

HEBREWS 4:12

Fundamental to operating successfully across the full range of military operations is an understanding of the Army's doctrinal foundations—the principles of war and the tenets of Army operations.

FM 100-5 OPERATIONS,
DEPARTMENT OF THE ARMY, 1993

The [soldier's evaluations] are based upon the employment of sound doctrinal principles.

U.S. ARMY RANGER
HANDBOOK, U.S. ARMY
INFANTRY CENTER,
FORT BENNING, GA, 1998

OUR FIELD MANUAL

S
oldiers live and die by the book. The "employment of sound doctrinal principles" determines success or failure on the battlefield. It's true for the active duty infantryman, and it's even more relevant to the spiritual warrior.

Last spring I stood on the edge of the grassy, neatly kept assembly area of one of the U.S. Army's elite special operations units. Many consider the Seventy-fifth Ranger Regiment to be the finest light infantry unit in the world. I certainly do. On this typical Pacific Northwest morning—somewhat breezy, partly cloudy—the Second Battalion of the Seventy-fifth was offering her final salute to the senior enlisted soldier in her ranks. The battalion Command Sergeant Major was retiring after more than two decades of sterling service to the nation. In the time-honored and solemn ritual, with measured movements he passed the unit colors to his replacement, another experienced CSM wearing a few scars of his own.

The old Sergeant Major got hold of my heart strings. Hearing his remarks and watching the chiseled noncom saying good-bye to his soldiers was potent enough to, as the stoic Rangers might say, "make your eyeballs sweat."

But the emotional peak was yet to come.

The Second Battalion is the Pacific theater's quick reaction infantry element. On virtually no notice, these guys can fly out of their base at Ft. Lewis, Washington, and parachute into any hot spot in the hemisphere. Highly trained, exceptionally skilled, and unswayed by the rigors of combat or threat of death, they do their job with vigor and professional focus.

You saw the Rangers at Point du Hoc on D day. You saw Rangers operating in Korea, Vietnam, Granada, Panama, Iraq, and Somalia. Their motto says it all: "Rangers lead the way!" Any soldier wearing the Ranger tab on his shoulder and the distinctive beret on his head is a soldier to be respected.

That morning on the assembly area, seven hundred Rangers in BDUs (battle dress, utility) were standing tall. The formation was tight and professional. Just the sight of it was deeply moving to me. But when the battalion said their final good-bye, it was in a manner I will never forget. With the old soldier standing at attention in front of them, hundreds of men spoke from memory with one voice. As though they were reciting Scripture, their singular message boomed across the parade grounds. Here is what I heard the seven hundred men broadcast from their hearts and souls that day:

Recognizing that I volunteered as a Ranger, fully knowing the hazards of my chosen profession, I will always endeavor to uphold the prestige, honor, and high esprit de corps of the Rangers.

Acknowledging the fact that a Ranger is a more elite soldier who arrives at the cutting edge of battle by land, sea, or air, I accept the fact that as a Ranger my country expects me to move further, faster, and fight harder than any other soldier.

Never shall I fail my comrades. I will always keep myself mentally alert, physically strong, and morally straight. And I will shoulder more than my share of the task, whatever it may be, one hundred percent and then some.

Gallantly will I show the world that I am a specially selected and well-trained soldier. My courtesy to superior officers, neatness of dress, and care of equipment shall set the example for others to follow.

Energetically will I meet the enemies of my country. I shall defeat them on the field of battle for I am better trained and will fight with all my might. Surrender is not a Ranger word. I will never leave a fallen comrade to fall into the hands of the enemy, and under no circumstances will I ever embarrass my country.

Readily will I display the intestinal fortitude required to fight on to the Ranger objective and complete the mission though I be the lone survivor.

Rangers lead the way!

It is the Ranger Creed, the beating heart of Ranger doctrine. Webster defines a creed as a "brief, authoritative formula of religious faith; a summary of principles professed and adhered to." He's got that right. Every good soldier understands he is lost without clear doctrine.

The Army so believes in sound doctrine that TRADOC (Training and Doctrine Command)—the fountainhead for all Army battlefield principles, doctrine, and training—is one of the few major commands of the U.S. Army headed by a power-packed four-star general.

Any army worth its salt is governed by carefully developed training and doctrine, which is encapsulated in written form and distributed faithfully to the troops. Oh, soldiers may enjoy the age-old ritual of griping about regulations, but when push comes to shove, they do understand the importance of the unit integrity and cohesion produced by sound doctrine.

Every soldier recalls the Field Manual library. Even the lowliest ROTC cadet becomes intimately familiar with *FM 22-5*, the Field Manual for close order drill. Without it he wouldn't know the difference between a left oblique and a right face. Without the Field Manuals there would be no army, only a loosely formed mob of renegades capable of little else but chaos.

It's always been that way. Soldiers learn early on that they must live "by the book!"

Probably one of the earliest codifications of U.S. military doctrine occurred even before there was a United States. "Rogers's Rangers" was organized in 1756 during the French and Indian War. In 1759, Major Robert Rogers issued his famous standing orders. Over two hundred years old now, they apply as accurately today as they did then. They still appear at the front of the latest edition of the *Ranger Handbook.* Just for fun, here are a few of the nineteen original standing orders:

- Don't forget nothing.
- Have your musket as clean as a whistle, hatchet scoured, sixty rounds of powder and ball, and be ready to march at a minute's warning.
- Tell the truth about what you see and what you do.
- When we camp, half the party stays awake.
- Don't ever march home the same way.... [Vary your] route.
- Don't cross a river by a regular ford.
- Let the enemy come 'til he's almost close enough to touch. Then let him have it...and finish him with your hatchet.[1]

It's not a lot different today. Every Ranger is familiar with the contents of the pocket-size *Ranger Handbook*. The current issue's preface reads this way in part:

> This publication is both an extract of doctrinal publications and a compilation of tactics, techniques, and procedures taught in the U.S. Army Ranger School.... Students' grades are based on the employment of sound doctrinal principles, not on the employment of a specific technique.[2]

The handbook deals with the "doctrines" of patrolling, small-unit tactics, ambush reaction, bunker elimination, breaching obstacles, equipment, aviation, first aid, mountaineering, demolitions, waterborne operations, and "escape, evasion, and survival."

Did you catch the major point of the preface? Warfare is a *doctrinal* issue. Students' grades will be derived primarily from their grasp of "sound doctrinal principles." The *Ranger Handbook* makes it clear that technique and doctrine are two different concerns. The soldier's skills and techniques will improve with time and practice. But if he has not mastered sound doctrine, there is little or no hope for his success on the battlefield!

THE PARALLEL

Spiritual warfare is identical in its reliance on sound doctrine. Ultimately, all physical war is merely a mirror of the greater and often unseen spiritual warfare. That's why the Holy Spirit so vehemently insists that Christians become masters of sound doctrine. In one of many similar passages, the apostle Paul, in the specific context of spiritual warfare and "fighting the good fight," seems to shout it out like a spiritual drill instructor:

> I solemnly charge you in the presence of God and of Christ Jesus, who is to judge the living and the dead, and by His appearing and His kingdom: preach the word; be ready in season and out of season; reprove, rebuke, exhort, with great patience and instruction. For the time will come when they will not endure sound doctrine...and will turn aside to myths.
>
> 2 TIMOTHY 4:1–4

That's Paul's way of saying, "Christian soldier, live and die by the Book!"

In another place, when people were being misled by false teaching and were losing the spiritual battle to "doctrines of demons," Paul demanded that his young fellow soldier stick to the Book:

> In pointing out these things to the brethren, you will be
> a good servant of Christ Jesus, constantly nourished on
> the words of the faith and of the sound doctrine which
> you have been following.... Discipline yourself for the
> purpose of godliness; for bodily discipline is only of
> little profit, but godliness is profitable for all things,
> since it holds promise for the present life and also for
> the life to come.
>
> 1 TIMOTHY 4:6-8

Again and again the spiritual Command Sergeant Major of the New Testament insisted that Christians engage by the Book:

> If anyone advocates a different doctrine and does not
> agree with sound words, those of our Lord Jesus Christ,
> and with the doctrine conforming to godliness, he is
> conceited and understands nothing.
>
> 1 TIMOTHY 6:3-4

The spirit warrior is to live by the Book. Unfortunately, many of the so-called spiritual warfare experts wandering about are doing just that—wandering far outside the Scripture and creating entire manuals of their own that bear little or no resemblance to the actual statements of Scripture. Spiritual warfare is to be conducted by the Book, the one Book—the Bible, the whole Bible, and nothing but the Bible. Period.

Spiritual warfare is to be conducted by the Book—the Bible.

Now hear this! The Christian soldier's success on the spiritual battlefield will be evaluated by the Commander of heaven based strictly upon his adherence to sound doctrine—and not the application of some personal, goofy, customized ritual or highly stylized technique.

It's the Bible, soldier! Nothing but the Bible. Not this brother, or that sister, but the Bible. Not this televised spiritual warfare expert or that one, but the Bible. The Bible. The Bible. The Bible.

OLD BLACKJACK'S LEGACY

For the thinking Christian, the Bible and warfare go hand in hand.

For the thinking Christian, the Bible and warfare go hand in hand. A strange statement, you say? Perhaps. But it does get your attention, doesn't it? Let me tell you about one old soldier who believed it.

General John J. "Blackjack" Pershing was one of the great military leaders of the twentieth century. He was a "dirt soldier," coming up the hard way to his celebrated five-star rank. His career as a simple soldier saw him engaging the Apaches in the Southwest, being decorated for gallantry at San Juan Hill, fighting the Moros in the Philippines, and chasing Pancho Villa away from Texas.

But his greatest achievement was reserved for the Great War, World War I. Starting from virtually nothing (a tiny, active army of twenty-five thousand men and no reserve), within eighteen months, John Pershing had established and trained an army of two million soldiers. This was the force that brought the stalemated World War I to a close in less than two hundred days. Pershing had to build the modern American army almost single-handedly. He is the only American to be named "General of the Armies" by a special act of Congress in his own lifetime, one rank above such five-star generals of World War II as Eisenhower, Bradley, and MacArthur.

Some say General Blackjack Pershing was at times an austere man. I suppose he had reason to be. He had experienced more than his share of pain in this war zone called life. Some of it was intensely personal and utterly devastating, more so than most of us will ever experience. In 1915 while he was stationed at the Presidio in San Francisco, a fire broke out in the officer's housing. General Pershing's dear wife and all three of his much loved little daughters died in the flames. Only his six-year-old son, Warren, survived.

The General's heart was broken. For more than a year he thought he might be losing his mind. But he regained mastery of himself and his heart. The tragedy shaped the silent dignity of the man. A clue to the strength of the five-star soldier's soul is found in a message he gave to his World War I troops, just two years after the fire.

In April of 1917 our nation had declared war on Germany. The Americans were pouring into Europe. General Pershing believed that the Bible had a great deal to say to his soldiers on the front. He knew it would shape the warrior's soul. In fact, he presented a copy of the New Testament to each of his troops, along with a personal handwritten message. I have one of these cherished "Pershing Bibles" in my possession. Its cover identifies it as the World War I "Active Service Testament." On the worn and yellowed inside front cover, in his own script, the general had recorded his heartfelt message to his soldiers, who would soon face the horrors of the trenches:

> To the American Soldier:
> Aroused against a nation waging war in violation of all Christian principles, our people are fighting in the cause of liberty.
> Hardship will be your lot, but trust in God will give you comfort; temptation will befall you, but the teachings of our Savior will give you strength.
> Let your valor as a soldier and your conduct as a man be an inspiration to your comrades and an honor to your country.
> Pershing
> Comdg
> Aug 10, '17

You should take Blackjack's words personally. Because it is *warfare* you're facing, you need to face up to reality—you could get shot up out there! Blasted. Blown away. You could become a casualty! I see it every day in the ministry. And this could be incredibly costly to you.

Warfare, by definition, implies losses. Ultimately, the loss for the non-believer is eternal separation from God in hell. For the believer, the loss is diminished eternal reward. And in the events of *this* life (our responses to which determine the quality of our eternal life), the losses include every variety of pain and suffering and diminished effectiveness imaginable. From simple disappointments to disease and loss of health to the trauma of children killed in fires—all the terrible, horrible, no-good days that everyone experiences along the way are part of the process in a sin-stained world. It is war!

The last book of the Bible shouts the message across the millennia:

> And I saw heaven opened, and behold, a white horse, and He who sat on it is called Faithful and True, and in righteousness He judges and *wages war*. His eyes are a flame of fire, and on His head are many diadems; and He has a name written on Him which no one knows except Himself. He is clothed with a robe dipped in blood, and His name is called *The Word of God*. And the armies which are in heaven, clothed in fine linen, white and clean, were following Him on white horses. From His mouth comes a sharp sword, so that with it He may strike down the nations, and He will rule them with a rod of iron; and He treads the wine press of the fierce wrath of God, the Almighty. And on His robe and on His thigh He has a name written, "KING OF KINGS, AND LORD OF LORDS."
>
> REVELATION 19:11–16, EMPHASIS MINE

This is war, soldier, and the Bible says it over and over. Here it is again from a passage a little later.

> Then He said to me, "It is done. I am the Alpha and the Omega, the beginning and the end. I will give to the one who thirsts from the spring of the water of life without cost. He who *overcomes* will inherit these things, and I will be his God and he will be My son."
>
> REVELATION 21:6–7, EMPHASIS MINE

How Do You Become an Overcomer?

Just how do we overcome? How do you and I as Christians build our warriors' hearts to win? How do we best prepare for this war? What is the single greatest key to preparing the soldier for battle? Here's the short answer:

Everything you need to know is in the training manual. Complete familiarity with the field manual, the Bible, is the soldier's greatest asset. There was a critical clue in what we just read: "His name is called the Word of God." His name and His Word are inseparable. His name represents everything He stands for: His heart, His character, His reputation, His integrity, His manner, and His standing orders. It's all in the name.

The single greatest key to your spiritual combat readiness rating is the Word of God, your soldier's field manual, the sword of the Spirit, the Bible.

When you're in a war, especially of this magnitude, you'd better carry your Bible close! Very close. Blackjack Pershing knew that. *For the thinking Christian, warfare and the Bible go hand in hand.* The Christian soldier takes his orders straight from his Commander in Chief, the Lord of hosts.

God Himself makes the case for the critical place of the Word of God in the battles we face every day:

> All Scripture is inspired by God and profitable for
> teaching, for reproof, for correction, for training in
> righteousness; so that the man of God may be adequate,
> equipped for every good work.
>
> 2 TIMOTHY 3:16–17

Inspired is an incredibly graphic word meaning "God-breathed." The Bible is the very breath of God. It shares the life-breath and character of God Himself. What are the enormous implications of this astonishing claim?

Just this: Throughout the entire history of the world, and among all the written documentation of all civilizations of all time, the eternal omnipotent Creator of the Universe, God Almighty Himself, who will one day judge every human being that has ever lived, has given the human race just one volume of His written words. This is it! There are no others! It is unique! This Book. The Bible. There are no other written words of God anywhere else in all of human experience. So, soldier, live by the Book!

The Bible is completely sufficient to tell us everything we need to know to be up to any and every task God asks of His soldiers. This Book alone has a fundamentally different character from every other bit of writing in all the world and all of history.

Now here are some key questions for every Christian soldier:

Do you act like the Bible is sufficient for all your needs?

Do you treat it that way?

Do you read it?

Do you study it?

Do you *treasure* it?

In Psalm 119, the longest chapter in the Bible (176 verses!), the psalmist spends every verse talking about the great love and passion of His life: the Word of God. In verse 162, he writes: "I rejoice at Your word, / As one who finds great spoil."

Great spoil? That calls up a picture of an invading army sacking a city and taking all the valuables within. In the psalmist's day, that would have included piles of costly clothing and great chests of silver, gold, and precious stones. Can you picture a room stuffed with such treasure? Can you imagine all it would buy? That's "great spoil."

And the psalmist says, "Yes, that would be nice. But I'm every bit as excited about having a copy of God's Word in my hand and in my heart."

In verse 11 that same man wrote: "Your word I have treasured in my heart, that I may not sin against you."

If you don't treasure the Word of God in your heart, you quite literally haven't got a prayer when it comes to spiritual battle. If you don't constantly immerse yourself in His truth, turning it over and over again in your mind through what the Bible calls meditation, you leave yourself defenseless and unarmed, thoroughly ill equipped to meet and defeat the formidable opposition you face every day.

The Bible alone must be the only authoritative source of instruction for Christian soldiers involved in spiritual warfare.

How well do you even know God's Word?

Do you take it to heart?

Do you turn the words over in your mind?

Do you let it roll across your taste buds like the finest food or wine?

Do you consult this Book in all your life decisions?

If you cannot answer these questions in the affirmative, you can assume that you will become a casualty in this spiritual warfare.

Did you notice something else in 2 Timothy 3:16? That little verse insists that you don't need any other source of information but the Bible to be *all* that God intends you to be. Adequate...thoroughly adequate...fully equipped. The Bible and the Bible alone must be the only authoritative source of instruction for Christian soldiers involved in spiritual warfare.

Maybe you had some kind of "power encounter" in your Aunt Bessie's attic when you were a kid. I don't care what it was; it is in no way normative. The Bible and the Bible alone is our source of information in spiritual warfare.

Second Timothy 3:16–17 teaches us that the Bible is absolutely sufficient for the Christian. The Bible is enough for knowing everything God wants us to think or do. Think carefully through some of the amazing principles derived from the concept taught in this passage.

The sufficiency of Scripture...

- means that Scripture contains all the words of God we need for salvation, for trusting Him perfectly, and for obeying Him perfectly. There is no "good work" that God wants Christians to do that is not provided for in Scripture. There is nothing God wants you to do that is not taught in Scripture.
- should encourage us to discover what God would have us *think* about a particular issue or *do* in a particular situation. Everything God wants to tell you about a particular issue is to be found in Scripture. Guidance for anything of importance to a well-lived Christian life is provided for in Scripture.
- reminds us that we are to add nothing to Scripture and that we are to consider no other writings of equal value to Scripture. Every cult and sect violates this reality: Mormons, Christian Scientists, and Jehovah's Witnesses are prime examples.
- tells us that God does not require us to believe anything about Himself or His redemptive work that is not found in Scripture.
- shows us that no modern "revelations" from God are to be placed on a level equal to Scripture in authority. Whatever the charismatic movement claims as additional revelations must be subjected to the

scrutiny of Scripture. God doesn't expect you to believe anything that is not revealed in His written Word. Much of this televised Christianity is simply not biblical Christianity. If any such so-called modern revelation adds to or contradicts Scripture, it is clearly not from God.

• tells us that nothing is required of us by God that is not commanded in Scripture either explicitly or by implication.[3]

The clear focus of our search for God's will is to be the Scriptures. Rather than seeking guidance through prayer, changed circumstances, altered feelings, or even direct guidance from the Holy Spirit Himself, we are to rely upon the Scriptures. If God wants you to know it, have it, or experience it, it's there in the Bible. If it is not clearly there, don't seek it.

Without an intimate knowledge of the Field Manual, the Christian soldier will never thrive on the battlefield. That's why it's so critical that the soldier begin his every day with "spiritual reveille." When the sun comes up, the Bible comes open. Call it what you want—devotions, quiet time, spiritual reveille—it is food for soul-thought. It is biblical meditation, turning it over in your mind, chewing on it throughout the day until you've reached the point of assimilation.

My friend Steve Farrar illustrates it graphically when he says meditation is a bit like chewing tobacco. In the morning you take "just a pinch 'tween your cheek and gum." And then, as you go about your tasks, you turn it over and over again along the way. There's something to that illustration (if you can get past the spitting!).

Every day the warrior must feed his soul on the Commander's standing orders.

Every day the warrior must feed his soul on the Commander's standing orders. Hiding the Word of God in your heart is the path to victory in spiritual warfare.

Can your Lord handle the spiritual battles you face? Do you think His resources, strength, and wisdom are up to the challenge of winning the battles in your life, given the kind of spiritual, mental, emotional, and physical challenges you're up against? Of course! He insists on it. Read these two passages:

His divine power has given us everything we need for life and godliness through our knowledge of him who

called us…. He has given us His very great and precious
promises, so that through them you may participate in
the divine nature and escape the corruption in the
world caused by evil desires.

2 PETER 1:3–4, NIV

Even youths grow tired and weary, and young men
stumble and fall; but those who hope in the Lord will
renew their strength. They will soar on wings like
eagles; they will run and not grow weary, they will walk
and not be faint.

ISAIAH 40:30–31, NIV

Careful meditation on His Word allows you to see Him with increasing clarity. When in the midst of battle you see your Lord leading the way,
you fight so much more effectively. Seeing your Lord with clarity provides
a cleansing, a refreshing of heart, and a deep, soulish determination to
fight on. And then in the midst of the battles, you find yourself joyfully
overcome by awe, wonder, joy, intimacy, conviction, brokenness, repentance, refreshment, hope, and strength. You are not alone on the battlefield. The King fights beside you and within you!

Oh, how I love Your law!
    It is my meditation all the day.
How sweet are Your words to my taste!
    Yes, sweeter than honey to my mouth!

PSALM 119:97, 103

How many times during the course of life's battle has the living Word
of God touched my soul? I recall one time when I was feeling hard pressed
by a number of factors. There were external pressures professionally, there
were some difficult family circumstances, and it was a season of increased
pressure for Linda and me in our marriage.

Then, to top it all off, I received some criticism from a very close
friend. It felt like the proverbial straw that broke the camel's back. I
wanted to strike back. I wanted to defend myself. I wanted to toss spiritual maturity out the window and throw a tantrum. But to my mind came
the words that I'd been reading earlier in the day: "Better is open rebuke

Better is open rebuke

than love that is

concealed.

Faithful are the

wounds of a friend.

PROVERBS 27:5-6A

than love that is concealed. Faithful are the wounds of a friend" (Proverbs 27:5–6a).

The Spirit of God used the Word of God at the right time and under the right pressure to make the right verse come to mind—and my soul was quieted. I honestly believe that if I had not experienced a little spiritual reveille that morning around that very verse, I would've become a casualty in the spiritual battlefield of that day.

Thanks, Lord, for the spiritual disciplines of the morning and the power of the Spirit throughout the day.

SUGGESTIONS FOR SPIRITUAL REVEILLE

Here are a few suggestions to get you started in a regular plan of spiritual reveille:

1. Plan a time. Be as consistent as possible every day, whether morning, noon, or night works best for you. Find a time that is least likely to have the "press" of dailyness squeeze it out. That's why early, before the world starts moving, is usually best.
2. Pick a place. This will usually be in your home. But perhaps in your car, at a site with a view, near a park, in an open field, or somewhere else will work best for you.
3. Come thirsty. Cultivate a *desire* to meet with Him. Yes, read Scripture. But love Him, your Savior-Warrior-King. Keep the living Jesus before you. Be still.
4. Come with an approach. Maybe decide to read through the Bible in a year; maybe study an accompanying devotional booklet; maybe take a "read 'til I hit the point of underlining" approach.
5. Memorize portions of His Word. Pick the length, the theme, the passage, and so forth, and then stick with it enough days in a row that it becomes "yours."
6. Periodically, take a little retreat. Take a hike with a pocket Bible, sit under a tree or beside a stream. Worship.

Bottom line: We are Bible people. The Word of God is our sole authority; it contains our only standing orders. *Sola Scriptura* (Scripture alone) is our unit motto, flying like a battle streamer from our unit battle flag. The Bible alone, in its entirety, is our field manual.

It contains nothing less than the standing orders of our Commander in Chief.

*There are two kinds of information that no commander can be without—
information pertaining to the enemy... 'combat intelligence'—
and information on the terrain. Both are vital.*

MATTHEW B. RIDGEWAY,
SOLDIER

*Be of sober spirit, be on the alert. Your adversary, the devil, prowls about like a
roaring lion, seeking someone to devour.*

1 PETER 5:8

*And there was a war in heaven, Michael and his angels waging war with the
dragon. The dragon and his angels waged war...the serpent of old who is called the
devil and Satan, who deceives the whole world.*

REVELATION 12:7-9

MEET THE OPPOSITION

D o you remember some of your childhood imaginations? They were graphic, virtual-reality adventures of all sorts! Most of us can recall them vividly. I can still picture certain rooms and particular hours of the day (bedtime!) when a whole new and fearsome world confronted me.

Some of the adventures we all imagined were light and happy. Those were usually the ones you dreamed up during the daylight hours—like trips to Disneyland, riding magnificent stallions across the terrain, stealthy adventures in the woods, or flying like the hawks circling high in the sky.

But childhood imagination *at night*—that's another story! Terrifying.

I can recall some of my childhood fears as though it were last night. They were fearsome. Monstrous and threatening. Only by summoning all my strength and determination could I hold them down. I fought my way through many an imaginary battle in the dark recesses of my lonely upstairs bedroom.

In fact, I remember two seasons of such battles during my childhood. They took place in two different bedrooms in two different houses. The scenes were set either by the long climb up the stairs to my second-story bedroom in my preschool years or the torturous walk descending the long staircase into the basement where my bedroom was located when I was in my early elementary school years.

Either way, it was a treacherous route of passage for this youngster. At times it required great determination to run those gauntlets. After all, there were monsters in them there shadows.

Upstairs in my hometown of Cle Elum, Washington, the beasts were wolverines. Humpbacked, teeth-baring, young-boy-shredding wolverines! Downstairs in Yakima, they were alligators. And these weren't your ordinary lay-around-in-the-sun-at-the-zoo alligators, either. While recognizable as alligators, they were horribly deformed. Hunched and unnatural in appearance, they had unusual limbs and sharp angles, vicious, snarling teeth and dark, unsettled eyes.

They lived under a guy's bed.

The word was that if you let your foot unwittingly drift over the edge of the bed while asleep, they'd grab it and pull you down, tear you to pieces. They pretty much stayed under the bed during daylight, but they moved about in the dark. That's why you never actually *saw* one, but you knew very well they were there. If you were to quickly flip the lights on and off, you might be able catch them briefly out in the open. I never did catch them out there, and from time to time I'd let my foot slip ever so slightly over the edge of the bed to see if they'd take the bait. They never did get me, but, of course, I never left that foot there long enough to really test 'em!

Sometimes life can be like your worst childhood nightmare. Only it's not a dream. There *is* an evil, dark world out there. And it *is* full of disfigured alligators and demented wolverines.

It seems you're always living right on the edge of their world. And if you're not careful, if you allow yourself to drift, those creatures of the night will grab you, pull you down, and tear you to pieces. You seldom see them coming. They love darkness rather than light, and they don't always look like alligators or wolverines. Sometimes they actually appear as angels of light. But light or dark, seen or unseen, recognized or not, they are capable of destroying you.

That's why the apostle Peter warned you and me to stay alert, to avoid walking too close to the edge: "Be of sober spirit, be on the alert. Your adversary, the devil, prowls about like a roaring lion, seeking someone to devour" (1 Peter 5:8).

The devil.

Everyone believes in him (sort of). But no one *really* believes in him. Surveys indicate that almost three-fourths of the American public believe he is real. But few *act* like it. One thing is certain: Science will never find him. But then, science can't find a lot of things that are real—like love, for example. The fact is that the evil one is a powerful spirit being occupying a world beyond our own. The Bible is so full of references to Satan and his dark realm that a person who does not believe in him really is not qualified to claim the title Christian. If you can't trust the Bible's word about a personal devil, how can you trust the Bible's word about a personal Savior?

Jesus certainly insisted the devil was real and personal, and He constantly warred against him. One day Jesus will end Satan's existence by casting him into the lake of fire prepared for him. But until then we face a living and vicious adversary.

Indeed, we are at war with a very real enemy! This is no childhood dream. This is no dream at all. It is a very real, very dark world.

You don't have to dig too deeply in the Bible to understand that this world we live in is not the real world. It is only temporary. Planet earth is not our eternal home. Someday soon this whole place is goin' up in smoke. And that's when the real world will take shape. The real life—eternal life—and the real world—eternity—are ahead of us. The life we live now is but a shadowlands, a doorway to the better country yet to come.

The Bible teaches us that the quality of our life after death is determined by the quality of our life before death. How you live now determines your reward in heaven.

Now hear this: That same Bible teaches us that the quality of our life after death is determined by the quality of our life *before* death. How you live now determines your reward in heaven. Our Lord intends to reward us for "fighting the good fight" in this life. The New Testament is full of such teaching, encouraging Christians to be "overcomers" and "victors."

Here's the point: We want to win in this life so that we might enjoy what Peter calls a "rich welcome into the eternal kingdom of our Lord and Savior Jesus Christ" (2 Peter 1:11, NIV). This life, lived in a war zone called planet earth, is merely a preparation for the real life and real world yet to come.

As Christian men and women, we live in the crosshairs! This is big. Bigger than you are! You could get shot out there! Devoured! There are creatures out there who don't want you to live for the glory of God. Satan the adversary and his dark angels will stop at nothing to bring you up short.

You have a dark and deformed enemy who seeks to consume you. If you are not alert, you could become a victim, not a victor. A casualty, not a conqueror. When you enter eternity, you want to be what the Scripture calls an overcomer. Listen to how the last book of the Bible describes such victorious Christians:

> "And they overcame him [Satan] because of the blood of
> the Lamb and because of the word of their testimony, and
> they did not love their life even when faced with death."
>   REVELATION 12:11

We've already understood that, for a thinking Christian, war and the Bible go hand in hand. We also know that the way a Christian soldier stays alert, or keeps his way pure, is by immersing himself in the Scriptures, by treasuring God's Word in his heart. You must be meditating on the all-sufficient Word of God—turning it over in your mind to the point of assimilation, until it's part of who you are. By internalizing God's thoughts into your heart and mind, you can experience genuine transformation and win both the internal and external battles.

IDENTIFYING THE ENEMY

One of the most basic principles of warfare is stated in three words: Know your enemy. It carries with it this strong corollary: Never underestimate your enemy.

Never underestimate

your enemy.

Years ago, while serving on active duty with the U.S. Army, I found myself in a nine-week tactical-intelligence course designed for one purpose: to convince us of the absolute necessity of accurate intelligence. Nine weeks just to be sure we caught this principle: If you don't understand the enemy's situation, you're going to get slaughtered! They seemed to think it was important. And it is.

Without a clear and accurate picture of the enemy situation, it isn't likely you'll come out on top. And, much worse, you and a lot of your buddies could come home in body bags.

It's no different in spiritual warfare. If you don't have a basic under-standing of what you're up against, you are very likely going to wander into an ambush somewhere along life's journey. And ambushes, by their very nature, are vicious, destructive, and deadly. We've got to be intelligent about the enemy and alert to his tactics.

David, the warrior king, knew the enemy well. He stated in Psalm 143:3, "The enemy pursues me, he crushes me to the ground; he makes me dwell in darkness" (NIV). We've got to know about him and how to deal with him.

Please note that my purpose here is *not* to give the devil undue atten-tion. Nor do I wish to scare you sufficiently that you live in dread of him. But I do want you to know enough so as not to get caught off guard, but to "stand firm against the schemes of the devil" (Ephesians 6:11). We're going to spend this chapter taking a good look at our ultimate arch-enemy—the devil himself. In another chapter we will look at his army of demons.

As we dive in to take a closer look at the devil himself, let me offer a couple of qualifying statements.

AVOID THE EXTREMES

People in our day tend either to ignore the devil or to be infatuated with him. Neither is any good. As usual, C. S. Lewis said it best:

> There are two equal and opposite errors into which our
> race can fall about the devils. One is to disbelieve in
> their existence. The other is to believe, and to feel an
> excessive and unhealthy interest in them. They them-
> selves are equally pleased by both errors, and hale a
> materialist [nay-sayer] or magician [enthusiast] with the
> same delight."[1]

Whether you deny his existence or obsess over his existence, the devil has you right where he wants you. You're either ignorant and therefore in danger of ambush or preoccupied and therefore neutralized. Some Christians, particularly in the Western world, pooh-pooh the demonic spirit realm. Other Christians take the opposite approach, developing a curious fascination. Neither is healthy.

Frank Peretti's popular works of fiction (*This Present Darkness* and others) have been widely read. These books can be helpful, serving as a healthy warning to those who have taken the dark side too lightly. They are also fiction. F-I-C-T-I-O-N. Just so we don't forget, let's refresh our familiarity with Webster's definition of fiction: "that which is feigned or imagined; invented." Fiction is just that, fiction. Peretti's books and similar ones by other authors are not necessarily unbiblical, but they are often extrabiblical.

Some Christian fiction writers are better than others at reflecting the Scriptures. In my opinion, Randy Alcorn is one of the best. See his book *Lord Foulgrin's Letters.*[2]

For the purposes of this book, we'll stick to the Scriptures themselves. The Scriptures alone and in their entirety are sufficient. In the process, then, we will avoid our own imaginations. And we will not form our doctrine, teaching, or tactics from any of the many sensational stories that represent either the experiences or the imaginations of other people. What may have happened in Aunt Bessie's attic in past decades is hardly a foundation for clear thinking about the dark world.

I'm working hard at trying to make a balanced statement here. Spiritual warfare is real, but it is not silly. It is actual warfare, not showmanship. It is real battle, not entertainment. It is never to be sensationalized. One writer summarized it like this:

> Spiritual warfare is not the mumbo-jumbo incantation
> of spooky experience, but the Christian's daily (and
> often rather mundane) battle to die to self and live for
> Christ…. The dangers of sensationalizing spiritual war-
> fare beyond its biblical paradigm can devastate a
> person's life—spiritually, emotionally, and, all too often,
> even physically.[3]

WHERE DID THE DEVIL COME FROM?

We first meet Satan in the earliest pages of Scripture. In Genesis chapter 3 we come upon an evil, malignant being in the form of a serpent. This creature is full of lies and hate and is clearly the bitter enemy of God, which makes him the archenemy of God's image—mankind. Then, in the last pages of the Bible, we meet him again. Scripture identifies him as "that old serpent, called the Devil, and Satan" (Revelation 12:9, NKJV). From the first pages of Scripture to the last, Satan is the adversary. Where did that snake come from?

Originally, God created hosts of spirit beings with high intelligence and moral judgment. These were the angels, and they were all good. We know that Satan was the senior of the angels. At the time he was called Lucifer, the star of the morning, the son of the dawn. The entire universe was in harmony then. There was no evil. No pain. Only peace and harmony. Lucifer was the magnificent, radiant leader of the angelic world.

Satan is clearly the bitter enemy of God, which makes him the archenemy of God's image—mankind, namely you.

But at some point in the halls of heaven, the senior angel, the Son of the Morning, exerted his will in defiance of God's will (see Isaiah 14). His sin was self-assertion and pride—what C. S. Lewis called "the national religion of hell."

He rebelled from God's authority and was followed in his rebellion by some unknown number of other angels, thereafter referred to as fallen angels. These treacherous angels, Satan included, are referred to in Scripture as demons. Demons are angels who have sinned against God and who now continually work evil.

Satan, then, is the personal name of the head of the demons (Job 1:6). He is the originator of sin (1 John 3:8), and his every fiber—not to mention his every follower—opposes God and seeks to destroy His work.

THE BAD NEWS

Yes, we are in a war. From before the beginning of time—and every single day since—the adversary has marshaled his forces against the living God. The devil will stop at nothing, will do anything that is effective, to destroy the intentions of God. Satan's heart is filled with unbridled rage and hatred toward the living God—and therefore he hates you. At the very heart of Satan's strategy is the destruction of the image of God—the human being.

SATAN HATES GOD—AND YOU!

You, your life, your marriage, your family, and your church are at the very center of the battle. And if you just lay there, you're going to lose them all! There is absolutely no place for passivity in this spiritual battle. Neither are there any neutrals.

Bottom line: Satan is a God hater and human basher. He is the author of terror and destruction, and he will stop at nothing in his attempt to supplant the glory of God.

In the final days of earth, Satan's last-gasp attacks from his bottomless pit will be filled with horror. Revelation describes the hideous plagues that will strike people and cause them to "seek death but not find it." All of these terrors are ultimately Satan's tools. The Book describes it this way: "They have as king over them, the angel of the abyss; his name in Hebrew is Abaddon [Destruction], and in the Greek he has the name Apollyon [Destroyer]" (Revelation 9:11).

Since Abaddon means destruction and Apollyon means destroyer, you know that this is an enemy to be taken seriously. Wake up, soldier: A spiritual being named Destruction the Destroyer hates you and is out to take you down.

SATAN IS PERSONAL

The devil is a person, an individual. He is not some indefinable force or vague influence. He is very real, intense, and personal. He has a name.

Scripture refers to him with a variety of terms, each of which in some way describes his character. He is referred to as the devil...the serpent...the great dragon...the accuser...the murderer...the liar...the deceiver...the tempter...the ruler of this world...the evil one. The two most common names, both of which occur over thirty times in the New Testament, are Satan (meaning adversary), and the devil (meaning obstructer). He is also identified as an angel of light.

SATAN IS SUPERNATURAL AND POWERFUL

Satan operates in the heavenlies. That is, he is a *super*natural creature, otherworldly in his power and capacity. Using the terms of Ephesians 6 we can describe Satan with such words as "principalities and powers...and forces." These are potent words, words of authority, might, intelligence, and vast energy.

This enemy is sinister and wicked. His realm and his specialty is darkness. He does not deal with light or truth except deceptively. His specialty is twisted truth, half-truth, and falsehood. John 8:44 states he was a murderer from the beginning. He is the father of lies. There is no truth in him. He is utterly deceitful and never to be trusted. He is the ultimate narcissist, having deluded himself into the utterly irrational hope that he will replace God. And he remains to this day compulsively self-driven to recruit us to believe his lie.

He Is Scheming and Strategizing

This enemy is intelligent. He is cunning personified. He has perfected schemes, wiles, and strategies. In other words, he uses plans and tools and seductions and deceits, all of which Satan much prefers over frontal attack.

There are, however, elements in his tactics which have an established pattern. We know he is observant and alert, but his lies have a consistent thread or two running through them. Some have suggested that he or his lieutenants are aware of our habits, patterns, weaknesses, and vulnerabilities.

Years ago, there appeared in *Christianity Today* the following imaginary but all too possible dialogue between Satan and one of his underlings, a demon named Fireball. It may well be illustrative of Satan's deceptive tactics. They're talking about their attempt to undermine the Easter season and its emphasis upon Christ's resurrection. The title of the article was "Dark Counsel at Easter."

> The devil's look pierced thin smoke-ribbons and fell on his underling, Fireball. "How are things shaping up this Easter?" he asked.
>
> Fireball shrugged. "Normal. Lots of nice outfits being assembled. Florists doing a big business. Choirs tuning up on the old hymns about victory over the grave."
>
> "Anything serious to our cause?"
>
> "No more than usual. Some of them are always a problem. They *mean* that creed they repeat. But millions of them probably never dig this Easter thing.... Lots of Christians appear to like their ideas better than those in the New Testament. Many of them seem to be taking less and less to the Resurrection."
>
> "Hmm. Very interesting. Immortality is fine. Let them talk about it. But muddy the theme as much as possible.... Try to keep the word *justification* out of their minds. They are not to realize *why* He arose from the dead. And keep them from studying Paul too much, especially where he insists that if Christ did not rise

from the dead, then mankind cannot be saved."

"Noted, Majesty."...

"Deflect them from connecting the Resurrection with stewardship also."

Fireball beamed. "You mean like when Paul comes up with that poetry about the Resurrection, then winds up referring to the passing of the collection plate for the needy?"...

"What really matters, little brother, is that we make *immortality* becloud the issue. Hide from them that awesome blow to our cause when He quit that grave. The Church today must not feel the force of this thing. Never forget how the young Church felt it—they overrode all our philosophical arguments with their very *glow!* Easter shone out of them. You can't stop people who actually believe that death has been done in.... We have to keep the Resurrection out of history so we can keep it out of human personalities. Ethics is involved, spirituality, stewardship, evangelism—everything!"

"Unquestionably."...

"Keep a blanket over that open grave! Never let them peek in and see that it's empty. Let the clergymen copy one of their famous and fluent preachers who said that His body lies in a nameless Syrian tomb but His deathless spirit goes marching on. That sort of thing! Only *outside* that tomb does He have the keys of death and hell! Understand?"

"Understand, Majesty. My assignment is quite clear. I have to steal Easter."

"Go steal it, then. Swallow up the Resurrection in undefined immortality! Keep *Him* locked in that tomb and you can keep Christianity locked up there with Him!" Smoke floated about Satan's grimace. "If the theologians ever really let Him out of that tomb—hell help us! All heaven might break loose!"[4]

Bottom line: Satan uses a thousand tactics in his attempts to thwart God's intentions and destroy human beings, God's image bearers. Satan's tactics have left humans in this world utterly shell-shocked...mentally confused...emotionally needy...sexually disoriented. And, most basically, spiritually bankrupt.

THE GOOD NEWS

Yes, the enemy is powerful. And he's actively scheming to take you out. But take heart, Christian! Greater is He that is in you than he that is in the world (1 John 4:4). Here's some good news for you.

SATAN IS NOT ALL-POWERFUL

Satan may attack you, but he cannot possess you. You must believe Jesus meant what He said when He stated, "All authority in heaven and on earth has been given to Me" (Matthew 28:18). You are Christ's possession and no one can pluck you out of His hand (John 10:28, NIV). You must have confidence in the Scriptural assurance that if you resist the devil, he will flee from you (James 4:7).

All of this means that as powerful as the devil or any other principality and power may be, that power is rendered utterly toothless against you because of the Cross of Jesus Christ. If the Creator of the universe says you are free in His Son, then you must believe it and disregard any teaching that suggests otherwise.

As one astute observer noted: "Too many Christians are forgetting this truth and surrendering to a disarmed and defeated enemy. They regard the emotional weight of an experience to be more truthful than the Word of God, and they stumble in their fear and confusion...."[5]

SATAN IS NOT ALL-KNOWING

We know he has been defeated, but he has not yet been executed. He is no weakling. He is nothing to be trifled with. At the same time it is important to remember that he is a created being, subject to the limitations of his creation. He is neither all-powerful nor all-knowing. Only God is.

This is good news. It means Satan doesn't have the deck stacked against you. It means that he can't see or know the future except as God has revealed it to mankind. He schemes against us and sets us up for attack, but not knowing the future, he can never be certain his plans won't backfire. Instead of taking his bait we can run to God or a friend and actually gain strength rather than lose it. This is a risk he takes again and again with us. We can actually thrive against him. God has a way of using even Satan's evil to advance His own divine story.

SATAN CANNOT ACT OUTSIDE THE KNOWLEDGE AND PURPOSES OF GOD

God is with you at all times. Satan cannot take you where you are not willing to go. God has him on a leash, so to speak. You can bear it.

Can you see in these passages God's authority over the devil's activity?

- Then Jesus was led up by the Spirit into the wilderness to be tempted by the devil (Matthew 4:1).
- Then the LORD said to Satan, "Behold, all that he has is in your power, only do not put forth your hand on him" (Job 1:12).
- "Simon, behold, Satan has demanded permission to sift you like wheat, but I have prayed for you, that your faith may not fail, and you, when once you have turned again, strengthen your brothers" (Luke 22:31–32).

Here's the point: Nothing the devil can throw at you can overpower you if you walk with Christ. "Greater is He who is in you than he who is in the world" (1 John 4:4b).

NEVERTHELESS, THE BATTLE RAGES ON

Simply put, the devil is a defeated foe. Scripture makes it gloriously clear that Satan's defeat is guaranteed. Never forget that, spirit warrior! While Christians must be alert to his schemes, we are never to live in dread of him. He is a defeated enemy.

Think of it this way: The war's outcome is secure. Final victory is guaranteed. The decisive battle has already been fought—and won. Christ's victory was won not on Pork Chop Hill or Hamburger Hill or San Juan Hill or some other piece of famous high ground, but on a hill called Calvary, the most decisive battlefield in all of history.

But that does *not* mean the bullets have stopped flying. As we pointed out before, D day is one thing; V day is something else.

Satan's defeat is certain. But, like Hitler directing the war out of his Berlin bunker, he still rages in his defeat. He is still a fierce fighter. His fiery darts are still real. And people still go down.

Yes, the victory is secure, but the battle is unfinished. On a day yet future, the victorious Christ will cast Satan headlong into the eternal lake of fire, and at last it will be over.

That day is coming.

But it isn't here yet.

THE CASUALTIES CONTINUE TO MOUNT

In the violence of Satan's death throes, he still manages to take plenty of people down with him. Unfortunately, many Christian people still:

- fall into temptation,
- quench the Spirit of God,
- isolate themselves from the church,
- don't control their own appetites,
- fail to resist the evil one, and
- make extremely poor choices that leave them victims rather than victors.

Christian people still go down as casualties on the battlefield, ambushed and beaten up by the evil one. Some are violent and direct attacks. But most are more subtle—devious ambushes of the mind and soul. All are destructive. And, unfortunately, in many cases Christians actually *cooperate* with the enemy. Rather than being soldiers on alert, they act like partygoers who've had a powerful drug slipped in their drinks. Dreamily looking for personal happiness, they wander down dangerous side trails. Arriving thoughtlessly at the edge of the precipice, they throw themselves into the sinkhole of sin.

Such self-inflicted wounds do double damage to the kingdom. They not only consume the self-shooter, they destroy the morale of other soldiers in the unit.

I am so painfully aware of Christian people in my own church family who, thinking they are entitled to complete personal happiness, walk away from their mates and families. Then they distance themselves from their friends. And the pain spreads, seeping like toxin into the soil of surrounding lives.

Self-inflicted wounds do double damage to the kingdom.

- The wounds go deeper.
- The kids fall apart.
- More lives take the shrapnel.
- The church suffers.
- Eternal reward is lost.

And many of these people—in the very process of such overt, unre-pentant sin and disobedience—have the audacity to say they "feel closer to God than ever before." Wrong. That is only because they have redefined God and their relationship to Him. They have allowed themselves, like Adam and Eve before them, to fall victim to a satanic twisting of God's Word and a devilish contorting of human emotions.

A couple of fresh casualties come vividly to my mind right now. These individuals were involved in the process of divorcing their mates without a shred of biblical justification. They clung to the usual, baseless, cultural norm—"My first concern is my own welfare." Translate that, "I want to be happy as I define it at the moment. Nothing else matters." Nothing matters, such as God, His Word, or submission to Him.

These people were not yet divorced. Christian brothers and sisters wept with them and begged them to reconsider. But their decision had been made. Their language was chosen. Their attitude was sealed, and their ongoing pursuit of divorce constituted clear and undeniable sin. And one day, at the heavenly battlefield awards ceremony, they will be passed over.

One of the casualties even had the clarity of mind to recognize his bla-tant sin. The precise words were: "I have not abandoned my faith. Even through all this cynicism. I will return. Not to church, and probably not to my wife. But I still love the Lord deeply and cannot abandon Him. I am in sin. I am taking advantage of grace. Each day, even my next breath, I owe to His love and forgiveness. My days are numbered living like this. But one thing I do know, what I have found here [in this extramarital affair] I will never experience with my wife. It is not possible."

To which all of God's people must shout, "So what?"

Where is it written that the purpose of your life is to feel happy? Everywhere it is written you must keep your covenant. Choose this day whom you will serve! Your Lord or yourself? If you choose self, count on the necessary consequences in this life and in the life to come.

In such ugly cases where there is no repentance, there is no heart to deal with the plain meaning of the Scriptures. Such people know perfectly well that what they are doing is absolutely contrary to God's will. Still they tend to state in vague, almost syrupy, and most certainly self-deceiving terms that even though they know they are sinning, they "feel" closer to God than they ever have before.

Let me tell you a secret, friend: *It is impossible to get closer to God by sinning.* To the contrary, Scripture suggests that people engaging in such direct, open-eyed, willful "sin of the high hand" are in danger of God's direct judgment. Some died because of it (Acts 5:1–10; 1 Corinthians 11:30). And the devil wins another skirmish.

We twist the Word to our own liking. We question the plain meaning of Scripture. We convince ourselves, "Oh, He couldn't have really meant *that.*" And as Satan's lie is believed, another marriage dies. Another family dissolves, slowly and internally. Another small civilization withers. And eternal reward is lost. The casualties are strewn all about. That's what's so horrible about war! And it's only made worse when the wounds are self-inflicted in order to avoid the real battle.

Refuse it, my friend! Fight it! Stand firm! Be victorious soldiers. Be overcomers. You cannot expect to walk closely with Jesus without getting into a fight for your faith.

That's the purpose of our considering these truths together. When spirit warriors across this nation and throughout the world open their eyes and submit their lives to the power of the living Christ, heaven will break out across our poor, broken planet.

And heaven knows we need that!

Do not neglect to show hospitality to strangers,
for by this some have entertained angels without knowing it.

HEBREWS 13:2

The empire of angels is as vast as God's creation.

BILLY GRAHAM

And there was war in heaven, Michael and his angels
waging war with the dragon. The dragon and his angels waged war, and they were
not strong enough, and there was no longer a place found for them in heaven.

REVELATION 12:7-8

DON'T FORGET YOUR ALLIES

Don never thought much about angels, one way or another. But that was before he learned that angels could swim. And it was before he realized that, for whatever reason, God had plans for his life.

I met Don a few years ago while I was speaking at a conference. After the first afternoon session an impressive-looking man in his sixties approached me and invited me to his room to talk. Don was tall, tanned, and physically fit, with intense blue eyes and striking silver hair trimmed close. Turns out he had done a stint in the Marines as a fighter pilot, but had spent the last thirty-five years in a successful business.

But Don didn't want to talk about his business or the Marines. He wanted to tell me about how he came to faith in Jesus Christ. He wanted someone who understood the Bible to listen to his personal story and give an opinion. Here's the essence of what I heard that afternoon.

Don and a man named John, Don's most trusted employee and an experienced seaman, had been ferrying a yacht down the Atlantic coast from South Carolina to Florida. The only two crewmen on this large vessel, they were having a ball out under the bright sun on that wide-open blue water, far out at sea.

During the afternoon, while John was at the wheel on the bridge, Don occupied himself coiling ropes on the fantail. The sea was choppy, but nothing the men were particularly concerned about. Then, without warning, a freak wave slapped Don right off the deck into the sea. Completely unaware of Don's desperate plight, John stayed at the wheel and continued to steam ahead.

You and I can only imagine the horror and hopelessness Don experienced—treading water as best he could while watching his only hope cruise toward the horizon. Don's lean body was not well suited to floating. And dressed in shorts, he didn't even have the option of making a refillable flotation balloon out of his trousers. To top it all off, the area was known to be infested with sharks.

Nevertheless, Don's marine discipline (something that never quite leaves you) enabled him to fight off the urge to panic.

Time passed, and the yacht disappeared from sight. Three quarters of an hour went by. Don grew tired, but fought on. He had managed to keep his mind and emotions under tight control, but the temperature of the water began to take its toll on his body. At 98.6 degrees, the body is normal. At 90 degrees, it's starting to shut down. At 86 degrees, you're dead. Hypothermia quite literally kills you by degrees.

Eventually too weak to tread water with his head above the surface, Don resorted to gasping for air and letting his body drift downward in the water several feet below the surface. Then he would fight desperately to the surface again to refill his lungs. Only to repeat the process. This went on for a long time.

But Don was gradually losing the battle.

He wondered how long he would be able to hold off hypothermia. Eventually, he became so weak it was difficult to even get his arms to move. There were moments when he wanted desperately to just quit. To give up. To yield to the quiet of death.

At more than one point Don heard an all too audible voice. Rough, raspy, and void of emotion, the voice told him that it wasn't any use—that he might as well give up. Don is reasonably confident he was hearing the voice of the devil.

But the former fighter pilot refused to surrender. He actually shouted back in defiance...and continued to fight for life. Then, as Don surfaced for what he thought must be the final time, he heard a boat engine.

John, aboard the yacht, had finally missed him. Fortunately he knew enough to execute an accurate 180 degree turn, and follow a strict back azimuth on his previous course in an attempt to locate his missing shipmate. From the bridge he scanned the water systematically from side to side with his nautical binoculars. Nothing.

Meanwhile in the water, Don heard the approaching yacht.

But he had no strength to shout.

He couldn't even raise an arm.

By this time the troughs in the waves were deep enough that he was completely out of sight more than 50 percent of the time. His desperate mind formed a plan. He would wait until the engine sound was as loud as possible. He would wait until his body was carried by the wave action from the trough to the crest of the wave. At the crest he would muster his final ounce of energy and attempt to flop his arm, since he was no longer able to wave.

Just as he crested a wave he flopped his arm across his head. In the providence of God, his friend's binoculars crossed that point in the borderless ocean just as Don made his last, desperate move. John did what Don calls a "Hollywood double take." He'd spotted his friend.

But in some ways, the trials were just beginning.

The tricky part would be hauling an exhausted, water-soaked man up over the fantail of the yacht while it rode the Atlantic swells. Don recalls thinking, *I sure hope he doesn't jump into the water for me without a line securing himself to the boat.*

Don distinctly heard the welcome splash, but he was so weak he couldn't make it to the boat's fantail. He remembers sinking in the water, seeing sunlight through seawater and the bubbles from his friend's splash. But exhausted as he was, he had no strength to even stay afloat until his friend could reach him.

Suddenly—and with vast relief—he felt his friend's strong hands on his back. John's forceful shove propelled Don forward enough through the water to allow him to grip the fantail.

But there was no strength to get his leg up onto the yacht to make that last, desperate lunge to safety. Again, it was his friend's hand on his buttocks and leg that thrust him up onto the fantail and completed the rescue.

The nightmare was over. The Coast Guard helicopter arrived and rushed Don to the hospital.

The next morning, having piloted the boat to harbor, John entered Don's hospital room. They laughed and rejoiced that it had all turned out just great. They talked about the whole ordeal, from the freak wave to the long, lonely struggle to how to skillfully run a back azimuth. The whole nine yards.

At one point Don said, "Well, I was sure hoping you had sense enough to tie yourself to the boat when you piled into the water to save me. Without that line we could both have been lost, unable to reach the boat in that turbulent sea."

That's when they realized something strange was up.

John's face creased in confusion. He said, "Don, I never left the boat. I'm just glad *you* had enough strength left to make it those last few yards. I thought I'd never get you pulled up onto the fantail, but you sure pulled it all together with your final lunge. I guess a desperate man can muster some kind of special reserve strength."

"John, I had *no* strength," Don said. "None! I couldn't possibly have made it to the boat on my own—let alone climb onto it. You shoved me to the boat with your hand on my buttocks. And *you* pushed my leg up onto that fantail!"

"No, Don, I never left the boat."

"Well, then *who did?*"

"No one did. There was no one else out there on that ocean. It was just the two of us."

That's when Don realized he must have been aided by something or someone supernatural. He must have been the beneficiary of an angel's work. As a result of that encounter, that tough ex-marine subsequently surrendered his life to Jesus Christ.

Angels. What do you think? Are they real? Do they do things like that? Was Don saved by an angel? I think so. I know Don well now, and I can tell you he's not a man given to excess or delusion. He is a man, a marine, with his wits very much about him.

We'll probably never know precisely what happened out there on the blue Atlantic that day. Not this side of heaven. But you can know what the Bible says about angels. And that's what this chapter is all about.

ANGELMANIA

The New Testament says it this way in Hebrews 13:2: "Do not neglect to show hospitality to strangers, for by this some have entertained angels without knowing it."

Of course angels are real. Scripture clearly indicates they have been

frequent visitors to our embattled planet, sometimes visible as mighty spirit beings and sometimes
in human form. Yes, angels, the bright hosts of
heaven, are very much a part of spiritual warfare.
The holy angels are God's personal messengers.
And they are the Christian's allies in this very real
spiritual war.

> *Angels are real.*
>
> *But don't believe*
>
> *everything you hear*
>
> *about them.*

But don't believe everything you hear about
them.

Many today are fascinated by stories, myths,
legends, and testimonies of angel sightings.
Consequently, most of what you hear espoused today is based on myth,
misinformation, and outright deception. The angels of our current popular culture are more like the fairies in fairy tales, rather than the radiant
beings of biblical revelation.

Angels are incredibly popular these days, especially to those who are
attracted to the peripheries of spirituality and the spirit world. *Time* magazine reported in the nineties that 69 percent of Americans believe in the
existence of angels. The craze is real. People produce bimonthly newslet-
ters about angels. For example, "Angel Watch" is free-thinking Eileen
Freeman's newsletter out of New Jersey. She believes that "angels tran-
scend every religion, every philosophy, every creed. In fact, angels have no
religion."[1]

You can find all kinds of Web sites related to angels, including one I
stumbled onto called "The Temple of Angels." The site claims to be "dedicated to the glory of God and to the glory of angels."

There's a big red light right off the top. God shares His glory with no
one.

Christians and non-Christians alike are drawn to the subject of angels.
And as you might expect, there's a ton of books out there: *Where Angels
Walk, Angels Watching Over Me, A Rustle of Angels, Ask your Angels, 100
Ways to Attract Angels, Angel Walk,* and more. There's even one entitled
The Angel Book: A Handbook for Aspiring Angels.

The great bulk of the popular books about angels have everything to
do with anecdotal experiences and seemingly little to do with scriptural
exposition.

You'll find angel images everywhere. Angel bookends. Angel candle
holders. Angel ashtrays. Angel card decks, calendars, cookies, and coffee

mugs. There are even entire stores given over to angel books and souvenirs—like the one in the Hawthorne district in southeast Portland, Oregon. The Hawthorne district is notorious for being the center of much of Portland's "New Age-granola-far-out" culture. The location there ought to tell us something about the craze. Angels are a hot topic among the biblically illiterate.

During one television ratings week, the program *Touched by an Angel* ranked third with a 16.6 Neilsen rating—meaning more than 16 million households were tuned in to watch the three angels depicted there. *TV Guide* magazine even felt compelled to do a featured special report on "God and Television."

The program *Touched by an Angel* is not a bad program. Basically, it portrays *some* biblical truths. The show's producer, Martha Williamson, says it the best way she knows how: "Our show [portrays] that God exists. God loves us. God wants to be part of our lives." Della Reese, one of the actors, adds that God "has a plan."

Yes, the program is good in that it does offer a view of life which competes with sheer naturalism. It supports the notion that there is a personal, caring God, and that faith has a legitimate place in our lives. But the critical viewer needs to ask, *"What* God?" The program does not necessarily elevate the God of Scripture.

Della Reese insists that their show is not about religion but only about a "supreme being." As a matter of fact, it is reported that Della (whose character Tess was voted the person parents would most want as their kids' Sunday school teacher) is the pastor of a metaphysical congregation in west Los Angeles. She is an active participant in what is called the "New Thought Movement," which prefers to describe itself as "creedless" and "celebrates individual freedom." Be careful you don't follow Della's angelic caricature.

My point is this: Don't believe everything you hear about angels. Don't form your doctrine of angels from popular sources, even reasonably healthy TV programming. Get your information on angels strictly from Scripture. Without a personal saving knowledge of Jesus Christ, all the angel talk in the world is valueless. We human beings need a Savior, not an angel!

Following are three constant cautions—three hazard lights for your internal dashboard—when it comes to considering the topic of angels.

*1. Never let your imagination shape your under-
standing of angels.*

Broadly speaking, most of what you will see, hear,
and read concerning angels in contemporary litera-
ture is the product of active human imagination—
not solid biblical reality. If you want the straight
scoop on these powerful allies of God's people, go
directly to the Bible, not coffee table books, maga-
zines, or tabloids.

*Never let your
imagination shape your
understanding of angels.*

2. Never let your heart pursue angels in place of God in your life.

This is a constant temptation for people because of our natural fascination
with the unseen world around us. Angels are real. They are also created
beings. They are not God. The first of the Ten Commandments makes it
clear that you must have "no other gods" before Him! Know God, not angels.
Study your Lord, not His messengers. And that leads to the ultimate caution.

3. Never let your soul worship angels.

Never give them glory, honor, or worship. They are mere creatures. The evil
one, himself an angel (albeit fallen), would love to divert you from the Living
One. That is the story of Romans 1: We tend to worship the created thing
rather than the Creator. Never allow your fascination to drift in that direction.

Larry Libby, in his excellent book for children entitled *Somewhere
Angels,* catches the right spirit when he asks:

> Would angels like this book? One thing you can be
> pretty sure about…angels aren't too excited about angel
> books. Angels, you see, don't like to be the center of
> attention. Angels may not even like having people *think*
> about them very much. Do you know why? Because
> angels live for only one reason. With all their angel
> hearts, they long to please and serve God. Angels live to
> obey God's command and do EXACTLY what He says
> as fast and well as they possibly can…. "What's the
> point of a book about *us?*" an angel might say. "We're
> only God's helpers just like you. We do only what *He*
> says. We go only where *He* sends. We say only what *He*

tells us. Write your book about your heavenly Father
and king Jesus—if you have to write another book at
all. Why get all excited about the King's messengers
when you could talk about the King!"[2]

So we'll go where the Bible goes—and we won't go beyond it.[3] Just
what, then, *does* the Bible say about angels? It says a great deal. In the few
pages that follow we'll seek to survey the mountain peaks, rather than
attempting to chart a much wider biblical terrain. Ready to fly?

ANGELS ACCORDING TO THE BIBLE

The Bible is our only authoritative source of information regarding spiritual realities. It is divinely inspired revelation—information we would
have no other way of knowing. And, yes, the Bible speaks about angels.
The Bible was into angels before angels were cool. God's Word offers a
wealth of rich teaching about angels, but it does not tell us everything we
would like to know. The Bible was not given to satisfy our curiosity but to
stimulate our pursuit of solid, authentic, spiritual truth and life.

Billy Graham says it this way: "The empire
of angels is as vast as God's creation. If you
believe the Bible, you will believe in their ministry. They crisscross the Old and New
Testaments, being mentioned directly or indi-
rectly nearly three hundred times."[4] To be more
specific, angels are referred to in thirty-four of
the sixty-six books of the Bible. They are mentioned 108 times in the Old Testament and 165
times in the New Testament.[5]

"The empire of angels is as vast as God's creation."

John Calvin wrote: "Angels are the dispensers and administrators of
the divine beneficence toward us. They regard our safety, undertake our
defense, [and] direct our ways."[6]

In Scripture, angels act as God's messengers, His emissaries. Clearly,
holy angels are our allies in this spiritual warfare. We are on the same
team—the winning team.

Obviously, we can't examine all three hundred biblical references to
angels here in a single chapter. But we can take a look at a healthy sampling.
Let's learn a bit about them.

What follows is something of a "crash course" in angelology. It's adapted from Wayne Grudem's *Systematic Theology: An Introduction to Biblical Doctrine.*

Grudem gives us a simple, clear, biblically precise definition of angels: "Angels are created, spiritual beings with moral judgment and high intelligence, but without physical bodies."[7]

ANGELS ARE CREATED

They have not always existed. According to Colossians 1:16, the angels were created by and for Christ. While they are supernatural, they are not divine.

ANGELS ARE SPIRITUAL BEINGS

They do not ordinarily have physical bodies (Luke 24:39). They are therefore invisible to us (Psalm 34:7; Hebrews 1:14; 12:22) unless God makes special provision for them to be seen (Numbers 22:31; Luke 2:13). Sometimes they do take on the bodily form of adult human males to appear to people in Scripture (Matthew 28:5; Hebrews 13:2). Interestingly enough, angels in the Bible never appear in female form.

What angels really look like is a major point of our curiosity. And their different biblical appearances are far from uniform. But we can say this: Like so many of the created world's great wonders, angels are awe inspiring.

Recall the overwhelming sensation of standing at the edge of a towering cliff overlooking a wilderness vista or being deafened by the roar of a huge, thundering waterfall. Remember how you felt? Remember the fearsome beauty? Remember the majesty and power that seemed to pull the air right out of your lungs? So it is with the appearance of angels. Fresh from the presence of our awesome God, their appearance stops us humans in our tracks. And the record of those encountering them usually registers some form of fear.

Listen to Daniel's experience:

> I looked up and saw a man dressed in linen clothing,
> with a belt of pure gold around his waist. His body
> looked like a dazzling gem. From his face came flashes
> like lightning, and his eyes were like flaming torches.
> His arms and feet shone like polished bronze, and his
> voice was like the roaring of a vast multitude of people.

I, Daniel, am the only one who saw this vision. The
men with me saw nothing, but they were suddenly terrified and ran away to hide. So I was left there all alone
to watch this amazing vision. My strength left me, my
face grew deathly pale, and I felt very weak. When I
heard him speak, I fainted and lay there with my face to
the ground.

DANIEL 10:5-9, NLT

ANGELS HAVE A VARIETY OF NAMES OR TITLES

The term *angel* means "messenger." Sometimes angels are referred to as
"sons of God" (Job 1:6), "holy ones" (Psalm 89:5), "spirits" (Hebrews
1:14), "watchers" (Daniel 4:13), "thrones, dominions, rulers, authorities"
(Colossians 1:16), and "powers" (Ephesians 1:21).

THERE SEEM TO BE SPECIAL CATEGORIES OF ANGELS

Cherubim guarded the entrance to the Garden of Eden (Genesis 3:24).
God Himself is sometimes described as traveling in the company of cherubim (Psalm 18:10; Ezekiel 10). Two golden angelic forms stretched their
wings above the ark of the covenant where God met with His people
(Exodus 25:22).

Seraphim (from the verbal root meaning "to burn"), mentioned only
in Isaiah 6:2–7, are stationed in the throne room of heaven worshiping the
Lord and calling His glory out in foundation-shaking decibels.

THERE APPEARS TO BE RANK AND ORDER AMONG THE ANGELS

Only one angel, Michael, is called an archangel (Jude 1:9), a title which
suggests his rule over other angels. He appears to be a warrior commander
among the angels as well (Daniel 10:13). Paul tells us the Lord Himself
will return from heaven heralded by the triumphant shout of the archangel
(1 Thessalonians 4:16).

ONLY TWO HOLY ANGELS ARE NAMED IN SCRIPTURE

Michael is mentioned in Daniel 10, Jude 9, and Revelation 12:7–8. In the
last passage, he is called "one of the chief princes." The angel Gabriel

(whose name means "mighty one of God") is mentioned in Daniel 8:16 and 9:21, where he is depicted as a messenger who addresses Daniel the prophet. He is also the messenger to Zechariah and Mary in Luke 1:19 at the birth of Christ.

ANGELS ARE NOT OMNIPRESENT

They are described as traveling from one place to another. For example, Gabriel was "sent from God to a city in Galilee called Nazareth" (Luke 1:26).

ANGELS ARE INNUMERABLE

Scripture gives no specific total, but we know there are a very large number of angels.

Deuteronomy 33:2 notes at Sinai that God "came from the midst of ten thousand holy ones; at His right hand there was flashing lightning for them." Psalm 68:17 (NIV) tells us that "the chariots of God are tens of thousands and thousands of thousands." (Doesn't that make you wonder about all of those heavenly horses pulling those chariots?)

In the New Testament, Hebrews 12:22 (NKJV) speaks of us one day coming to worship in the presence of "innumerable...angels." Jesus tells His disciples there were at least six legions of angels (72,000) stationed in proximity to His crucifixion. Revelation simply refers to their numbers as "myriads of myriads, and thousands of thousands" (Revelation 5:11).

DO PEOPLE HAVE INDIVIDUAL GUARDIAN ANGELS?

Angels do protect God's people (Psalm 91:11–12). Jesus hints that children may have special cohorts watching over them: "In heaven their angels are always in the presence of my heavenly Father" (Matthew 18:10, NLT). While there is no convincing proof in Scripture of every individual Christian having a guardian angel per se, it can be said in general that angels do protect God's people. Some have suggested the angelic cohorts may be playing zone defense rather than man to man.

When Corrie ten Boom arrived at Ravensbruck, the Nazi prison camp to which she'd been sent, she believed that an angel blocked the eyes of the Nazi guards to keep them from finding the Bible hidden under her clothing. The guards found everything else which others attempted to conceal, but Corrie miraculously walked through two complete searches with her Bible intact. Did an angel block the guards' eyes? The whole camp certainly benefited from Corrie's presence and faith in that wretched place.

There are many other similar incidents on record and no compelling reasons to doubt them.

I sometimes wonder if there isn't some kind of angelic protection in effect outside my office window at the corner of Haley Road and U.S. 26, the major intersection near our church. Highway 26 is a four-lane, full-speed freeway. But it is not limited access. Farm roads, like our own Haley Road, cross it regularly. There is no traffic signal, only a blinking yellow light. Over the twenty years we have been at our current location, our church people have certainly been delivered! Think of it: Over twenty years of incredible traffic along a notoriously dangerous section of highway, and virtually "zero defects" so far as our church people are concerned. Yes, I believe in angels.

SOME CAUTIONS

The Bible warns against believing any doctrine that does not square with Scripture, even if it appears to come from angels (Galatians 1:8). The apostle says, "Even if we, or an angel from heaven, should preach to you a gospel contrary to what we have preached to you, he is to be accursed!" Satan, a fallen angel himself, can still appear as an angel of light in order to deceive God's own (2 Corinthians 11:14). Further, we are never to worship or glorify an angel (Colossians 2:18). Those honors belong to God and God alone (Revelation 19:10).

We are never to pray to angels (contrary to the instruction of some "angelic" Web sites). "There is...one mediator between God and men, the man Christ Jesus" (1 Timothy 2:5).

Angels certainly made spectacular appearances in biblical history—and will do so again in the biblical prophetic future. There is no compelling reason to rule out the possibility of angelic appearances today, although the sufficiency of Scripture and the closing of the canon seem to argue against a high frequency of appearances today.

Believers should use extreme caution in receiving any so-called guidance from an angel today, should such an unusual occurrence take place. An angelic appearance would be highly unusual in our day and should be carefully and critically evaluated against the Scriptures in the presence of wise, biblical counselors who are not given to exaggerated or showy flamboyance. Scripture is our only authoritative guide and is sufficient to render every believer "adequate, equipped for every good work" which God expects of him (2 Timothy 3:17).

TO SUM IT UP....

Angels are created beings with moral judgment, high intelligence, and fearsome supernatural power. Their purpose is to serve the Creator as His attendants and messengers. They patrol the earth as God's representatives (Zechariah 1:10–11), and they conduct warfare operations against Satan's minions (Daniel 10:13; Revelation 12:7–8).

Angels advance His kingdom purposes on earth by guiding, comforting, protecting, and enlightening His people. They do battle in His name and for His purposes. They are sometimes involved in punishing unbelievers (Acts 12:23). They will act as heavenly reapers at the end of the age (Matthew 13:39). Angels are magnificent warrior beings who serve as the agents of God's judgment (2 Chronicles 32:21; Acts 12:23; Revelation 16:1), divine wrath, and power.

Angels are never the smiling, chubby-cheeked cherubs pictured on modern greeting cards. To the contrary, the sheer power of angels is immense—and the response of those who face it is generally one of overwhelming terror (Luke 1:28–29; Matthew 28:4; Revelation 19:10; 22:8–9). They are called "mighty ones who do his bidding" (Psalm 103:20, NIV).

On a day yet future a mighty angel will seize Satan, bind him for a thousand years, and throw him into the abyss (Revelation 20:1–3). What a day that will be!

THE "RIGHT KIND OF EYES"

Remember, then, angels are real, and they are at work, whether we have eyes to see them or not. Just remember that they are merely agents of the living God. They serve to advance His kingdom by assisting His people at strategic points. We are normally unaware of their presence or effectiveness. And when we are aware, it is only because God has given us special sight to see for a moment beyond our physical world.

Angels are real, and they are at work, whether we have eyes to see them or not.

Scripture tells us how the prophet Elisha and his servant were granted such special vision. The experience grew out of some very dark days in Israel's history.

> Now when the attendant of the man of God had risen
> early and gone out, behold, an army with horses and
> chariots was circling the city. And his servant said to
> him, "Alas, my master! What shall we do?" So he
> answered, "Do not fear, for those who are with us are
> more than those who are with them." Then Elisha
> prayed and said, "O, LORD, I pray, open his eyes that
> he may see." And the LORD opened the servant's eyes,
> and he saw; and behold, the mountain was full of horses
> and chariots of fire all around Elisha.
>
> 2 KINGS 6:15–17

Elisha had the right kind of eyes! Occasionally, I believe God may give us special sight for a moment of personal encouragement at a major life crisis—such as facing our own deaths. The Apostle Paul writes:

> I pray for you constantly, asking God, the glorious
> Father of our Lord Jesus Christ, to give you spiritual wis-
> dom and understanding.... I pray that your hearts will
> be flooded with light so that you can understand the
> wonderful future he has promised to those he called.... I
> pray that you will begin to understand the incredible
> greatness of his power for us who believe him.
>
> EPHESIANS 1:16–19, NLT

Like Elisha and his servant, we need the right kind of eyes—eyes of the heart, flooded with the light of biblical hope and reality! And some-times, I believe, God does just that in our own day and age. He gives us a temporary optical adjustment to see what we could never see apart from His enabling. As I mentioned, I think this may be particularly true as we draw near to our time of passing from this world.

The Bible says, "Precious in the sight of the LORD is the death of His godly ones" (Psalms 116:15).

In this regard, let me offer a personal observation garnered over more than a quarter-century of full-time ministry. *People die like they live.* If you live in your own wisdom and poor attitude, you'll reflect that on your deathbed. Complainers die complaining. Bitter folks die in a black swamp of bitterness. But if you live by God's wisdom and His perspective, you'll reflect that in your parting moments. People who walk with Jesus die with Jesus.

Those with eyes and hearts to see, often do. And it seems He often gives them a glimpse of what awaits…the presence of angels, heaven, and His own magnificent Person. Remember Evelyn Hofeld's story in chapter 3?

Angels, however, have a great deal more to do than appear in human visions. Whenever Scripture mentions them, they always seem to be on the job—and busy as can be. Let's take a brief stroll through the pages of Scripture and highlight some angelic "special operations" in the kingdom's battles.

SPECIAL OPERATIONS

Our own nation's Special Ops units are those military forces highly trained to operate behind enemy lines—and particularly in precarious situations. They include such units as the SEALs, the Rangers, and the Green Berets.

Angels operating on planet earth are certainly behind enemy lines. Whenever God's angels step into this earthly airspace, they must in some sense contend with "the prince of the power of the air…the spirit that is now working in the sons of disobedience" (Ephesians 2:2; see also Daniel 10:4–14).

The purposes and activities of angels might be categorized in many ways. For our intentions, we'll group them into just two very general categories: angels as messengers and angels as ministers. They are messengers of God's information and ministers of God's operation.

Both the Hebrew and Greek words translated *angel* mean simply and plainly "messenger." In other words, one of the primary functions of angels as they relate to our world is to provide God's people with care and information.

This "messaging" function of angels is on a grand or strategic scale, in contrast to a personal or tactical scale. That is, God has used angels to communicate His intentions at critical junctures in the progressive development of the kingdom program on earth. Angels are not used to respond as personal message boys for your individual questions or concerns. Angels report to God alone.

ANGELS AS MESSENGERS

Let's do a quick walk-through of a few typical biblical examples of angels as messengers—providing communication and information at critical points in the kingdom's advancement. An angel was sent:

- *To Abraham...* An angel brought the supernatural announcement of the Messiah's line through a son, delivered by God Himself and two angels at the tent near the oaks of Mamre (Genesis 18:1–19).
- *To Moses...* The angel of the Lord announced the deliverance of the chosen people in Exodus 3:2–8. The people of Israel knew it too. Numbers 20:16 (KJV) states: "When we cried unto the LORD, he heard our voice, and hath sent an angel, and has brought us forth out of Egypt."
- *To Mary...* This is the extraordinary visit of a mighty angel to a private home in a little town of Galilee. His announcement was like no other: "Now in the sixth month the angel Gabriel was sent from God to a city in Galilee called Nazareth, to a virgin engaged to a man whose name was Joseph" (Luke 1:26–27).
- *To Joseph...* An angel used a dream to convey an urgent message: "And Joseph...being a righteous man and not wanting to disgrace her, planned to send her away secretly. But when he had considered this, behold, an angel of the Lord appeared to him in a dream, saying, 'Joseph, son of David, do not be afraid to take Mary as your wife'" (Matthew 1:19–20).
- *At the resurrection...* An angel at Jesus' tomb, seated on the rock in front of an open grave, terrified a squad of Roman guards. "And behold, a severe earthquake had occurred, for an angel of the Lord descended from heaven and came and rolled away the stone and sat upon it. And his appearance was like lightning, and his clothing as white as snow. The guards shook for fear of him and became like dead men" (Matthew 28:2–4).
- *In the prophetic future...* A soaring angel in the heavens will again announce the kingdom's next step of advancement. "And I saw another angel flying in midheaven, having an eternal gospel to preach to those who live on the earth, and to every nation and tribe and tongue and people; and he said with a loud voice, 'Fear God, and give Him glory, because the hour of His judgment has come; worship Him who made the heaven and the earth and sea and springs of waters'" (Revelation 14:6–7).

ANGELS AS MINISTERS

Now let's take a quick jog through a few biblical examples of angels as "ministers"—providing comfort and protection—at crucial stages in the kingdom's advancement.

- *Ministering spirits:* "Are [angels] not ministering spirits sent out to render service for the sake of those who will inherit salvation?"(Hebrews 1:14). Often in such ministry, the angels take the role of strong warriors. Ministering angels advance the kingdom by aiding God's people in doing battle on the kingdom's behalf.

- *Special forces commander:* Picture an ancient walled city in the Middle East—hot, dry, and surrounded by palm trees swaying in an early morning breeze. See a lone man, a scout, crouched in the brush at a distance from the city. An enormous battle is about to be joined. As he leans forward to part the brush for a better view of the walls, he is startled to notice a fierce warrior standing nearby. Our scout freezes, for the lone figure has his sword drawn. The warrior introduces himself as the captain of heaven's special forces command. He instructs the scout, Joshua, to take off his sandals, for he is on holy ground. He assures Joshua that victory is his. And he proceeds to issue to Joshua a multiparagraph operations order for the battle about to unfold (Joshua 5:13–15).

- *Special delivery:* Picture the high walls of a prison. See the foreboding gate: bolted, barred, and chained shut. Visualize a cold, damp, bug-infested prison cell filled with the sleeping forms of several men. See one of the men with his arms bound in chains. Shortly before, one of his faithful companions has been beheaded with the sword. Our lonely friend sleeps surrounded by four squads of soldiers, also sleeping. Picture the man's friends in another part of town on their knees in prayer for him. Now see the dark prison chambers aflame with white light. Amazingly, none of the sleeping soldiers stir. See a large angelic figure appear in the light. He bends over Peter and thumps him in the side. Groggy with sleep, Peter stirs and hears a voice say, "Get up. Quickly." The chains fall from his wrists and ankles, clinking to the ground. "Get dressed. Put on your shoes," says the angel. Peter follows his rescuer past two guard stations in the hallway. As though with an intelligence of its own, the iron gate swings open before them, and they slip into the street. Peter looks about. The angel is gone. (See Acts 12:4–11.)

- *In the prophetic future:* Picture a man blinded by a light like the sun, shielding his eyes. Hear ear-splitting, ground-shaking thunder. See a mighty being soaring high in the sky, dressed in a cloud, and wearing a rainbow on his head. See his face shine and his feet aflame. And see the little book he carries in his hand. See him straddle the earth, with one foot on the sea and one foot on the land. Visualize his hand raised…and picture the final and magnificent completion of the "mystery of God" in time and space. (See Revelation 10:1–10.)

CHRIST IS GREATER

What, then, are the most important truths we can learn from angels?

- Do as they do! Obey God immediately and fully! Do *what* He says, *how* He says it, *when* He says to do it.
- Worship God with all your heart. Bow before Him alone. Render *all* glory to Him!
- Remember what the holy angels never forget: Angels—and human beings—are nothing compared to Christ! This is the most critical point to remember when considering angels: Jesus Christ, our mighty Lord and Savior, is infinitely greater than the angels!

Thinking about angels in our day has gotten so outrageously out of hand in some Christian circles. So it was in the first century. The book of Hebrews was written, in part, to correct the churches that had gone bonkers in their fascination with angels. This is a book that declares the sheer superiority of Christ in every way. Hebrews 1:1–4 contains the theme. All the rest of chapter 1 and much of chapter 2 is dedicated to setting the record straight about angels and their utter puniness in comparison to Jesus Christ!

It all boils down to *who* Jesus is—the name that is His. He's better than angels because His identity is far superior. He is by name and identity God Himself.

So move over, angels. Step aside, Mohammed. Forget it, Jehovah's Witnesses. Write it off, Mormons. We're declaring Jesus Christ as God of the Universe, worshiped by angels and every other creature under heaven. Jesus is the King, and angels are "ministering spirits" (Hebrews 1:14) who do His bidding to advance His kingdom.

Jesus has created angels for Himself and for His bride—to follow His every command in advancing His kingdom through the church in our day.

This universe is filled with "myriads of myriads, and thousands of thousands" of helpers. They will serve Christ and they will serve you, His bride. Ultimately, they will bring you safely home to His heavenly kingdom.

Spirit warrior, don't ever become fascinated with the messenger. Rather, grasp the message— Jesus is Savior and Lord. Trust Him! Put aside your curiosity about angels, and test your relationship to Christ today. Do you know Him? Do you believe Jesus is God Himself? Have you trusted Jesus for your soul's eternal salvation? Do you live and act like Jesus is your God? Do you worship Christ? If you don't, angels are the least of your worries.

Jesus has created angels for Himself and for His bride.

But if you do love and serve Jesus, then be greatly encouraged. You're not alone in this war. You've got more powerful allies than you could ever imagine. But as my friend Don might say, "Even one of 'em is mighty welcome when a fella finds himself in over his head!"

My name is Legion; for we are many.

When in difficult country, do not encamp....
Do not linger in dangerously isolated positions....
In a desperate position, you must fight.

SUN TZU, THE ART OF WAR

[Israel] mingled with the nations,
And learned their practices,
And served their idols,
Which became a snare to them.
They even sacrificed their sons and daughters to the demons...
And the land was polluted.

PSALM 106:35-38

SATAN HAS ALLIES TOO

Sometimes you'll receive advice that doesn't seem right at the time, but then later you realize how true it was. When I was a green officer, my old brigade commander gave me just such a word of wisdom. What he said made no sense…at first.

Keep in mind that angry intimidation has been a stock-in-trade military motivator for centuries. As a young officer, I'd seen leaders blowing their stacks all the time. I thought that was just how it was done. It always seemed to pick up the pace of whatever task was at hand. I was even beginning to use it with my own men now and then.

But my brigade commander, "the old man," told me something that went completely against the grain. He said, "There is a place for anger, but it is rare. Commonplace, angry displays of temper are more often than not actually a substitute for a lack of leadership skills on the part of an insecure leader."

His advice didn't fit with what I'd seen. In fact, I questioned it completely. But the more I watched the officers around me, the more I realized he was right. I discovered that over the long haul, leadership will be more respected—and therefore more effective—when it is consistent and even tempered.

I'm glad I listened to "the old man" instead of just blindly going with the conventional wisdom.

When it comes to the devil and his minions, we too have to listen to something besides conventional wisdom. It is precisely because we take the Bible seriously that we do not take the devil and his legions of

Because we take the Bible seriously, we do not take the devil and his legions of demons lightly.

demons lightly. Unbelieving skeptics will tell us that there are no such beings as demons. The sophisticated man on the street tells us that this whole devil idea is a leftover from the myths and superstitions of an ancient, ignorant world. Demons, they say, belong only in the world of imagination, myth, and entertainment.

The Lord Jesus, however, has taught us in His Word that Satan is a real and personal enemy, and that he rules over a kingdom of evil beings sometimes called demons. He has taught us that spiritual warfare is real and personal, with real casualities, real dangers, and real forces to reckon with.

I don't know about you, but I'm going to side with Jesus Christ.

When it comes to matters physical or spiritual, life or death, present or future, heaven or hell, I'm going with the Son of God. I've already staked my eternity on His Word, so why shouldn't I hang my hat on His teachings about the devil and his fallen angels? If Jesus gives me the scoop on life, that's all the scoop I need. If He tells me I need to be on guard, then point me toward my sentry post, because I'm there.

NOT FOR ENTERTAINMENT!

Demons are "in" these days. Television, movies, and novels—not to mention those looking to explore the supernatural world—love to dabble in the demonic. To see the way demons are treated in the media, you'd think they existed pretty much for entertainment purposes.

They do not.

The study of demons is solemn, even frightening, business. Any careful reader of the Bible must eventually take demonology, the study of demons, seriously. The great theologian G. C. Berkouwer put it in right perspective: "There can be no sound theology without a sound demonology."

Randy Alcorn, my friend of thirty years now, says it well in the afterword to his marvelous novel, *Lord Foulgrin's Letters:*

> Some deny the existence of demons, regarding them as symbols of man's inhumanity to man. But even those who believe the Bible tend to develop sloppy demonology. Often our understanding of fallen angels is

based more on superstition, tradition, and assumptions
than the Scriptures.

Our adversary is the ultimate con artist.... Satan is
a liar.

Demons are masters at deceit.... They are intelligent beings portrayed in Scripture as rational and com-
municative.... Demons are fallen angels, a high order of
God's creation. They are spirits, and therefore not subject to the sensory limitations of human bodies. They
are stronger and more intelligent than we are....

Though Scripture doesn't suggest they can read our
minds or know the future, demons are certainly aware
of much truth we aren't. Their modus operandi is to
twist, deceive, and mislead, but they are intimately
familiar with the truth they twist. In fact, they may
even quote Scripture in their attempts to mislead us, as
Satan did in his temptation of Christ.[1]

We're dealing in this chapter with a potent reality: the demonic enemies
of our souls. It is therefore critical that we rely fully upon God's Word in
understanding them. We will endeavor at every point to be faithful to the
Bible—and we will seek to avoid taking even one step beyond it.

People are naturally interested in the invisible. We're drawn to the idea of
other worlds, particularly the dark world. Just look at the entertainment indus-
try. And, frankly, look at Christendom! Some of the Christian world's "shows"
dealing with demons are almost cartoonlike in their drawn-out dramatics.

This chapter is necessary for a couple of reasons. First, any biblical study
on spiritual warfare cannot omit demons, and second, given the many biblically abusive excesses that Christians are prone to develop in this subject area,
we probably need some kind of caution or corrective.

So, what are we supposed to think about demons? This chapter will
be perhaps more didactic than normal. *Dragnet*'s Sergeant Joe Friday used
to be famous for his gruff line: "Just the facts, ma'am." That's what we're
after here: nothin' but the facts. There's already enough showmanship and
razzle-dazzle in the Christian media, so maybe we'll just settle down in
these few pages and uncover some facts together. No, it's not very glam-
orous. But what we uncover will leave us with a stronger grip on what the
Bible actually has to say about demons.

THE DARK SIDE IN A NUTSHELL

Let's begin with a quick march through what Scripture says about the dark side. Following that overview, we'll develop a simple and straightforward practical theology regarding demons. These will be principles to help us deal biblically with demon activity in daily life.

As I did in the chapter on angels, I've again adapted for this chapter material from what is perhaps the most readable contemporary systematic theology text available today—that of Dr. Wayne Grudem.

THE ORIGIN OF DEMONS

Since God pronounced His created world "good," it is reasonable to assume that somewhere between Genesis 1:31 and Genesis 3:1, where Satan appears, there was a rebellion in the angelic world. In this rebellion, approximately one-third of the good angels turned against God and became evil (Revelation 12:4).

THE LEADER OF THE DEMONS

The word *Satan* (which means "accuser" or "adversary") is the personal name of the head of the demons (Job 1:6). The New Testament refers to him as "the devil." Satan was the originator of sin (2 Corinthians 11:3), and has been a "murderer from the beginning" and "a liar and the father of lies" (John 8:44).

THE MISSION OF THE DEMONS

Demons oppose and try to destroy every work of God. To do so, they use lies (John 8:44), deception (Revelation 12:9), and many other devious means to turn people away from God and destroy themselves. The work of demons is to blind people to the gospel (2 Corinthians 4:4) and to keep them in bondage to things that hinder right response to God (Galatians 4:8). They use temptation, doubt, guilt, fear, confusion, sickness, envy, pride, slander, and many other means to hinder a Christian's life and witness.

THE LIMITATIONS OF DEMONS

Demons are limited by God's control and limited within their own power (Jude 6; James 4:7). They do not know the future. They are neither omniscient, omnipotent, nor omnipresent (Isaiah 46:9–10; Daniel 2:27–28; Mark 13:32). And they cannot read minds.

THE STAGES OF DEMONIC ACTIVITY IN HISTORY

In the Old Testament we see demons working quite effectively in the proliferation of false, idolatrous religions (Deuteronomy 32:16–17; Psalm 106:35–37).

During the years of Jesus' ministry and that of the apostles, demonic activity appears to have been at a peak. Jesus demonstrated complete power over demons, a power shared to a lesser degree by His apostles (due to their human frailty). Jesus Himself indicated that the purpose of His first coming was largely to bind the power of Satan's demonic forces (Matthew 12:29). Christ's triumph on the cross guaranteed the ultimate defeat of Satan's dark kingdom.

The ongoing advancement of the kingdom of God frees people from satanic bondage. At the final judgment, Satan's house will be completely and finally "plundered" (Revelation 20:1–10).

THE RELATIONSHIP OF DEMONS TO US AND OUR WORLD TODAY

Demons continue to be active today. Their evil influences governments, corporations, religions, and institutions. They also impact individuals. It is important, however, to recognize that not all evil and sin is from Satan and his demons. Some of that evil originates out of our own human flesh.

In marked contrast to the practice of those who today emphasize what they call "strategic level spiritual warfare," in absolutely no instance in the New Testament does anyone—our Lord, His apostles, or otherwise—(1) summon a "territorial spirit" before preaching in a community, (2) demand information from demons about a local demonic hierarchy, (3) say that we should believe or teach any information whatsoever which is derived from demons, or (4) teach by word or example that certain "demonic strongholds" over a city have to be broken before the gospel can advance there. Rather, Christians are simply to preach the gospel and live out God's Word.

CAN A CHRISTIAN BE DEMON POSSESSED?

There is no such language in Scripture. People may "have a demon" (see Matthew 11:18), but there is nowhere any language that suggest demons can possess someone. The real problem with the commonly used terms *demon possessed* or *demonized* is that they are used today in such a way that seems to imply that the person under demonic attack has no choice but to succumb to it. But that is not the general impression left by the New Testament.

And certainly that is not the case with a Christian. Christians can come under strong attack

No truly born-again believer is ever necessarily helpless before Satan or his demons.

and may be particularly vulnerable if they are not living holy lives, but no truly born-again believer is ever necessarily helpless before Satan or his demons. Jesus gives all believers authority to command demons to leave (2 Corinthians 10:3–4; Ephesians 6:10–18; James 4:7; 1 Peter 5:8–9).

In summary, Christian, you are not powerless before the devil and his demons. You need not succumb. Quite the opposite. Satan's defeat is already guaranteed. When you resist him, he will flee. That's the promise of Scripture.

You recall the story at the start of chapter 7 about my friend Don falling overboard and floating for what seemed like an eternity in a lonely, overpowering ocean. Don would tell you that at one point he felt like he actually heard a voice say, "Give up, buddy. Your days are over." Whether or not it was an actual voice is immaterial. It was an actual battle. In response to these instructions, Don heard himself shouting, "No, I won't give up! You're not going to have me. Go away!" And that's precisely what happened. The battle ended. Don continued to tread water. And in the end, he was delivered.

Bottom line: The only thing you need to say to a demon is, "Just go away!" No prolonged conversation. No fancy technique. No exchange of names or calling cards. No long list of protocol. Just "Get outta here in the name of Christ!" I've noticed that virtually every long, drawn-out "deliverance conversation" I've come across ultimately ends with words to that effect anyway: "I command you in the name of Christ to leave!"

May I offer a novel suggestion?

Why not *start* there?

It saves a lot of time and energy, and it's more clearly biblical in the first place.

PRACTICAL DEMONOLOGY

What follows in the remainder of this chapter is what I call a bit of "practical theology" in dealing with the dark side. It may seem too short to be complete, but I assure you that it's all you really need to know about demons to handle their impact in your daily world. Ready? Here are my three big points:

- Demons are real—don't toy with them.
- Demons are defeated—don't sweat them.
- Demons are not a biblical emphasis—don't make them one.

DEMONS ARE REAL—DON'T TOY WITH THEM

Demons are mighty spiritual beings who fell from heaven in cooperation with Satan's rebellion. They are personal, evil, supernatural spirits, and they are frighteningly real. They represent about one-third of the angelic population. They are called "unclean" or "wicked spirits" (Matthew 12:45), and the Bible insists we are to have nothing to do with them.

Scripture suggests that demonic forces are united and organized (Ephesians 6:12) under Satan (Matthew 12:24) in his drive to destroy the works and glory of God. Demons are subtle, sinister, malicious, and potent in their attacks (Daniel 10; Jude 9).

The Gospels record several instances in which the devil or his demons apparently took control of a victim's personality (Mark 5:1–19 is one of the longer and more detailed accounts). Jesus dealt with such demons by dismissing them.

But the Bible never instructs Christians to hang around demons, engage them in lengthy conversation, or do personal battle with them. Though Jesus did ask on one occasion, we are never told to try to learn their names, discern their assignments, or catalog their organizational hierarchy. To do so is pure arrogance and the height of presumption. And nowhere are we told to aggressively and offensively pray against them.

So what do we do when actually faced with demons? Consider doing the same thing the Bible instructs us to do with their leader: Resist!

If all we have to do to make Satan himself flee from us is resist him (James 4:7), then it stands to reason that nothing more elaborate should be required to send his underlings packing. Nowhere does the Bible encourage a Christian to focus on demons or go "demonhunting," as it appears some current ministries are doing.

Please take note of the fact that most of the New Testament cases of demonic possession took place prior to the death, resurrection, and ascension of Christ. Christ's work on Calvary and His resurrection dealt a potent—and ultimately fatal—blow to the effectiveness of the forces of evil.

Demons are most effective where Christ's message is absent, ignored, perverted, or rejected.

Where Christ reigns supreme in a life, demons do not. Where Christ enjoys a strong influence in a culture because of the effectiveness of His message in His people's lives, demonic activity seems to cower in the shadows. Conversely, it would appear that demons are most effective where Christ's message is absent, ignored, perverted, or rejected.

Demons take on different disguises and tactics based on their environment. Where animism is dominant, demons use animism. Where the false theology of Mormonism dominates a community, the dark side puts on shirt and tie and sings hymns with empty lyrics. In an intellectual culture, Satan will happily twist intellectualism. In a materialistic culture, the dark world capitalizes on materialism. In any religious culture, the enemy will distort and bend that religion away from the true and living God.

Interestingly, there are very few cases of demonic activity recorded in the book of Acts. In the few examples there are, the demons are usually encountered in the earliest stages of evangelistic activity in any given area. The New Testament seems to indicate that demonic activity peaked during Jesus' ministry, then diminished after His crushing victory at Calvary and the empty tomb. And please note that none of these cases in Acts (5:16; 8:7; 16:16–18; 19:11–12) involved a demon-possessed believer.

It is clear from the text that, even if one accepts Ananias and Sapphira as true believers, the issue here is one of Satan filling or controlling their minds. This would appear to be in complete cooperation with their own attitudes and bents. The matter of demonic possession or ownership is not at issue. But the matter of influence on their thinking, deciding, and acting is.

Also, observe that there is no biblical record of Jesus ever instructing His followers on understanding demons or engaging in exorcisms. On those occasions when the disciples seemed to be asking for more detailed information, He briefly commented on it and moved on. For all the examples in the Gospels of the Messiah and His apostles casting out demons, there is absolutely no emphasis anywhere on long, drawn-out, specific, technical methodology.

When it came to demons, Jesus and the apostles simply threw them out and moved on. There was no showiness. No elaborate displays. No prolonged conversations. The demons were simply told to leave! And they did.

That is a solid pattern. Today people should be very careful about prolonging any contact whatsoever with demons. Avoid feeding any curiosity with the demonic. Overattention can easily lead to unhealthy fear or fascination. Go as far as Scripture, no further. Do not read anything into the "white spaces" between what is actually said in the biblical text.

Bottom line: The Bible insists that Christ's followers avoid every contact with demons or demonic practices. And when they are unavoidably encountered, they are to be resisted or simply ordered to leave. Such dark practices as astrology, so-called magic, divination, séances, Ouija boards, or attempts to contact the dead are emphatically forbidden (Leviticus 19:26, 31; 20:6, 27; Deuteronomy 18:9–13; Jeremiah 27:9–10).

If the Bible commands Christians to avoid demonic contact, then it stands to reason that we ought to avoid watching movies, reading books, or listening to music that in any way highlights the dark side or demonic activity.

The believer's focus is always to be on Christ, Christ's power, and Christ's provision. If more Christians would fall deeply in love with the Savior, demons would not stand a chance. Our focused attention is never to be on Satan or his schemes.

The Bible insists that Christ's followers avoid every contact with demons or demonic practices. When they are unavoidably encountered, they are to be resisted or simply ordered to leave.

DEMONS ARE DEFEATED—DON'T SWEAT THEM

Never, never, never forget that God's reign over the universe is absolute and supreme (Psalm 33:10–11; Isaiah 14:24–27; Ephesians 1:11). At Christ's first coming, He effectively bound "the strong man." At the Second Coming, He will completely "plunder his house."

Jesus' reference to "binding" Satan (Matthew 12:29) was never intended to be applied as some kind of a formula for verbal rebuke of the devil. His simple word picture in no way instructs believers to run around the world seeking to change it through some verbal rebuke of Satan.

Similarly, the bindings in Matthew 16:19 and 18:18 have nothing to do with what is currently called binding Satan. Rather, these references speak of believers having authority to bind or arbitrate things on earth that have to do with doctrinal truths revealed in God's Word and particular judgments in church discipline. These passages have nothing to do with what is commonly called "strategic level spiritual warfare."

The Christian fights Satan by living a holy personal life in obedient faithfulness to God. Christians should forget toying around with formulas, shows, and stagecraft, and concentrate instead on personal holiness. Unfortunately, much of Christian television's emphasis on the more showy forms of what they call spiritual warfare resembles actual biblical spiritual warfare about as much as the World Wrestling Federation resembles actual competitive wrestling.

In other words, hardly at all.

Nowhere in the Bible do we see Christians using sacred objects, holy water, wooden crosses, keychains, or other trinkets to combat the devil or demons. There is no hocus-pocus, no mumbo jumbo, no bargaining or engaging in conversation with demons. In the Bible, demons are simply sent packing by the power of God based on the triumph of Christ. And nowhere in Scripture is there any example or model for spitting out demons, choking them up, or coughing them out as seems to be increasingly popular in some deliverance ministries.

Sometimes well-meaning Christians get together in weekly prayer meetings to "bind Satan" from their community. As much as our communities need prayer, I'm afraid their binding efforts are not supported by Scripture.

A FEW TRUSTY TRUTHS

I believe in traveling light through life, don't you? Why get bogged down with a bunch of heavy stuff that only slows you down and doesn't do you any good? So here are some nuggets of truth about spiritual warfare that you can easily tuck into a backpack. Basically, this is all you need to know.

Jesus Christ decisively defeated all the powers of darkness. His triumph at the Cross was utterly disarming (Colossians 1:16; 2:13–15; 1 Peter 3:22). There is not the slightest chance of an eventual Satanic victory (Romans 8:38–39; Ephesians 1:20–22). That battle is determined. Christians should act in that light. Christians need to focus on Christ and never on the devil or his minions.

Believers share in Christ's victory over Satan and his dark forces (Colossians 2:9–15). When a person is saved, God transfers that person from the kingdom of darkness (Satan's realm) into the kingdom of light—Christ's kingdom (Acts 26:18; Colossians 1:13).

At the moment of conversion the new believer becomes a child of God, experiences full forgiveness, is completely justified before God, and shares in the inheritance of Christ Himself. From that moment on, the purpose of his life is to be conformed to Christ (Philippians 2:12–13).

The Bible clearly teaches that the Christian belongs to Christ. He is Christ's property, His possession, and no one—not even Satan or his demons—can pluck him out of Christ's hand. It is impossible for a believer to be demon possessed!

DEMONS ARE NOT A BIBLICAL EMPHASIS—DON'T MAKE THEM ONE

The Gospels and Acts are the historical books of the New Testament. Their primary purpose is to record what actually happened during the ministries of

Jesus and the apostles. It is not the primary purpose of these books to teach doctrine. Such doctrinal teaching is, however, the express purpose of the epistles. The epistles were written to the church to teach Christians what was important to believe, to understand, and to live out.

In light of this distinction, note this almost startling fact: The epistles make no mention whatsoever of demon possession, nor give any instructions for exorcism.

If demon possession were an issue for the Christian, it would be reasonable to expect that the epistles would have dealt with the matter in detail. If exorcism were to be a major emphasis of the church, the epistles would certainly have at least touched upon the subject.

The epistles make no mention whatsoever of demon possession, nor give any instructions for exorcism.

They do not.

In contrast to many of the detailed and showy practices we observe among some Christian groups today, the New Testament epistles don't even deal with the subject! Even in the historical books, the Gospels and Acts, there is no mention of anyone "summoning a territorial spirit" before preaching the gospel in a given area.

Jesus didn't do it.

The apostles didn't do it.

So why do Christians do it? Why do modern teachers create entire strategies and ministries around it?

So what am I saying? That we shouldn't pray prior to an evangelistic campaign? Of course we should pray! Prayer is a critical spiritual weapon. But an elaborate and specific antidemon machinery seems out of place.

Further, there is simply nothing in Scripture indicating that Christians should carry on conversations with demons. The somewhat awkward "arguments" you sometimes see between so-called televangelists, demons, and their victims have no clear basis in Scripture. In fact, such contact seems to fall under the category of what is forbidden in Scripture (Leviticus 19:26, 31; 20:6, 27; Deuteronomy 18:9–13; Jeremiah 27:9–10).

The only time attention ought to be given to demons is when a Christian is rejecting them. The brief encounter recorded in Mark 5 is dramatically different from the long, drawn-out, fact-finding conversations conducted today.

The spiritual warfare emphasized in the New Testament is not a showy kind of fooling around with demons. It is proclaiming the gospel to the unsaved and teaching the believer to submit to God, stand firm in his faith, put on the armor of God, and live a holy life. Period. New Testament spiritual warfare consists of humbly and prayerfully practicing the disciplines of spiritual growth along with other believers in the body of Christ. That's what "putting on the full armor of God" is all about.

Believers may be tempted or deceived by Satan, but they need not be defeated by him. So-called deliverance ministries as observed today are largely unnecessary. A believer can be delivered from any temptation or sin simply by obeying the Spirit and Word of God. A ritualistic prayer to "expel" or "rebuke" a demon is no more effective than a prayer to God for power to resist temptation and sin in the first place.

Prayer for wisdom and strength is more effective than a prayer to rebuke Satan. Beginning a service with a prayer for Christ's reigning in the service is much more biblically appropriate than beginning a worship service with a prayer to rebuke Satan.

Further, when it comes to personal behavior, no believer ever has the right to say, "The devil made me do it." It is simply not true. It smacks of a "victim" posture which is patently unbiblical.

Any contemporary deliverance procedure that involves naming demons, questioning demonic hierarchies, or conversing with demons should stand itself up against the Scriptures. Any practice not observed in Scripture is at best suspect and is probably unbiblical.

WHAT ABOUT TERRITORIAL SPIRITS?

The increased public curiosity regarding Satan has sparked all kinds of extra-biblical conjecture about demons and their activities. The church certainly ought not to lead in the direction of cultural curiosity by developing elaborate (and imaginary) descriptions of demonic organization and assignments. The idea of territorial spirits is, in particular, an area in which caution should be exercised. While the Bible hints at the possibility of geographic influence, it certainly refrains from spelling it out.

So why in the world should we attempt to spell something out that Scripture deliberately avoids?

In Daniel 10, there is a reference to the "Prince of Persia," who may have been a demon. Many have taken this to mean that Satan has organized his demons into geo-political or territorial areas. Unfortunately, that singular clue, when coupled with another even more vague metaphorical reference or two (such as Revelation 2:13), has become a major springboard for human imagination. Whole doctrines, systems, tactics, movements, and exercises—not to mention innumerable sermons—sprout up around these few hints.

Moses had it right: The things revealed belong to us and to our children; the secret things do not (Deuteronomy 29:29). So let's gravitate, Christian soldier, toward what is clearly revealed. And let's avoid experimentation in the things that are not.

Time and again I've heard the theory put forward (without substantive biblical support) that territorial spirits are responsible for certain geographical areas. According to this theory, if you want to minister in their jurisdictions you need to get to know these territorial demons, learn their names, garner information from them, bind them, and exorcise them.

Some teachers take the scant biblical support for the idea of "territorial spirits" and conclude that there must also be demons assigned to individual tribes, families, generations, or religious organizations. It then follows, in their minds at least, that it is important to identify these additional evil spirits and expel them in deliberate, intentional, almost ritualistic ways. So whole organizations and ministries grow up around exorcising different kinds of evil spirits.

But....

The prophets never did it.

Jesus never did it.

The apostles never did it.

So why do we do it?

WHAT ABOUT GENERATIONAL CURSES?

Whenever Christians step beyond the clear teaching of Scripture, there seems to be no place to stop. Such behavior often throws open the door to a contagious rash of unusual thinking and sometimes bizarre behavior. Take, for example, the increasingly popular concept of generational curses. What is the scriptural basis for this?

Very little, if any.

There is one somewhat vague reference in Genesis 9:25 to Noah's son Ham being cursed, and how that curse affected his family. Beyond that, there is no development of the matter, no further explanation, and no clear teaching regarding it in any other passage. But some preachers have developed elaborate and very frightening doctrines around the subject. They are speaking where Scripture does not.

The tragedy is that some well-meaning people are quick to follow such teaching. For example, one Christian man reportedly struggled with significant sexual lust toward a child or children. He then claimed to have later discovered that his great-grandfather was a child molester. He concluded he must be suffering under some kind of generational curse. To his mind this fully explained his sinful temptations.

Because of certain teachings regarding breaking generational curses, he believed it was necessary for him to attend a series of meetings on the subject. In those meetings, he reportedly learned how, through specific techniques and prayer, to renounce the sin of his ancestor and break the curse.

But where, oh where, is this kind of pattern taught in the Bible? It isn't there. What must we conclude? It's extrabiblical at best. At worst, it's pure human invention.

I need to acknowledge that the Old Testament does state at least five times that "the sins of the fathers are visited to the third and fourth generations" (see Exodus 20:5–6; Numbers 14:18; Jeremiah 32:18).

But this is not about generational curses. The intention of this phrase should not be hard to grasp. It seems clear that it's teaching what we all know when we think about it: that certain learned behaviors or lack of disciplines tend to run in families.

It's about *character,* not curses.

Parents who are liars and thieves tend to raise children who are liars and thieves. Parents who engage in sexual immorality tend to raise children who engage in sexual immorality.

But to believe in a doctrine of generational demons requires us to take a significant interpretive jump from these texts of Scripture. Simply put, there is no compelling biblical evidence that demons curse generations.

In fact, Scripture teaches that God does not punish innocent children for what their fathers, let alone their more distant ancestors, have done. Whenever children are involved in a related discussion there is some indication that the children themselves were, by their own attitudes or actions, deserving of punishment. In other words, their fathers' sins worked their way out in the children's own lives as well.

But even if such a concept as generational curses were clearly taught in Scripture, the real leap for some of our Christian friends is in their follow-up ministries. There is simply no biblical precedent for developing whole training programs centered on exorcising certain kinds of demons or renouncing certain kinds of curses. Not ancestral demons. Not tribal or national demons. Not ethnic demons. Not any kind of particular behavioral demons. Jesus didn't do it. Neither did the apostles. Neither need we.[2]

When men and women choose to step beyond the clear teaching of Scripture, there is no logical place to stop. Imaginations run free. Have you noticed, for example, that before long in this evolving extrabiblical cycle, everything becomes a demon? There seems to emerge classifications of demons that are pretty ridiculous.

Is there really a demon of homosexuality?

The Bible teaches that homosexual behavior is wrong and sinful, but it never holds a demon accountable for it. It is a human sin and a clear human responsibility, not a demonic problem.

Is there a demon of Islam, or sexual abuse, or anger, or alcohol, or lust? Certainly the Bible teaches these things are wrong, but Scripture describes many of them as simply "works of the flesh" or the "old self." We are never instructed to exorcise the "demon spirit of lust" or the "spirit of alcohol" or the "spirit of abuse." No one needs to attempt to learn the name of the demon of alcohol. They just need to steer clear of Jack Daniels and his pals.

The Bible does indicate that many of our sinful motives are derived from the devil (ultimately, all evil is). For example, Jesus told His enemies that their desire to kill Him was from their father, the devil (John 8:44). But there is no indication here that some "demon of homicide" was involved.

Paul warned Timothy not to fall into "the trap of the devil...to do his will" (2 Timothy 2:26, NIV). Yes, there may often be demonic influence in personal decisions to sin. Some repetitive sinners even become, in effect, the devil's slaves. But that is a long way from saying that particular sins are the works of particular demons or that we escape such sins by rebuking those particular demons. That is extrabiblical nonsense. We are trapped by sin because we choose to sin. "The devil made me do it" went out with Flip Wilson's comic character Geraldine.

So let's take the clear biblical approach toward demons: Dismiss them and move on. No deferring or cowering. No chatting or toying. Our emphasis, like the New Testament's, should always be on putting on the full armor of God and walking in personal holiness. After all:

Demons are real—don't toy with them.

Demons are defeated—don't sweat them.

Demons are not a biblical emphasis—don't make them one.

'Nuff said.

We don't want Satan to win any victories here,
and well we know his methods!

2 CORINTHIANS 2:10-11,
PHILLIPS

Do not give the devil an opportunity.

EPHESIANS 4:27

OUR ENEMY'S STRATEGIES

s a young Green Beret officer during the Vietnam War, I sat in on countless military briefings. We discussed our "friendly forces" situation and the disposition of the enemy. I watched as senior officers pored over maps, charts, photos, and intelligence information.

Where were the vulnerabilities?

Where should we commit our next operations?

How could we catch the enemy off guard?

Where should we prearrange artillery targets?

What kind of air support do we have available?

The United States military commanded an awesome array of lethal force during the height of that war. We had everything from tanks to fighters to B-52 bombers to aircraft carriers—and even the storied battleship *New Jersey* steaming somewhere offshore.

Still, our leaders had to carefully strategize how to use those forces to best advantage. Where and when should we strike? How should we counter the enemy's offensives? How could we bring confusion and despair to enemy commanders and troops in the field? In short, how could we whip those guys?

Planning for operations was systematic, detailed, and very deliberate. It had to be; lives were at stake.

Christian soldier, have you ever thought about yourself as the target of such strategies? Have you ever thought about your own picture and vital statistics sitting on a table in the war room of some demonic gathering?

It isn't fantasy, my friend. It's solemn truth. You do have an enemy—one who employs battle strategies and tactics to bring about your destruction.

In 2 Corinthians chapter 2, Paul speaks of countering Satan's attempts to take advantage of a tragic situation in the church at Corinth. In effect, he tells them, "We're aware of what he may be attempting. We're not ignorant of his schemes and tactics!" To put it another way, "We're not wide-eyed Cub Scouts on a campout here. We know about this enemy, and we're cognizant of his devious methods and designs."

Satan uses a thousand tactics in his attempts to thwart God's intentions and destroy human beings, God's image bearers. The enemy's strategies have left humans in this world dazed and devastated. Mentally confused. Emotionally needy. Sexually disoriented. And, of course, spiritually bankrupt.

When it comes to temptations and evil in our lives, we would probably all like to claim the excuse Geraldine continually employed: "The devil made me do it!"

It's just not that easy.

We are responsible moral agents with capacities for choice. And we will give account for our actions quite apart from the devil. Even so, Flip was onto at least a half-truth. We can attribute the ultimate origin of evil in the world to the devil. And he is still very much alive and functioning. We do know, on sound biblical statement, that the devil and his legions are active in our world.

And even though the devil doesn't "make us" get tangled up in the bad decisions and sinful habits that afflict us from time to time, he certainly encourages the process! As western writer Louis L'Amour might have said, "He's out there greasin' the skids." He has schemes and wiles and specific strategies to trip us up, pull us down, and blunt our edge. In chapter 6, we learned about who Satan is, what he can and can't do. In chapter 8 we looked at his allies, the demonic hordes who follow his lead. Now we're going undercover to expose some of his most successful tactics, to steal his playbook. To arm ourselves not only with knowledge about our enemy, but about his plans and means.

Paul Harvey, syndicated columnist, has Satan's number. He described him and his tactics quite well in a piece called "If I Were the Devil."

> I would gain control of the most powerful nation in the
> world. I would delude their minds into thinking they had
> come from man's effort, instead of God's blessings. I
> would promote an attitude of loving things and using
> people, instead of the other way around. I would dupe

entire states into relying on gambling for their state reve-
nue. I would convince people that character is not an
issue when it comes to leadership. I would make it legal to
take one's own life, and invent machines to make it convenient. I would cheapen human life as much as possible
so that the life of animals are valued more than human
beings. I would take God out of the schools, where even
the mention of His name was grounds for a lawsuit.

I would come up with drugs that sedate the mind
and target the young, and I would get sports heroes to
advertise them. I would get control of the media, so
that every night I could pollute the mind of every
family member for my agenda. I would attack the
family, the backbone of any nation. I would make
divorce acceptable and easy, even fashionable. If the
family crumbles, so does the nation.

I would compel people to express their most
depraved fantasies on canvas and movies screens and call
it art. I would convince the world that people are born
homosexuals, and that their lifestyles should be accepted
and marveled. I would convince the people that right and
wrong are determined by a few who call themselves
authorities and refer to their agenda as politically correct.

I would persuade people that the church is irrelevant and out of date, and the Bible is for the naive. I
would dull the minds of Christians and make them
believe that prayer is not important, and that faithfulness and obedience are optional.

I guess I would leave things pretty much the way
they are.[1]

We do have reason to believe these evil powers are capable of studying
our individual game films (as with Job), reviewing our patterns and habits,
and striking us at points of vulnerability. The dark side is incredibly active.

This is nothing to get spooky, goofy, or silly about (as some Christians
are wont to do with spiritual warfare). Satan absolutely loves to confuse us at
the emotional, gut-feeling affections level so as to bend our choices—which,
in turn, serves to pervert our morals, dilute our loyalties, twist our ethics,
erode our commitments, and break our covenants. So we lose, our families

lose, and the human race loses. In some sense, God loses, too.

Right now you may be asking yourself, "Okay, if Satan and his troops have tactics prepared to assault my life, how can I prepare myself? How and where is this snake most likely to get *me?* What is his modus operandi? What do I need to be especially alert to?"

Let me give it to you in a nutshell: Keep your eye on the way you respond to God's Word. That will tell everything.

SATAN'S NUMBER ONE STRATEGY

Most Christians know that the greatest asset we have in this spiritual war is God's Word. Does it not stand to reason, therefore, that the enemy of God would do all in his power to distort, discredit, and undermine the Word of God? Of course. How obvious!

The devil's first and most basic scheme is to twist the Word of God.

Obvious or not, that very tactic remains in Satan's frontline arsenal. Why? Because it continues to be so effective. Never forget it: The devil's first and most basic scheme is to twist the Word of God so as to confuse, disorient, disarm, and destroy the Christian soldier.

That was his first line of attack in the Garden of Eden. That was his ongoing assault on the people of God throughout the Old Testament. It was his strategy of approach on the Messiah Himself. And it is his ongoing battle tactic targeting your life and mine. It follows, then, that the less familiar you are with the Scriptures, the more vulnerable you are to Satan's direct attacks against you and your family.

You really don't have to go much farther than the first few pages of the Book to view Satan's basic strategies in action. Let's take some time together and revisit that familiar encounter with the serpent way back at the dawn of human history.

> Now the serpent was more crafty than any beast of the field which the LORD God had made. And he said to the woman, "Indeed, has God said, 'You shall not eat from any tree of the garden'?" The woman said to the serpent, "From the fruit of the trees of the garden we may eat; but from the fruit of the tree which is in the middle of the garden, God has said, 'You shall not eat from it or touch

it, or you will die.'" The serpent said to the woman, "You
surely will not die! For God knows that in the day you
eat from it your eyes will be opened, and you will be like
God, knowing good and evil." When the woman saw
that the tree was good for food, and that it was a delight
to the eyes, and that the tree was desirable to make one
wise, she took from its fruit and ate; and she gave also to
her husband with her, and he ate.

GENESIS 3:1–6

The devil spun God's words at Eve in such a way that His original meaning was lost. Unfortunately, that is not unlike what a lot of Christians do
today. If you question God's Word hard enough and long enough, you'll
begin to hear what you want to hear, rather than what the Word actually says.
The devil's first and most common scheme, then, is to make you doubt your
understanding of what God has said.

QUESTION THE UNDERSTANDING OF GOD'S WORD

Satan doesn't have to attack the authority of God's Word when he's dealing
with one of God's children. All he has to do is twist the understanding of
God's Word just enough to let us justify for ourselves our own desired behavior. Human beings, like the devil, are incredibly adept at twisting the words
of God to their own selfish ends. Peter tells us that the "unstable" distort
Scripture "to their own destruction" (2 Peter 3:16).

Have you ever found yourself there? Have you ever taken note of your
own incredible ability to reinterpret the perfectly plain and simple meaning
of Scripture? Most of us, at one time or another, have proven very agile—
almost athletic—in our ability to twist the Bible in order to justify some dark-
hearted appetites of our own.

That twisting is usually progressive in nature. We start out by interpreting Scripture broadly and vaguely, until we manage to sear our consciences a
bit. That accomplished, our interpretations become even more bizarre.

I can't help but think of the man who gave me his "biblical" rationaliza-
tions for divorcing his wife for another woman. To hear this guy tell it, he was
pursuing God's will with all his might! His reasoning went something like this:

1. God invented marriage as an expression of relational intimacy, or one-
    ness, to glorify Him.

2. Since I experience no deep relational intimacy or oneness with my wife, I do not have a marriage, and am not glorifying Him by pretending I do. In fact, my marriage is a lie and God hates lying.

3. Since I do not have a marriage in God's eyes, I am free—no, *compelled*—to divorce my wife in the eyes of the state. It's purely a civil and legal issue perfectly in keeping with both God's intentions and man's law.

4. Since I will then have no marriage in either the eyes of God or the state, voilà! I will be free to marry the woman with whom I'm having a sexual affair.

5. Isn't God good? I've never felt so close to Him or so cared for by Him! He is blessing me by giving me my dreams.

Amazing, isn't it? This man's twisted logic is satanic to the core. It defies God and destroys human lives. Before this reasoning has run its course, life itself will have been stripped of value and meaning.

Through my years of pastoring, I've seen this sort of thing happen again and again. You begin by experimenting with the language. You toy with the words. You shade meanings. Then, having changed the language in subtle ways, you begin to redefine reality to your own satisfaction. That done, you kid yourself into believing you're not going to answer to God for it.

That's just what our culture has done on the issue of abortion. You begin with a living baby in the womb. Of course it's a baby! Of course it's alive. Of course it's human. Of course it has a right to be born. But over time, you teach yourself to think of it as a "fetus," not a baby, per se. Later it becomes simply the "product of conception," which finds its way into the trash can of the surgi-center as "discarded tissue."

How did we get from a living human being to a random piece of discarded tissue in a dumpster?

It happened when truth was redefined, stripping life itself of its value. And before long, after we've lowered the bar on the value and meaning of life, we've got legalized suicide pills for senior citizens and kids killing other kids in the school yards.

You might expect such rationalization and linguistic gymnastics from the secular culture, but it's doubly revolting when Christians follow the same serpentine line of reasoning.

Here's another example. Think of the Christian man's progression from pornography to full-blown sexual addiction. The early rationalization is easy enough: "I mean, after all, God invented the female body. He pronounced it good. He sculpted every line and made it incredibly beautiful. It is glorious to behold. And He gave me, as a man, a great appreciation for and attraction to that female form. So...I'll just go ahead and enjoy these artful representations. What harm could it do? After all, it's pretty soft stuff. I'm not after the hard-core stuff."

Ah, but before many such encounters have passed, we've traveled a long, long way down the very slippery slope of twisting God's Word and its clear intentions. In fact, we've just taken a bullet, and we're down, a casualty on the battlefield! All because we, like the devil, twist the Word to our own destruction.

You see, the desire to sin is aroused in the human heart. Sin and destruction begin with a simple suggestion that causes the believer to question the plain meaning of Scripture.

Remember how Satan came against Eve? Paraphrase: "Indeed...? Has God really said you shall not eat from *any* tree you wish? Are you reading that passage correctly, Eve? Have you double-checked that translation? Are you sure you have the right context?" And the debate is on. The questions flow. Our own depraved minds snuggle into the assumption that God's Word is somehow subject to *our* judgment.

- "Indeed, has God really said no sex before marriage?"
- "Indeed, has God really said no divorce?"
- "Indeed, does God really expect me to live an unhappy life?"
- "Indeed, does God really intend for me to give a tithe...or more?"
- "Indeed, did God mean I should literally submit to my husband?"

The devil begins by challenging our understanding of God's Word. If that doesn't produce casualties, he attempts to lure us into the next step.

QUESTION THE MOTIVES OF GOD AND HIS WORD

You can read it between the lines of the serpent's conversation with Eve. Raised eyebrows. Incredulity. Amazement. "My, oh, my. Are you telling me you can't eat the fruit from any tree in the Garden? Really? The Creator said *that?* You must have misunderstood Him. He must have intended to say something else."

Eve picked up on it right away, adding her own blatant exaggeration of God's directives. "God has said, 'You shall not eat from it or touch it, or you will die'" (Genesis 3:3).

Touch it? When did God say anything about not touching the fruit? By exaggerating the commands of God, we end up trivializing them, trying to take them to some self-serving extreme that the Lord never intended.

"Wait a minute. You're telling me that God put you in a beautiful Garden (true) loaded with beautiful, luscious fruit trees (true), and then told you you couldn't eat from any of those trees (not true) or even *touch* the tree? (not true at all). Are you kidding? What harm is there in such a simple thing? He couldn't have meant something so picky as that. Sounds a bit overcontrolling to me. Even dominating. In fact, it's just plain legalism."

So we begin to build a straw God—a phony caricature—by magnifying His strictness disproportionately. Before long we've succeeded in remaking Him after our own image and our own self-centeredness. We twist God's Word and God's character to make it appear absurd.

And before long, we feel free (in our own deluded thoughts) to take the next fatal step.

BLATANTLY DENY THE TRUTH

Once you've questioned your understanding of God's Word and twisted your view of God's intentions, you're ready to accept absolute lies about Him. "The serpent said to the woman, 'You surely will not die!'" (Genesis 3:4).

Then, once you've moved from the plain truth of Scripture to a big lie, God's clear standards are no longer an issue for you.

For example, the Bible clearly condemns homosexual behavior. It's hard to imagine it being stated more plainly. But humans—even some claiming to be Bible-believing Christians—twist the plain meaning to their own purposes:

"Homosexuality is not unbiblical," some say. "Nor is it sin. It's just a natural orientation. So long as it's faithful and monogamous, it's perfectly in keeping with God's intentions for human relationships."

Why stop there? Some don't: "God would never create something so ugly as the 'hell' some Bible-abusers espouse. He's much too loving to do something so barbaric. Hell is simply a metaphor, a figure of speech illustrating the misery we sometimes create for ourselves."

We reap what we sow—and the result is a mental, emotional, and spiritual disorientation that renders the believer a useless casualty on the field of battle today and a tragically unrewardable occupant of the kingdom to come.

Beyond twisting and undermining God's Word, what are some of the other weapons in the arsenal of hell? I can think of a couple of his "big guns" right off the top.

DEPRESSION AND DISCOURAGEMENT

The father of lies doesn't waste his ammo. He holds his stock of fiery arrows in reserve until we are most vulnerable to his onslaught: those moments when we're weary…drained…frustrated… careless…reckless…emotionally flat. In those times, Satan pulls out two of his favorite arrows: depression and discouragement. With them he has won many battles by convincing Christians that they were defeated and beyond hope.

Just remember: He's a liar. Always has been, always will be. When he lies, he's simply speaking in his own language. In Poland, they speak Polish. In Afghanistan, they speak Afghan. In Satan's realm, falsehood is the native tongue. You should expect nothing else.

The great liar knows that every person will eventually find himself singing the blues. Disappointment, discouragement, grief, and failure are part of every person's life.

When those times come and you want to sing the blues, you've got a crucial choice to make. You've got to decide which music you'll listen to. You can tune in to the sour notes of the ancient liar, who hates you and lusts after your destruction, or you can listen to the sweet music of the *lyre* of Scripture.

If you listen to the strum of the liar, you'll hear things like: "You're a loser forever because you made that mistake. You've failed and you can never regain what you've lost. If you failed once you'll always fail. Don't even try."

The liar will have you humming negative details. He'll have you focusing on negative, critical thoughts until you're convinced everything really is negative.

The liar will sing a forlorn but curiously inviting tune: "Isolate yourself. No one wants to be with you. You're no fun! You're not worth being with. You're just hurting people. Better to get away from people. Be alone."

The liar will sing, "Those who give you counsel are just trying to make you feel better. They're lying to you."

The liar will ask, "How do you know what's real? Are your feelings real or are you making all this up? Maybe you're just trying to get attention. Did God really say…?"

The liar will tell you, "Your life is of no value. Everyone, including you, would be better off if you were dead."

It's the mantra of the devil himself. The prototype nihilist. The one who wants to steal, kill, and destroy. Don't tune in to that pirate radio frequency! Don't lend your ears to that music.

The liar's favorite hymn is "Trust and Betrayed." If he can get you to sing that tune, he's persuaded you that you trusted God and then He turned His back on you. Bottom line? Better give up, because you're hopeless. Even God doesn't want you.

The liar's incredibly popular tune is played to the chords of self-pity. He'll get you to thinking you're unnoticed, undervalued, and underappreciated. People just don't affirm you enough. You're worth much more than you're getting. You really should be recognized for all you are and do.

My friend, when you start listening to that music, you're on the road to becoming a Judas...or a Benedict Arnold.

Let me tell you a bit about ol' General Arnold. You see, he felt he should have been more widely recognized for his part in, among other things, the Battle of Saratoga. When he felt underappreciated, he sold out to the enemy. Don't even think about playing that self-pity tune. It'll kill you on the battlefield. It may be the ultimate self-inflicted wound.

Fortunately, there's another kind of *lyre* in the Bible. A good one. The lyre was a musical instrument related to the modern guitar, common in David's time. As you're reading the Psalms you'll sometimes see this instrument mentioned in the heading. In fact, it was probably to the strum of the lyre that God's people sang the song David wrote while hiding in the depths of a limestone cave called Adullam. And it wasn't some funeral-like dirge at all.

David wrote: "Set me free from my prison, that I may praise your name. Then the righteous will gather about me because of your goodness to me" (Psalm 142:7, NIV). Did you see that? David had no intention of setting up permanent housekeeping in that cave! No self-pity here. No listening to the devil's rotten music. Even though his heartbreaking exile lasted fifteen years, David believed it was a temporary ordeal. In his heart, he believed that one day he would look back and call all this good. And he did.

The *lyre* plays different tunes than the *liar*. When you listen to the lyre you'll hear: "He leads me beside quiet waters. He restores my soul" (Psalm 23:2–3).

The lyre hums, "The law of the LORD is perfect, restoring the soul" (Psalm 19:7).

Listen to the lyre and you'll hear: "You have made known to me the path of life; you will fill me with joy in your presence, with eternal pleasures at your right hand" (Psalm 16:11, NIV).

The lyre's refrain goes, "My flesh and my heart may fail. But God is the strength of my heart and my portion forever" (Psalm 73:26).

The strum of the lyre declares with confidence that joy *does* come in the morning (Psalm 30:5).

Think about that nasty cave at Addulam. Think about David and how his life relates to yours. See if you can't see these five thoughts wafting down to you out of that cave.

1. Every child of God can expect a little disappointment in his life.

The most potent educational experience of my life was serving in the army in the 1960s. I actually loved it, as strange as that might sound. Afterwards I felt called by God to enter seminary and the local church ministry, but my love of the military remained. In the 70s, when we were starting Good Shepherd Community Church, I was invited to continue my military involvement by serving as a chaplain in the Reserves.

I desperately wanted to do it, but the elders felt it would be too significant an involvement for me, especially during the pioneering years of the church. Of course, I submitted to the elders and chose not to be involved in the Reserves. It was a great disappointment to me at the time. But I knew it was best for the church and therefore best for me.

But our Lord, in His matchless ways, has not left me without the opportunity to serve the military. Now, twenty years later, I find myself with numerous opportunities to serve our soldiers in a spiritual ministry, speaking virtually every month at some army post in the United States or overseas.

God does work all things out for good—even our disappointments. And when we are able to enjoy a godly perspective, we can see it quite clearly. As was once said, "Our first words in heaven will be, 'Oh, of course.'"

2. When discouragement comes, don't run. Look up and ask three questions.

We live in a culture that says you should never have to experience discomfort or pain. You have a right to immediately have relief, by whatever means necessary. But that's not the way God works. Ask Job. Ask Elijah. Ask Moses. Ask David. Ask Christ Himself, who agonized in prayer in the Garden of Gethsemane. He prayed earnestly for relief from pain. He was in such deep pain that He sweated blood. But He didn't run. He stood firm. He held His ground. Aren't you glad?

When discouragement comes to you, don't head for the hills. Instead, ask these three questions:

- What are You trying to teach me?
- What do You want to change in me?
- What are You trying to do through me?

I recall a season of pain in my relationship with one of the guys on staff here at Good Shepherd. As it turned out, there was nothing really serious that should've caused any kind of a breach. But we are humans. And as someone has said, "The great difficulty with human communication is the misperception that it's taken place." In our miscommunication, we had done just that—missed each other. It was painful enough to cause both of us significant confusion.

Don't bolt at the first twinge of pain. You may miss a wonderful lesson from God.

But we managed to hang on to each other—as we say, "Holding one another's ankles through the dark tunnels"—so that today we are closer friends thant ever. And, of course, far more effective together in ministry. All in all, it was a terribly difficult season for both of us, but we're glad we stuck it out. And so is the church and the kingdom.

Don't bolt at the first twinge of pain. You may miss a wonderful lesson from God.

3. Sometimes disappointments will feel overwhelming, but they are not. God is in control.

Years ago when one of our sons was in middle school, he developed a friendship with a young man whose choices were raising our eyebrows as parents. Linda and I finally decided that the friendship was risky enough that we needed to reduce its impact in our son's life.

When we told our son that he would no longer be able to regard this person as his closest and dearest friend, it was extremely difficult for all of us. He couldn't believe we had butted in to his life so forcefully. And, frankly, we had a hard time dealing with it, too. But we felt in our souls it was the right thing to do. Through all of the disappointment, confusion, and emotional flip-flopping, we stayed the course.

Just a few years later, when the boys were college age, we received a letter from our son thanking us for terminating that friendship. He could finally see that his friend had continued down the wrong road and was paying the price. What had seemed like the end of the world at the time was now regarded as a very positive thing.

Disappointments may feel overwhelming, but they're not. God is still in control.

4. God doesn't set booby traps for His children. The liar does.

God's plan for you is victory. In His incredible sovereignty He can use any disappointment, any trial, any pain, any failure—even the enemy's snares—for your ultimate good.

Our church has felt like we've been through a few booby traps during our recent building program. Over the course of five years we have had to work our way through seven layers of government, wrestling with all kinds of "environmental issues," some of them seemingly imaginary.

While the process has been frustrating to all of us, and while we really don't like to admit that these kinds of difficulties can sometimes have positive ends, we do see the wisdom in the delay. We see it in our more carefully refined plans and in the specific designs of the buildings.

Yes, God can indeed use anything—even government bureaucracy or our own bad decisions—for our ultimate good.

5. Learn to sing the blues to the strum of the lyre.

No matter what comes our way, we can learn to sing that great old hymn, "It Is Well with My Soul." Becoming Christlike is the lifelong process of learning to sing the blues to the music of God's Word.

SELF-SUFFICIENCY

There is one more big gun in the devil's arsenal that we should examine in our survey. It is smoothed and worn from constant use since the beginning of time—but it's still lethal enough to cut down any one of us. It is extremely subtle, very effective, and counted among his favorite weapons. This tactic works so well against us because we never see it coming. Like a stealth weapon, it's on you before you know it. It causes things to explode around you before you ever sense its presence.

Watch how this destructive tactic of the enemy wrapped its tentacles around one of God's mighty men of old:

> Then Satan stood up against Israel and moved David to
> number Israel.
> So David said to Joab and to the princes of the

people, "Go, number Israel from Beersheba even to Dan, and bring me word that I may know their number."

Joab said, "May the LORD add to His people a hundred times as many as they are! But, my lord the king, are they not all my lord's servants? Why does my lord seek this thing? Why should he be a cause of guilt to Israel?"

Nevertheless, the king's word prevailed against Joab. Therefore, Joab departed and went throughout all Israel, and came to Jerusalem.

Joab gave the number of the census of all the people to David. And all Israel were 1,100,000 men who drew the sword; and Judah was 470,000 men who drew the sword.

But he did not number Levi and Benjamin among them, for the king's command was abhorrent to Joab.

God was displeased with this thing, so He struck Israel.

David said to God, "I have sinned greatly, in that I have done this thing. But now, please take away the iniquity of Your servant, for I have done very foolishly."

1 CHRONICLES 21:1–8

Joab knew there was a problem here. God had clearly stated that He intended His people to depend entirely upon Him and not the strength of their military. David insisted anyway. The act clearly violated God's intentions, resulting in severe discipline for both David and the nation.

The sin? Self-sufficiency. Call it self-reliance, seeking security on a human plane, pride in personal achievement, pride in kingdom size, or pride in human capacity and effectiveness. The psalmist tells us:

[The LORD] does not delight in the strength of the horse;
  He does not take pleasure in the legs of a man.
The LORD favors those who fear Him;
  Those who wait for His lovingkindness."

PSALM 147:10–11

Self-elevation is the national religion of hell. And it will kill you on the battlefield quicker than anything else.

Self-elevation is the national religion of hell.

I recall a time when Professor Howard Hendricks referred to a list naming scores of pastors who had experienced moral falls in one twenty-four month period. In seeking to discover some of the common elements in those fallen warriors' lives, Dr. Hendricks reported that every one of them had concluded, "It couldn't happen to me." That kind of pride gives the evil one opportunity to piece the heart. It kills quickly. It's even worse than failing to put on your armor.

Self-reliance is the marketing slogan for all of hell's corporate products. If hell ran a million-dollar Super Bowl TV ad, its motto would be: "Hell—where self-sufficiency has run its course."

Here's the point: Preparing for battle starts in the head and heart. Thinking accurately is a critical soldierly skill. Pride has destroyed a lot of God's finest spirit warriors. You toy with pride and your fellow soldiers will have to call a medevac right away.

The Lord told Jeremiah:

> "Let not a wise man boast of his wisdom, and let not the
> mighty man boast of his might, let not a rich man boast
> of his riches; but let him who boasts boast of this, that
> he understands and knows Me, that I am the LORD
> who exercises lovingkindness, justice and righteousness
> on earth; for I delight in these things."
>
> JEREMIAH 9:23-24

Scripture is replete with similar warnings to you and me. Paul wrote: "Let him who thinks he stands take heed lest he fall" (1 Corinthians 10:1, NKJV).

So here's a foundational question to ask yourself on the way to armoring up for the battlefield: What must I do to keep from getting ambushed by Satan?

If you're supposed to take an aggressive, stiff-armed stance in resisting the devil, how do you do that…without falling into the deadly trap of self-sufficiency? If this battle is no Sunday school picnic, how do you keep from getting caught unaware? How do you deal with the sheer shock of battle?

How do you prepare for battle without depending on yourself? How do you avoid getting knocked silly in this spiritual warfare?

Simply put, you trust in the provision of God.

You trust God's care and provision for you. He has issued you everything you need in order to succeed on the battlefield. It's up to you to put it on.

People, we've got to *fight* to win! If you have any desire to be effective for Christ in this world and rewardable in the next one, you must become intimately familiar with the Bible, God's Word, in order to resist the devil and be an overcomer. How do you beat an enemy as strong as the devil? In the words of Scripture, you "trust God." You "resist" Satan. And you "put on the armor" which God provides.

Read on, spirit warrior.

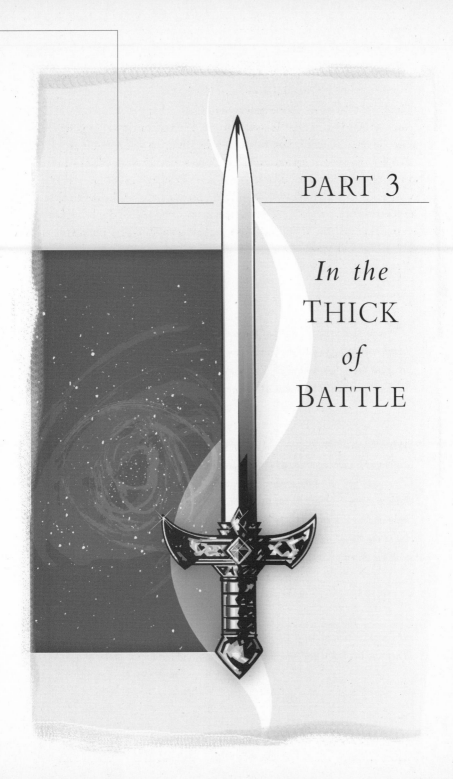

PART 3

In the
THICK
of
BATTLE

The good fighters of old first put themselves beyond the possibility of defeat.... To secure ourselves against defeat lies in our own hands.... Never forget—when your weapons are dulled, your ardor dampened, your strength exhausted, and your treasure spent, other chieftains will spring up to take advantage of your extremity.

SUN TZU

When, because of negligence and laziness, parade ground drills were abandoned, the customary armor began to feel heavy since the soldiers rarely, if ever, wore it. Therefore, they asked the emperor to set aside the breastplates and mail and then the helmets. So our soldiers fought the Goths without any protection for the heart and head and were often beaten by archers. Although there were many disasters, which led to the loss of great cities, no one tried to restore the armor to the infantry. They took the armor off, and when the armor came off—so too came their integrity.

FOURTH-CENTURY GENERAL
OFFICER OF THE ROMAN
LEGIONS

The night is almost gone, and the day is near.
Therefore let us lay aside the deeds of darkness and put on the armor of light.

ROMANS 13:12

ARMOR UP!

You may have noticed from photographs, paintings, and movies about the Civil War that the soldiers in that conflict wore no helmets. Just about any old cap or cloth rag served for headgear. Helmets were seemingly out of vogue in the midnineteenth century. Though indispensible in ancient warfare, helmets were initially considered useless against bullets.

If only they had known!

Just prior to the First World War—and quite by accident—a French soldier reported escaping death when a metal food bowl he had placed under his cloth cap actually deflected a rifle bullet. Just like that, helmets were in vogue once more!

The Kevlar helmet of the modern U.S. Army represents the zenith of research and development, and it is truly an amazing piece of armor. It weighs little more than three pounds and costs only ninety dollars each, but it's saved many lives.

On May 28, 1987, a soldier wearing his Kevlar helmet was on a training exercise when a 4.2 mortar round exploded nearby, sending shell fragments in all directions. The soldier, with his back to the explosion, was struck so hard in the back of the helmet by a chunk of shrapnel that he was knocked off his feet and rendered unconscious. The laminated Kevlar fabric was severely damaged (actually torn to shreds) but the soldier regained consciousness and returned to duty.

In December 1989, during Operation Just Cause in Panama, an AK-47 round struck Sergeant Howard Overacker in the helmet at point-blank range. The helmet literally stopped the bullet, and the sergeant's life was spared.

One U.S. Army manual states: "Casualty reduction is an occupational health issue." I would think so! If any soldier believes in the absolute necessity of "putting on the full armor," it is the battlefield medic. He's seen its effectiveness with his own eyes. As General Bruce Clark once said, "The first step in motivating soldiers is to tell them the reason why." Putting on the full armor serves to "enhance force effectiveness by reducing casualties while minimizing performance degradation."

That's the army's way of saying, "We're trying to keep you from getting slaughtered out there, so you better get motivated to keep your helmet on."

Beyond the helmet, a second major piece of equipment the modern soldier wears is what the Roman legions would have called the "breastplate." The formal name of the modern U.S. soldier's breastplate is the body armor, fragmentation protective vest, or what we commonly called the "flak jacket" in Vietnam.

The modern flak jacket is a direct descendant of medieval chain mail. In the history of warfare, chain mail, though expensive, was regarded as so effective it was issued constantly for almost two thousand years of warfare history.

The flak jacket consists of thirteen layers of fourteen-ounce, water-repellent Kevlar fabric designed to cover the upper torso. It weighs about nine pounds, costs about two hundred dollars, and is proven to decrease all shrapnel injuries by as much as 53 percent.

In Vietnam a pilot flying a Huey (UH-1) helicopter was at an altitude of just fifteen feet over a rice paddy when ground fire from an AK-47 round passed through the front of his chopper and struck him dead center in the chest. Wearing his ceramic "chicken" plate armor vest, the pilot, unwounded and unaffected, simply continued to fly his aircraft. Because one man wore his full armor, he saved the lives of others.

The routine of putting on the full armor significantly reduces the likelihood of fatal injury and greatly increases battlefield effectiveness.

Conversely, one man in less than full armor actually endangers the lives of those around him. When armor isn't put on, it is of no value at all. That's why the verb in Ephesians 6:11 is a command, not a request. It's a direct order to "put on" your armor.

Bottom line: The routine of putting on the full armor significantly reduces the likelihood of fatal injury and greatly increases battlefield effectiveness. We face an enemy that is a malevolent, God-hating, human-hunting, Christian-bashing machine. So let's get ready for battle, inside and out.

EQUIPMENT FOR RESISTING

Don't ever get tired of the armor passage in Ephesians chapter 6. Memorize it. Live with it. Quote it on dark nights when the fiery arrows are flying and on bright, blue-sky days when the war seems a thousand miles away. Forgetting this passage would be like falling asleep on guard duty, the almost unforgivable sin for a spirit warrior:

> Finally, be strong in the Lord and in the strength of His might. Put on the full armor of God, so that you will be able to stand firm against the schemes of the devil. For our struggle is not against flesh and blood, but against the rulers, against the powers, against the world forces of this darkness, against the spiritual forces of wickedness in the heavenly places. Therefore, take up the full armor of God, so that you will be able to resist in the evil day, and having done everything, to stand firm. Stand firm therefore, having girded your loins with truth, and having put on the breast-plate of righteousness, and having shod your feet with the preparation of the gospel of peace; in addition to all, taking up the shield of faith with which you will be able to extinguish all the flaming arrows of the evil one. And take the helmet of salvation, and the sword of the Spirit, which is the word of God. With all prayer and petition pray at all times in the Spirit, and with this in view, be on the alert with all perseverance and petition for all the saints.
>
> EPHESIANS 6:10–18

Let's take a quick look at that armor as a whole package. You'll note right off the top that there are six pieces, and that its role is primarily *defensive* in nature. We're given no indication in these verses that we're to go after the devil. No suggestion that we are to become aggressive demon hunters conducting major antidemon campaigns or deliverance meetings. No suggestion that we are to speak to his legions. No hint that we are to take authority over him. Not the slightest indication of a formula, or a prayer, or a command catalog. Just the armor…which is largely defensive and protective.

This is how you dress for success on the battlefield. This is how you beat the devil. This is how you win in spiritual warfare. This armored uniform was just as familiar to the Ephesian Christians as an NFL uniform is to a football fan today. The Ephesians saw the Roman legions regularly. Paul, a prisoner at the time, was likely chained to a Roman soldier while he was writing these words.

The equipment list is derived straight from the Roman infantry's equipment. Every legionnaire wore it. It was permanent attire for the soldier. One is never to face life's battles without it. One is never to be without it…period.

It's like in army basic training—you wear that helmet every day, everywhere. It's such a nuisance in the hot Georgia sun—and no one is even shooting at you there! Still, you wear it. Every day of your training.

So it is in the Christian life. Every day of your life you must put on your armor. It's part of who you are. It identifies you. It equips you. Satan is more afraid of and stymied by this magnificent armor than anything else you can be, wear, or do. In this armor you are to live—to stand, to watch, to never relax your vigilance.

THE BELT OF TRUTH

It's significant that the belt of truth is mentioned first: It is absolutely foundational.

This is a belt for function, not style. This is no designer belt to accent your outfit. This is the solid buckle of truth, the spiritual equivalent of the weightlifter's massive leather belt girded around the back and abdomen to hold everything together under stress. Without it, you will hurt yourself.

Every Roman soldier wore a tunic, a loose-fitting outer garment that was basically a square piece of durable material with holes in it for the head and arms. When draped loosely, it protected the Roman dogface from the elements. But it was a disastrous hindrance in the close hand-to-hand combat of the day. Without a belt, you'd be hopelessly entangled before you could even get to the battlefield.

If you weren't wearing your belt properly, your tunic would fly loosely, wrapping you up like an animal trapped in your own net. You would be helpless and defeated before you even engaged in battle. You would trip. You would fall. You would offer the enemy a place to grip. To enter battle without the belt girded was unthinkable!

The individual had to bend forward at the waist, extend an arm between the legs, and reach through the legs to grip the back lower fringe of the tunic. That back lower hem was then pulled forward through the legs and, with the person standing upright now, tucked into the belt in the front. Then the loose ends hanging to either side were pulled up from below and tucked into the belt. When all the loose ends of the tunic were carefully tucked in, the belt was cinched securely. The individual would then be girded for action.

It is indeed similar in function to the serious weightlifter's belt, but in the case of spiritual warfare, the belt is applied to your *brain* as opposed to your back. This spiritual war is brain over brawn, mind over matter. It is tucking all the loose ends of your life into the belt of truth. Girding up the loins of your mind in the belt of truth is refusing to think like the average human being. Refusing to let the world squeeze you into its mold.

This spiritual war is brain over brawn, mind over matter. It is tucking all the loose ends of your life into the belt of truth.

What kinds of loose ends might we be talking about here? Things like your personality, decisions, habits, work ethic, marriage, spending patterns, morals, parenting skills, giving amounts, sexual appetites, choices, and actions must all be tied together by and subject to God's truth. *Everything* in your life must be subjected to and held together by the truth.

The parallels to spiritual warfare are fairly obvious. If you are going to be an effective Christian, engaged in the spiritual warfare of everyday life, you must gather up the loose ends of your life and cinch your life securely with the belt of truth. *All* the elements of your life must be tucked into the securing qualities of the belt.

Read that list again, slowly. Pause for reflection on every one. Your personality. Your decisions. Your personal habits. Your work ethic. Your spending patterns. Your conversational style. Your marriage covenant. Your parenting skills. Your morals in every area. Your business ethics. Your giving amounts—a full tithe to your local church, and alms and offerings beyond. Your sexual appetites. Your eating habits. Your vocabulary. Your relationships. Your attitudes. Your choices. And, of course, all your other actions. Whew! The Holy Spirit takes this spirit-warrior stuff seriously!

The Roman's belt not only held the tunic together, it also carried the sword. It was the equivalent of today's soldier's LBE (load bearing equipment), a strong canvas harness to which is attached his handgun, ammunition, grenades, and knife. When a soldier buckles on his LBE it gives him a sense of security, a hidden and inner strength, and a personal confidence. It has a bracing effect. He is ready now to engage.

Your belt, Christian soldier, is one of truth. Christians in every age have regarded the "truth" here as the revelation of God through both the living Word, Christ, and the written Word, Scripture.

The Christian soldier must possess a strong, unshakable conviction in the reliability of Scripture and in its living power to impact the battlefield. You must not allow yourself to drift in your thinking, especially in this postmodern world that sees truth as individually centered, fluid, and culturally constructed. You must also demonstrate a facility with Scripture, becoming conversant with its pages and principles on a level that is wholly involved in the "dailyness" of life. Every good spirit warrior constantly asks himself, "What does the Bible say about this? About that? About anything and everything!"

If you want to survive the battle and weather the warfare, soldier, master the truth—the whole, comprehensive counsel of God, the truth of God's revelation. Are you involved in a regular, rigorous regimen of Bible study? If not, what in the world are you doing? Do you betray yourself by thinking Paul may have overstated the whole deal? Then you are incredibly vulnerable!

Your mind, your most critical weapon in battle, is braced by doctrine. Your soul is strengthened by biblical knowledge. Our Commander in Chief said it best when He faced off with the devil: "Man does not live by bread alone, but...by everything that proceeds out of the mouth of the LORD" (Deuteronomy 8:3). And the apostle caught it when he enjoined, "Be diligent to present yourself approved to God as a workman who does not need to be ashamed, accurately handling the word of truth" (2 Timothy 2:15).

Your mind, your most critical weapon in battle, is braced by doctrine.

So...read, read, read. Subscribe to a tape library...grow...firm up!

THE BREASTPLATE OF RIGHTEOUSNESS

The Roman soldier wore a molded metal chest covering that extended from the neck down nearly to the thighs, covering the entire torso. The breastplate covered the vitals—the heart, the lungs, and the viscera (bowels). Now this is an important recognition. Many ancient cultures centered the soul and/or heart in the viscera—literally, in the bowels! When truth had dropped the distance from the head to the heart, it was "owned."

In the Jewish culture, these visceral elements, particularly the bowels, were considered the seat of emotions and feelings. It was the seat of the affections, and the center of the conscience, the desires, and the will. It's where life made up its mind.

It is perhaps not unlike our own reference to "gut feelings," those strong mental-emotional convictions that govern our actions and behaviors. Sometimes we say, "I just have to go with my gut on this one." This, of course, can be good or bad, healthy or unhealthy. But the point here is that the breastplate of righteousness is intended to protect your visceral, soulish, and emotional makeup. In this way your personal behaviors can be appropriately righteous, *and you don't fall victim to emotional wounds.* It is at this visceral, emotionally needy level that we are often deeply wounded.

So many times we Christian soldiers fall right here. To my mind right now come the names and faces of many people in our own church who have, under the weight of emotional stress, made incredibly poor choices. This is so real. It is so personal. I'm tempted to write here a long list of actual names and addresses, together with full descriptions of the pain, wounds, and destruction of sin. If I did, it would break your heart as it breaks mine.

Satan's schemes appear to be so good and need-meeting, but they burn the soul with a painful fury. And these poor people have to live with the consequences of their choices for the rest of their lives. And not just them, but the people around them.

I know men who have borne significant emotional weight, only to eventually collapse and let their emotions seize the steering wheel. They run to another woman, somehow convincing themselves it is manly and virile. No! On the contrary, to cave in to one's emotional appetites is nothing less than rank emotional weakness. And it is the source of a thousand addictions.

To protect your mental-emotional vitals, you need to keep the breastplate of practiced righteousness polished to an incredibly high sheen.

Why is this a breastplate of righteousness? In Scripture, the term *righteousness* can refer to a variety of things: (1) your own self-righteousness, (2) the imputed righteousness of Christ, or (3) the believer's practical behavioral acts of righteousness.

The Christian soldier, based on his faith in positional righteousness, is then to behave righteously ("put it on") or practice righteousness on a daily basis. That is moral righteousness.

So when we talk about the breastplate of righteousness, let's add a word for clarity—the breastplate of *practiced* righteousness, which covers the vitals. The vitals are your viscera, the seat of affections, emotions, and conscience. That's where your appetites and your will meet—in your gut.

Will you allow your desires to rule you? Or will you rule your desires by act of will?

The answer rests in your quotient of practiced righteousness, your breastplate. If left unprotected, you *will* fall to deep emotional appetites. If you have not properly maintained your breastplate of practiced righteousness, the flaming arrows of appetite will penetrate. And you will be one more Christian on the growing casualty lists.

How many intelligent, thinking Christians have fallen to their deep-seated personal needs of the heart because they left their vitals unprotected!

Recently I was forced to announce the names of four members of our church who have become casualties. These were not bad people. To the contrary, these were stalwarts. Three of the four had formal ministry training and had actually served on church staffs in the past. And the fourth was one of the female "pillars of the church." Each was at one time an extraordinary example of committed Christian soldiering.

They are also human beings.

With normal human needs and desires.

After years of battling well, in a season of unguarded selfishness, they left their breastplates of *practiced* righteousness untended and fell in the darkness of the spiritual war. We pursued them following the Matthew 18 process of church discipline: there has been no apparent effect thus far. Three of the four have moved out of state and taken up with new "lovers." And the mates of their youth, to whom they gave their lifelong vows, are left behind. Aching. Their children are devastated and their families are destroyed.

All because their breastplates of *practiced* righteousness were allowed to rust like discarded antiques. They left their flak jackets stacked in the corner of their emotional tents when they went out on daily operations. Satan's fiery darts penetrated the unprotected soft tissue of their souls. And more lives and familes were blown apart, for failure to "put on" the flak jacket of practiced righteousness.

GERONIMO!

Maybe an analogy will help. Think of the paratrooper. Airborne! Do you know how long it takes the Army to teach a soldier how to jump out of an airplane? Three weeks! Three weeks of training just to jump out of an airplane, so gravity can take over.

It's not as simple as it looks. Oh, sure, gravity is gravity. You jump out the door and there's a 100 percent chance that you'll come down. The jumping and the descent are pretty much done deals. The critical point is the *landing*.

Falling a thousand feet through the air can be traumatic enough, but the landing even more so. And when you experience the traumatic point of impact, you'd best be trained to react rightly or you might just break both your legs—or worse.

Jump school is essentially three weeks of learning and practicing new behavior patterns. It's multiple days spent mastering the "parachute landing fall," or PLF. Hours and hours spent practicing for the moment of impact so it doesn't blow you apart. The goal is that under the pressure of a jump into combat you won't even have to think about landing—you'll instinctively move toward the right way of doing it. It's all a matter of practiced behavior.

Living by the word of righteousness has to do with time, custom, practice, and training. It is soldierly discipline practiced constantly so that at the moment of crisis—in that instant when the pressure's on—you'll know, almost instinctively, almost habitually, what you must do. Having learned new patterns, the breastplate of righteousness, which guards your vitals, will hold up during the battle. You will have so rehearsed the right thing to do that even under significant pressure, you'll just do it.

TRAINED FOR VICTORY

As a young officer in the war zone of Vietnam, I was not walking with Christ. The turmoil of the sixties had taken its toll on me to the place where, intellectually, I had left the faith. I was not sure God even existed. I tell you that to point out that my spiritual life was not healthy, to say the least. Even so, I managed not to succumb to many of the temptations practiced by a number of my GI friends.

At base camp, there were plenty of porn movies available for off-duty troops. And just a few miles away in town, all of the sinful pleasures of the East waited for any GI with a few bucks.

Now, why didn't I get sucked into the addiction like so many others did? It was certainly not due to a deeply vigorous spiritual life at the time. There was none. Nor was I immune to such temptation as a healthy young male far from home. I firmly believe that my ability to resist such things was the fruit of years of "practiced righteousness," learned under the tutelage of my father at home. I had no real strength in myself. But I did have training that managed to carry me.

We Weber boys were trained so consistently over the years at home in appropriate manly behavior that even without an active spiritual heart at the moment, the temptation did not penetrate. Even though I was spiritually disoriented for a lengthy season, the rehearsals of the years came through, and I didn't become a hapless victim of my own poor choices and appetites.

Heart issues are at stake here! We are called to live a devout and holy life of moral rectitude—whether we feel like it or not. Such a pattern of righteous habits, lived out by the grace of God and our diligent response to that grace, is worn like a breastplate, right over our vitals. This breastplate of practiced righteousness protects our vitals on the battlefield. So stand firm, soldier!

Just as the belt of truth overcomes the devil's deceits, so the breastplate of righteousness overwhelms his temptations. Apart from such a life of devout moral purity and holiness, the believer is subject to the whims of the evil one. By considering ourselves "dead to sin," we do not allow it to reign in our lives. We enjoy victory over the lusts of the flesh and other tools of the evil one. A clean conscience is a magnificent factor in carrying the battle. By consistently keeping short accounts and confessing our failings to our Lord and, as appropriate, to others, we keep the breastplate polished.

> Beloved, if our heart does not condemn us, we have confidence before God…because we keep His commandments and do the things that are pleasing in His sight.
>
> 1 JOHN 3:21–22

Such moral power clearly occupies the high ground and carries the day. A polished breastplate gives the Christian a life of joy, fruitfulness, and eternal reward.

Do right by your Savior and *nothing* else matters!

THE BOOTS

Footgear is absolutely critical to any strenuous activity, but most especially to war. Think of all the specialty footgear available today. Every sport—football, soccer, baseball, basketball, tennis—has its own unique, specially designed footgear.

I remember the day my parents presented me with my first pair of track shoes. It was a long time ago—and more than a few pounds back. I was just getting started in high school. The shoes were Adidas "three-stripers." White with three blue stripes. They fit tight, molded to the foot, and felt like a million bucks. And of course they were equipped with just the right length of spike to grip those cinders for the quarter mile. With those shoes I was prepared to run like never before.

Prepared. That's the key word when it comes to your footgear. The Christian soldier's feet are to be shod with the *preparation* of the gospel of peace. The key element in this piece of armor is the readiness derived from the gospel of peace. "Combat readiness" is a basic military term. Preparedness is the key element for any standing army. And if your feet aren't ready, you are not ready.

One of the most critical keys to the success of Caesar's legions was the ability of the Roman legions to move great distances, to move quickly, and to sustain the pace on the long marches. It's what the military calls "expeditious mobility."

Historically, far more soldiers on the battlefield have been immobilized by foot problems than have gone down from bullets. That was certainly true in Vietnam. Many a platoon sergeant in those jungles felt the most critical part of his job was to be a foot-care specialist. Sometimes he felt more like a nurse or a mother than he did the leader of a lean, mean, fighting machine. "Change your socks, boys" became his regular mantra. "Take your boots off. Dry your feet. And, yes, powder 'em, too, or you're no good to this unit. That powder is gooood for you. The Army wouldn't issue it to you if you didn't need it!"

Early in the Vietnam War, the troops wore the normal leather military boot the Army had used for years. But that had to change if the Army were to survive. The normal leather boot couldn't weather those jungles. Today when you think of the soldier in Vietnam you probably don't think of him wearing the black leather jump boot, but rather the specially developed, self-draining, self-drying "jungle boot" designed for the wet, humid environment of the jungles of Southeast Asia.

So it was with the roman soldier. Long marches and solid stances required what Josephus called "shoes thickly studded with sharp nails."[1] The Romans wore the right footgear. Boots are what advance the soldier on the battlefield, carry the soldier to meet the enemy, and ready the soldier for battle.

What is it that readies your heart for spiritual warfare? The gospel of peace! Being perfectly secure in life's battles because you are carried to war by the gospel of peace.

These first three pieces of armor—belt, breastplate, and boots—are foundational, long-range protection, never removed from the soldier. Now we come to three more pieces. Ephesians 6:16 says "above all" or "in addition to all" when it approaches the final three pieces of equipment. It is helpful to know that this "above all" is not stated in the sense that what follows is most critical, but more in the sense of "given all these basic elements above, a significant, even indispensable, addition follows."

THE SHIELD OF FAITH

The Roman soldiers had two kinds of shields in their armory inventory. One was an individual or personal shield. It was round, about two feet in diameter, and attached to the arm. It was lightweight and highly mobile—an individual shield. It is important to note that this personal shield is *not* the one referred to here in Ephesians.

The second Roman shield was a much larger shield: about two-and-a-half feet wide and four feet high. It was made of wood and usually covered with a layer of leather (often soaked with water, which served to deflect or extinguish any fiery arrows). This second shield, or *thurcos,* is the shield Paul names here. Though carried by an individual, it was not a personal shield, per se. It was always carried in formation. It was the shield intended to protect far more than the individual carrying it. It was intended to defend the group.

These larger shields were carried in such a way that they packed tightly together, virtually interlocking, to defend the whole unit formation.

This is the full-sized buckler which the Roman legions of infantry carried when the legions were marching as a unit. These larger shields were carried in such a way that they packed tightly together, virtually interlocking, into a large complex or "testudo" of shields. By virtue of their being tensely packed together with others, the shields served to defend the whole unit formation. The many became one.

Do you see the critical point here? This is the shield of faith, which, by design, is interlocked with the soldier next to you. This is the shield of faith utilized in community, the community of faith. In our spiritual battles, as is true in any combat environment, there is no room for lone rangers. If you expect to be protected, you've got to stick with the group, march with the unit, and live like a family.

The strength of locking arms or interlocking shields is an indispensable quality for the spirit warrior. For example, I believe if Jonathon had lived, there would have been no Bathsheba episode in David's life. We absolutely need the interlocking effect of "souls knit together" with fellow spirit warriors if we're going to survive and thrive on the battlefield. Left to ourselves we are picked off one by one. Get in a group! Form up! And lock your shield of faith with the soldier next to you.

What is the "faith" Paul refers to here? Paul is not here describing doctrine or systematic theology, the whole body of truth that we sometimes call "the faith." Rather, the faith here refers to a deep, personal, and total trust in God. It is the faith of personal trust in God and His sovereign care. It is the wonderfully freeing confidence of abandonment to God, trusting Him entirely with one's well-being, both present and future. This is the kind of faith which fosters rest in the shadow of the Almighty, that faith which confidently asserts, "Live or die, I am in the Father's hand. I trust Him with my life, my soul, my all."

It's the deep personal trust which Paul expressed in his letter to the Philippians. From prison, possibly chained to a guard whose equipment he described in Ephesians 6. In the first chapter of Philippians, Paul wrote:

> My imprisonment in the cause of Christ has become
> well known throughout the whole praetorian guard and
> to everyone else.... What then? [How am I to think
> about this battle?] Only that in every way...Christ is
> proclaimed; and in this I rejoice, yes, and I will rejoice.
> For I know that this shall turn out for my deliver-
> ance.... Christ shall even now, as always, be exalted in
> my body, whether by life or by death. For to me, to live
> is Christ and to die is gain. But if I am to live on in the
> flesh, this will mean fruitful labor for me; and I do not
> know which to choose. But I am hard pressed in both
> directions, having the desire to depart and be with
> Christ, for that is very [far] much [more]; yet to remain
> on in the flesh is more necessary for your sake.
>
> PHILIPPIANS 1:13, 18–24, BRACKETED WORDS MY ADDITION

THE HELMET OF SALVATION

There's a clear and straightforward purpose for the helmet—to protect the soldier from head wounds.

The Roman helmet was made of thick leather, sometimes covered with metal plates, sometimes with a molded bronze or iron shell, sometimes with extended cheek plates. It was intended to protect the head and face, and even the eyes, in battle.

Nothing is more important on the battlefield than perspective. Nothing

The head, including the eyes, is the centerpiece of perspective in battle. A helmet is indispensable to the soldier.

is more critical than having your wits about you and a clarity regarding what is happening. The head, including the eyes, is the centerpiece of perspective in battle. A helmet is indispensable to the soldier.

Have you ever had your "bell rung"? Believe me, it's not something to aspire to. It's totally disorienting. Even dangerous. That's why head slaps are outlawed in the NFL. Can you imagine playing football in full uniform, except for your helmet? Ouch! Your bell would be rung on the first play, and you'd be utterly useless for the rest of the game.

I had my bell rung one time. I was playing college football, at the wide receiver position. Seven minutes before halftime, the quarterback called a play in the huddle that gave me a particularly crucial, albeit inglorious, assignment—a crackback block on the defensive end. No problem. Well, yes, it was. This particular defensive end was huge—he stood six feet seven and weighed in at over 250 pounds.

It was a quick-developing play so I had to commit early. I moved with the snap, took a couple of steps, and loaded up for the block. I actually left my feet and was stretched out, fully committed to impact his knees from what I expected would be his blind side (legal at the time).

But there was a problem.

He'd seen me coming and turned full into me. In fact, he raised his knee as an offensive weapon. Having already left the ground, there were no alternatives left to me. The guy put his kneepad full force into my helmet and face mask. Boom! That was it. The last thing I remember seeing was his huge knee at point-blank range.

When the play concluded, no one seemed to notice, least of all me—but I was out cold though still on my feet. I had a fully functional body, but no head. A walking concussion. I collected myself after the play like everyone else and returned to the huddle. But I didn't know it. Later I would learn that only the sportscaster, from his perspective high in the booth, had noticed me taking a circuitous route back to the huddle after each of the subsequent plays. Fortunately halftime arrived soon.

The first thing I remember after seeing that knee headed straight between my eyes was "waking up" in the locker room at halftime, sucking on an orange and watching the coach at the board. No recollection of any subsequent plays. No remembrance of the halftime clock. No recall of the jog from the field to the locker room. I didn't even remember picking up the orange. Evidently the taste or smell of the citrus shocked me back into reality, and my senses gradually cleared.

I could hardly wait to see the game films on Monday. When I did it was like watching someone else in action. There were about eleven minutes of my life that even the film failed to bring back to memory.

Here's the point, of course: A blow to the head leaves you senseless and disoriented, perhaps able to appear functional, but absolutely oblivious to reality and perspective, and therefore utterly dysfunctional.

I wonder how many Christians in America are functioning right now with a cracked helmet. They may be walking about with the appearance of faithfulness, but they are utterly worthless to the kingdom in terms of impact and true function.

This spiritual warfare helmet, intended to protect the head and thereby preserve perspective in battle, is called the helmet of salvation. Since this passage is addressed to Christian believers, we know Paul is not saying, "Christian, get saved." Nevertheless, the Holy Spirit does want us to wrap our minds around the fullness of salvation. The "helmet of salvation" word picture suggests that Satan's head slaps are directed at the believer's security, his confidence, his orientation, his perspective.

Satanic head slaps come in a variety of forms. I'm thinking of one friend who went out of uniform, so to speak, to his twenty-year high school reunion. He's a good man. He's a family man. He loves his wife and kids. But it was a particular season in his life when he'd lost perspective. There had been some disappointments professionally, and, quite frankly, his marriage had come to one of those points that every marriage experiences: that time when things are a bit out of kilter.

He walked unprotected into that high school reunion, encountered an old flame from two decades prior, and almost walked off the cliff. His helmet of salvation had been twisted a bit on his noggin, and it nearly cost him dearly. But a fellow soldier saw what was happening, grabbed him by the belt, and pulled him from the edge. In his own discouragement and loss of perspective, he nearly became a casualty—all because he hadn't put his helmet on securely.

Satan's disorienting blows to the head impact the believer's ability to understand and appreciate the certainty and fullness of his salvation—not only his justification, but his sanctifying holiness, and his eventual and eternal glorification.

Look at it from another angle. The disorienting head blows from Satan often center around discouragement and doubt. We become deeply discouraged over our own failures to be all we want to be in Christ. And Satan, the accuser of the brethren, gnaws away at our confidence with his accusations. We begin to doubt not only ourselves, but our salvation, our faithfulness, our place in the kingdom, our role in the battle, and ultimately, the Lord Himself. Satan loves to get us feeling that we're not spiritual enough to serve Christ well.

Remember what we established a few chapters back? One of Satan's chief tactics is to get us to doubt God's Word and God's character. The most debilitating satanic attacks are those that tempt the believer to doubt his salvation, that say he is lost or could lose his salvation. The believer may indeed lose his effectiveness in the war—and even some of the battlefield decorations or eternal rewards he may have won—but he does *not* lose his salvation. Don't allow Satan to render you ineffective on the battlefield because you're not wearing your helmet securely.

An incident from two of my sons' days in high school comes to mind. Kent and Blake were with our student ministries group on a snow-day activity—skiing, snowboarding, and snowtubing in Central Oregon. The two were on the same tube, Blake on top. At a high rate of speed they hit a mogul; Blake flew high into the air and landed upside down with a terrific blow to his head on the ice. People raced to see if he was okay. He stood up, but it was immediately apparent he was seriously dazed. He was rushed to the hospital and diagnosed with a significant concussion.

The disorienting head blows from Satan often center around discouragement and doubt. The helmet of salvation is intended to protect us from such head wounds as disorientation, doubt, and discouragement.

All the while Blake carried on a running conversation with our student ministry pastor, Steve Keels. My middle son kept making the same statement over and over again. "Keels, what are you doing here? Keels, what am I doing here? How did I get up here? Keels, have you called my dad?"

Blake, thoroughly disoriented, repeated himself so many times, Steve simply anticipated his next question and gave him the answer before he could finish asking. At which point Blake would ask, "Keels, wow, how did you read my mind?"

Disorientation is...well, disorienting. Put your helmet on right. Protecting your head is absolutely critical if you intend to survive and thrive on the battlefield. Head slaps may be illegal in the NFL, but Satan never plays by the rules. And he loves to ring your bell.

The helmet of salvation is intended to protect us from the head wounds of disorientation, doubt, and discouragement. The helmet of salvation refers to the past, present, and future aspects of our salvation. It is the certain prospect of ultimate victory! The helmet of salvation is the assurance of future, full, and final salvation and victory.

The helmet of salvation, then, is the emblem of hope in the spiritual warrior's battles. Your salvation is your guarantee of ultimate victory. Our failures, our sins, and our unresolved problems are all cared for in the fullness of salvation. Listen to the Scriptures:

> Because God wanted to make the unchanging nature of his
> purpose very clear to the heirs of what was promised, he
> confirmed it with an oath. God did this so that, by two
> unchangeable things in which it is impossible for God to
> lie, we who have fled to seize the hope offered to us may be
> greatly encouraged. We have this hope as an anchor for the
> soul, firm and secure.
>
> HEBREWS 6:17–19, NIV

This passage tells us that God has already said enough to give us total encouragement. He's given us His Word, a clear and careful promise. But He wants to go another step. He voluntarily adds to His infallible promise an inviolable oath! Two unchangeable things: a promise and an oath—both based on the integrity and character of God Himself. Wow—that's strong encouragement! Encouragement to do what? To seize the hope! Get hold of it! It's incredible! It's true. It's certain. It's guaranteed. It's eternal. Seize it and hang on.

Put on the helmet of salvation!

An old friend and a fine pastor, John Piper, comments on this passage:

> There are good times in this life. But let's face it: The
> days are evil; our imperfections frustrate us; and we are
> getting older and moving toward the grave. If in this life
> only we have hoped in Christ we are of all people most
> to be pitied (1 Corinthians 15:19). There are good
> times yet to come in this life. But fewer. And even these
> are rubbish, compared to the surpassing worth of gain-
> ing Christ in death (Philippians 1:21). Even here we
> can rejoice with joy unspeakable and full of glory. But
> only because there is a "hope set before us." Reach out

and seize it. God encourages you to. Take it now. Enjoy it now. Be encouraged by it now. Be strongly encouraged. Because your hope is secured with double infiniteness: the promise of God and the oath of God."[2]

Seize the certain hope!

Seize is a potent word, isn't it? It's an aggressive word. A forceful word. It literally means "to take into custody; to apprehend; to grip with force." The Holy Spirit's point: Get a firm grip on the certainty of your future, your hope. God is shouting, "Get a grip on this, folks!"

Put on the helmet of salvation, the emblem of hope on the battlefield. Living without your hope is like running a race with no finish line…ever. There *is* an end to this battle. Persevere. Don't quit. Stay in the fight. Stand firm. Hold your ground!

Stay at it…when your marriage isn't fun.

Stay at it…when parenting is over your head.

Stay at it…when the job is crushing your spirit.

Stay at it…when your kids let you down.

Stay at it…when your mate betrays you.

Stay at it. Seize the hope! Don't go down!

Victory is certain. Put on the helmet of salvation: the full assurance of hope persistently embraced, the certain prospect of ultimate victory. Dress for success…on the battlefield.

THE SWORD OF THE SPIRIT

The sword of the Spirit is God's Word in its offensive posture. The belt of truth is the comprehensive, objective reality of truth from all sources, centered in the revelation of God, His Word. The belt of truth is centered in the Word, primarily in its inward orientation to your soul, in what you might call its preserving, protecting, defensive posture. The sword of the Spirit is the Word of God in its primarily offensive, thrusting posture, intended to penetrate the enemy's purposes. We wield this sword to penetrate the culture.

The sword is the typical instrument of the military culture. It is the offensive instrument of war, the principal means of dealing the telling blow to the enemy. The Roman soldier's sword, or *machaira,* was anywhere from six to eighteen inches long. It was primarily a thrusting weapon used in hand-to-hand combat. It was the warrior's primary weapon, and he was thoroughly familiar with it. The soldier and his weapon were so close that the weapon was like a member of the soldier's family.

I suppose you might compare it to the finely balanced pistol of the noble lawmen of the old West. How many great westerns have we seen in which the old warrior, having retired from the active battlefield, is now faced with a crisis of major proportions? He walks quietly to the back room where there sits an old trunk. Carefully he removes a bundle wrapped in soft cloth. It contains his trusty sidearm and leather holster. He turns the gun over in his hand, strokes it with his finger, hefts it in the palm of his hand. Then, with a dexterity beguiling his age, he spins the gun around his trigger finger and slips it back into its holster. Then he straps it onto his waist and heads out to do the right thing.

When I think of that scene in terms of spiritual warfare, I think of my own father. I remember very well the day when I was just a youngster that Dad was able to purchase his first Thompson Chain Reference Bible. It was, of course, in the old King James Version. It was thick and heavy enough to use as a doorstop in any mountain lodge. I remember thinking he needed a wheelbarrow just to carry it around.

Over the years that old Bible has become the most obvious symbol of my father's life. He never leaves home without it. He carries it faithfully to our elders' meetings. A strange sense of serenity falls over me when I watch him pick it up, open it, thumb through a couple of pages, and drop his finger on a well-worn spot.

If you were able to pick up that old Bible yourself, you would find that it was well-used, underlined, thumbed, and starred. And you would find in the margins—top, bottom, and sides—in the precious handwriting of a man I deeply love, those personal little notes that offer a spiritual insight and uplift. The Book has become a truly awesome weapon in Dad's hands.

Not bad for an old coal miner turned city fireman, wouldn't you say? Dad and I frequently have to chuckle because so many people who come to our church and see Dad and his Bible just assume he's a retired pastor. Nope. Just a Christian infantryman with a well-worn sword that balances beautifully in his aged hand.

When was the last time you picked up your sword, soldier? Why don't you go get it out right now? Put this book down, go find your favorite old Bible, and hold it for a while. Thumb through its pages and let its wisdom remind you of all the things that are right about life under the King's enlistment.

The sword of the Spirit is a powerful, culture-penetrating weapon. It is your primary offensive weapon. Get to know it. Become intimately familiar with it. Feel it. Feel its balance. Feel its edge. Eat with it, sleep with it, walk with it, live with it. Know it, love it, and use it...or make no difference on the battlefield.

Face the fire and go in where it is hottest!

GENERAL A. P. HILL,
MAY 1864

The weapons of our warfare are...divinely powerful
for the destruction of fortresses. We are destroying speculations
and every lofty thing raised up against the knowledge of God.

2 CORINTHIANS 10:4-5

Deliver those who are being taken away to death,
And those who are staggering to slaughter,
Oh hold them back.
If you say, "See, we did not know this,"
Does He not consider it who weighs the hearts?
And does He not know it who keeps your soul?
And will He not render to man according to his work?

PROVERBS 24:11-12

RUN TO THE GUNS: CHARGING THE ENEMY'S STRONGHOLDS

There is no place for passivity on a battlefield. War is vigorous, aggressive, and overwhelming. It's all out. In a word, it is offensive.

Battlefields are hot and hostile. Bullets fly. Casualties mount. People scream. The natural tendency in such a hot environment is to "go to the ground," as the infantryman would say. And it's okay to take a limited and protective moment to gather your wits and bearings.

But you can't stay there...immobile.

Any good soldier knows that the longer you just lay there, the greater the likelihood is that you will become a casualty. If you just lay there hoping the nightmare of the firefight will go away, you will be destroyed. Sooner or later, the soldier must get up and fight off the attacking forces—or die.

Every war movie you see has the leader urging his troops not to stay on the beach where they will be slaughtered, but to get up, to charge, to run toward the guns. Nations must seek to avoid war, but once engaged, war is no longer defensive but offensive in nature. It is the soldier's responsibility under oath to protect the homeland. It is the soldier's calling to, as the U.S. Army doctrine puts it, "close with and destroy" the enemy.

That is why Jesus came to earth—to close with and destroy the enemy. Scripture leaves no doubt at all. "The Son of God appeared for this purpose, to destroy the works of the devil" (1 John 3:8).

Jesus came to earth in order to run to the guns! At the Cross, He closed with the enemy and won the battle, thus guaranteeing total victory. At His second coming He will directly and violently destroy the evil one by casting him into the lake of eternal fire and destruction. Since the battle on Mount Calvary, the church has been engaged in mopping up operations, so to speak.

The object of spiritual warfare, then, is not just to survive, but to realize the victory. To win! To close with and destroy the works of the devil. General Patton, for all his legendary eccentricities, grasped this fundamental principle of war. It made him the greatest battlefield general of World War II. He pretty much summed it up when he implied there were really only three principles of war: "Attack! Attack! And attack!"

"We all know we are in a war. Our problem is that we are not at war!" The warrior spirit is ruled by a sense of duty, sacrifice, and devotion.

Bill McCartney, former football coach of the National Champion Colorado Buffaloes and well-known founder of Promise Keepers (PK), seconds that motion. He has said it well to hundreds of thousands of men at PK stadium rallies across this country: "We all know we are in a war. Our problem is that we are not *at* war!"

Coach is right. Knowing there is a war on is one thing. Signing up and soldiering is quite another. The critical difference is what we might call the warrior spirit.

THE WARRIOR SPIRIT

So many of the great ones seem to have had the warrior spirit: Abraham, Moses, Joshua, Caleb, Deborah, David, Peter, Paul, and countless others. The warrior spirit is a shielding, defending, guarding, protecting attitude. It is a spirit of disciplined, assertive, sometimes aggressive, action.

The warrior spirit does not love war. Real soldiers never do. The warrior spirit draws no pleasure from conflict or destruction, nor does it seek a fight. At the same time, however, it will not turn and run from a just cause. Highly principled and with deep moral commitments, the warrior spirit is ruled by a sense of duty, sacrifice, and devotion. This is the individual who steps out of his or her comfort zone and stands in the gap for the sake of those who cannot defend themselves.

This warrior spirit is invaluable in both physical and spiritual warfare.

The thinking Christian must live with a wartime mentality. The thinking Christian *must retain the warrior spirit.*

It takes a warrior to do battle. The warrior spirit is a spirit of intelligent risk, personal discipline, and willing sacrifice. David's clearest expression of that spirit may have come out of a conversation with King Saul just before the famous encounter with Goliath. The teenager—fresh from the backcountry and filled with the presence of the living God—calmly explained to the cynical king that every true shepherd was also a warrior:

> "When a lion or a bear comes to steal a lamb from the
> flock, I go after it with a club and take the lamb from its
> mouth. If the animal turns on me, I catch it by the jaw
> and club it to death. I have done this to both lions and
> bears, and I'll do it to this pagan Philistine, too, for he
> has defied the armies of the living God! The LORD who
> saved me from the claws of the lion and the bear will save
> me from this Philistine!"
>
> 1 SAMUEL 17:34B-37, NLT

The warrior spirit is a blend of responsibility, duty, courage, justice, and aggressive action. It accepts legitimate risks as part of the fiber of life on a sin-stained planet. It acknowledges the fact that risks, wounds, and sacrifices are part and parcel of its trade. It understands that there truly are some things worth dying for. It does not invest disproportionate amounts of energy and thought on self-preservation.

Jesus was reflecting such a spirit in His conversation with the disciples after Peter's great confession, "You are the Christ!" Jesus told them He would have to suffer and be killed (Matthew 16:21). Luke says He "set His face" (Luke 9:51, NKJV) to go to Jerusalem. A warrior is resolute, as Jesus was. When His disciples tried to convince Him there must be another way, that it just wasn't worth the risk, Jesus responded, in no uncertain terms, in the language of the ultimate spirit warrior:

> "You are not setting your mind on God's interests, but
> man's.... If anyone wishes to come after Me, he must
> deny himself, and take up his cross and follow Me. For
> whoever wishes to save his life will lose it; but whoever
> loses his life for My sake will find it."
>
> MATTHEW 16:23-25

184 | SPIRIT WARRIORS

That is the warrior spirit. In our peace-at-any-price, comfort-at-any-cost culture, this steely determination of mind, heart, and will is something not easy to maintain, let alone develop. We like everything neat and clean. Antiseptic. We shrink back from treading into messy, difficult, or possibly dangerous situations. We tend to go soft at all the wrong times. Let me try to explain by using one relatively recent but tragic and concrete example.

THE FOLLY OF PASSIVE CONTAINMENT

What happened at Columbine High School in Littleton, Colorado, has caused our country to reexamine many aspects of our culture. Most obvious, of course, is the question: Why are children killing children? But another troubling question—not as often discussed around the water cooler or in the chat rooms—surrounded the actions of the professional SWAT teams that day. Why did our SWAT teams, armed to the teeth and wearing flak jackets and helmets, take so long to get to the point of action?

Why did no one—not even our best—run to the guns?

Please understand that in no way do I wish to criticize our magnificent law enforcement agencies in this country. At Good Shepherd Church we go out of our way to honor our local police, spending thousands of dollars every year, for example, on our annual Police Appreciation Banquet. But I do think we need to carefully analyze our culture and its fundamental doctrines with regard to obvious risk and violence.

You know the story of what happened at Columbine on that infamous day. Two angry high school students entered the building, heavily armed and with full intent to kill. There was shooting. At least one school security officer on the scene exchanged fire with Harris and Klebold.

The incident was immediately reported to the police.

The shooting continued.

SWAT teams arrived.

The shooting continued.

For *hours* the police practiced their current doctrine: containment. It may not be a bad policy in and of itself when properly applied, but sometimes containment may be a convenient word for attempting to keep the violence wrapped up in a limited area while not getting hurt yourself.

Think it through now. Bullets are streaking through a public school building filled with students and teachers, and we are containing?

Containing! There may be a time to contain. But it is not when the fox is loose in the coop.

My friend, there is a time to run to the guns.

Gunfire in a public school chock-full of kids is probably not the time to contain. That's the time to stop the guns! End the damage. Cut it off. With shots ringing out in a public school and bleeding kids crawling out of second-story windows, do we really need to contain? No. It's time to run to the guns. It's time to put an end to the carnage.

Now don't be too quick to cast stones at the officers involved. They were practicing what their training had taught them: Don't engage. And their training reflects our increasingly weakening culture. Contain. Wait it out. Negotiate. Reason. Call in the trained talkers. You see the fallacy, don't you?

A similar fallacy is making inroads in the U.S. military. It's part of our broader cultural drift to risk-free living. The irony is that our efforts to be secure are actually guaranteeing the opposite—insecurity. With an overbearing aversion to risk, we expose ourselves to even greater long-term danger. So determined are we to avoid casualties that we increase the number of victims. In the U.S. military this same softer, more passive spirit shows itself in the practices of "risk analysis." Columbine clearly demonstrates that a risk-free mentality can be a killer. Long, drawn-out risk assessments, in many cases, can actually be impediments.

Warriors, by definition, are in a risky business. The profession of arms, in both the police and military communities, cannot allow the warrior spirit to erode. The willingness to sacrifice must still be very much a part of the soldier's life.

I was impressed recently when the city of Portland, Oregon, hired a new police chief, Mark Kroeker. I had never met the man previously, but his first on-air interview with a local television reporter reflected real wisdom and maturity. The reporter said, "Describe for us your ideal police officer."

The new chief, a believer, responded thoughtfully: "The ideal police officer is highly intelligent, with a bright and welcoming countenance. He loves people, engages easily in conversation, and can relate to all varieties of people."

Then, with his warm smile tightening a bit at the edges, the chief added, "And, when faced with no alternative, he must be a skilled gunfighter."

The chief is right. That is the balance. When faced with the destruction all too common in our world, the officer must be the man of the in-between and run to the guns.

More recent reports out of Columbine suggest that we ought to take some comfort in the fact that most of the students killed there actually died in the first few minutes of those long hours. Indeed they did. But that recognition is not only twenty-twenty hindsight, it is also irrelevant. The fact is that bullets were still flying for some time and that one teacher did, in fact, die because of the time allowed to elapse.

The point should be clear: In a firefight in which innocent, unarmed people are dying, you've got to be active. On the battlefield, you've got to run to the guns. You've got to close with the enemy and engage him. When a lion or a bear is among the sheep, it's no time to compose a psalm, it's time to *act*.

STAND IN THE GAP

Coach Bill McCartney is a spirit warrior. "Coach" was heavy-hearted for his country. He had traced that deep concern to the loss of biblical manliness in our culture. But Coach didn't stop with that knowledge. He took action.

Weighted down with our nation's loss of true Christian manhood, Bill prayed. He talked to a few friends. They got together. They invited a few more. Seventy-two became four thousand in 1992, fifty thousand in 1993, and hundreds of thousands more in a few short years. Promise Keepers and its vision of restored Christian manhood reached a high mark with over a million men assembling at the nation's capital to "stand in the gap." The reverberations are still being felt today.

That's the warrior spirit in a spirit warrior. Way to go, Coach.

Christian disciples are spiritual soldiers. Assertive, not timid. Active, not passive. Yes, it's is a metaphor, but it's more than that. Sometimes the physical and spiritual realities can blend into one very real battle.

Take, for example, Wedgwood Baptist Church in Fort Worth, Texas. To take the lesson a little closer to the sanctuary proper, picture yourself as a member of Wedgwood on that terrible Wednesday night when the services were invaded by a gunman.

On September 15, 1999, Larry Ashbrook walked into the church, guns blazing. He killed eight innocent people and wounded seven more.

Still, no one stopped him. Apparently there was no man of the in-between present. Who knows what would have happened had he not chosen, eventually, to shoot himself. The only thing that stopped the nightmare was his own suicide.

Take it out of the metaphorical. What if a gunman invaded your church this next weekend? What would you do? Plug your ears? Drop to the ground and hide? Crawl under a chair? Hope "someone else" will act? I'll tell you what—there shouldn't be any doubt whatsoever. Men, run to the guns! Stop it. Yes, even at great personal sacrifice, including, if necessary, your own life. The guy who invaded Wedgwood had time to reload multiple times because no one took action.

To be fair, I need to recognize that initially people did not understand what was happening. But let's also be honest: It doesn't take all that long to recognize real bullets and real blood.

Don't lay down.

Don't sit by and watch.

Don't hide under the pews.

Run to the guns.

Save the innocent.

Yes, some of us would likely pay a price, but in doing so we protect the lives near and dear around us. Is that not the most basic of warrior functions? Is that not the most basic intention of Christ, to save us from the enemy who would destroy us? And in so doing, it cost Him His life.

Too many spirit warriors in Christ's army tend to sit by and watch. Too many tend to hide in the pews. There's a war going on out there, and you're in it, people. Engage! Get serious. Take responsibility. Run to the guns.

Yes, we are in a war. From before the beginning of time—and every single day since—the adversary has marshaled his forces against the living God. The devil will stop at nothing, will do anything that is effective, to destroy the intentions of God. Satan's heart is filled with unbridled rage and hatred toward the living God—and therefore he hates you. At the very heart of Satan's strategy is the destruction of the image of God—the human being.

There is absolutely no place for passivity in this spiritual battle.

Your person, your life, your marriage, your family, and your church are at the very center of the battle. And if you just lay there, you're going to lose them all! There is absolutely no place for passivity in this spiritual battle.

STORMING THE FORTRESSES

That "get up and fight it" attitude is the Holy Spirit's point in a statement Paul makes in 2 Corinthians. It is a warfare passage. It is a call to take the offensive. Paul is insisting that he and any Christian must take an offensive posture with regard to the battle. It is Paul's battle cry, his charge to run to the guns—to overrun the enemy's high ground! Here it is:

> For though we walk in the flesh, we do not war accord-
> ing to the flesh, for the weapons of our warfare are not of
> the flesh, but divinely powerful for the destruction of
> fortresses. We are destroying speculations and every lofty
> thing raised up against the knowledge of God, and we are
> taking every thought captive to the obedience of Christ.
>
> 2 CORINTHIANS 10:3-5

Get up, take the initiative, and tear down the enemy's fortresses.

How do you muster your offensive courage? The Christian soldier's deepest well of strength for these battles does not lie in the normal, fleshly weapons of personal power, assertive charisma, impressive credentials, or psychological "pumping up," but in what the Bible calls "weapons...divinely powerful for the destruction of fortresses" (2 Corinthians 10:4).

Those weapons, and the instructions for their use, are carefully inventoried in the soldier's field manual, the Word of God. The believer's arsenal includes such divinely powerful tools as knowing the Bible and intimacy with God through prayer. Those weapons, when properly employed on the battlefield, dismantle the enemy's capacity for doing effective battle.

Paul uses these weapons for the "destruction of fortresses." Fortresses are enemy strongholds. They are simply positions of strength. Fortresses are the strongholds, the center points, of the enemy's forces.

In the ancient Near East, the chief cities were the walled cities. The only secure population centers were enclosed within walls that were not uncommonly fifteen to twenty-five feet thick and over twenty-five feet high. Trenches or moats were usually dug in front of the walls, and towers built at the corners and other strategic points in the wall. These fortified cities were regarded as utterly impregnable.

The Assyrian capital, Nineveh, a city of about eighteen-hundred acres, was surrounded with walls a hundred feet high. They were so thick at the top that three chariots could ride abreast on top. Additionally, the walls were fortified by twelve-hundred towers as strong points. The city was surrounded on three sides by a huge moat, and on the fourth side was the river. Nineveh was considered to be unconquerable.

The Bible is telling us that spiritual warfare involves offensively charging the enemy's strongholds…and taking them apart. Spiritual warfare involves aggressively dismantling the enemy's defenses, no matter how entrenched or formidable they may appear to our eyes.

And what are the enemy's fortresses or strongholds? What is the apostle insisting we target here? The enemy's strongholds are patterns of thinking. They are what the Spirit of God here calls "speculations and every lofty thing raised up against the knowledge of God" (2 Corinthians 10:5).

The enemy's strongholds are patterns of thinking— "speculations and every lofty thing raised up against the knowledge of God."

The Christian has to learn to get up off the ground and charge straight into the teeth of the enemy's grip on himself and on other people. The Christian has to use the divinely powerful weapons (the Word, prayer, love of God, fear of God, obedience to God) to dismantle the thoughts, patterns, philosophies, perspectives, and lifestyles that the enemy uses as strongholds over people's lives.

This passage insists that we, as my longtime friend and pastoral colleague Alan Hlavka said so well, are to "break down every deceptive argument and imposing defense that people erect against the true knowledge of God. We fight to capture every thought until it acknowledges the authority of Christ."

Paul uses these military word pictures metaphorically here to refer to any and all things which people run to—other than Jesus Christ—for their security or sense of protection and identity. Human beings raise such walls and towers of self-protection to stand defiantly between themselves and God. Paul is speaking here, then, of taking the offensive against all the personal and philosophical strongholds which keep people from coming to Christ.

Perhaps when he was writing this passage, the apostle had Proverbs 21:22 in mind: "A wise man scales the city of the mighty, and brings down the stronghold in which they trust."

Paul knew—and the evil one knows—that if you capture the mind, you've captured life. The fortresses Paul is speaking about are largely conceptual. It's about thoughts. The spiritual fortresses of that day and this are those things that challenge belief in, dependence upon, obedience to, and love for Jesus Christ and His view of every facet of life. He was and always will be the issue. Paul is saying that he, and we, must use divinely powerful weapons to dismantle the thoughts, philosophies, and lifestyles that stand up in defiance of the living God.

This is a call to aggressive battle with the spirit of this age—but not by demon bashing. We run to the guns by fighting to capture every pattern of thinking until it acknowledges the authority of Christ. Every thought, not just in our own heads, but in our whole culture! And the verb is in the present continuous sense. That implies an ongoing process, a continual struggle. Like warfare, it's not 9 to 5—it's day and night, 24/7, 365 days a year.

PRISONER SNATCH

At every level the Holy Spirit insists that Christians "take every thought captive to the obedience of Christ" (2 Corinthians 10:5). Taking a captive is no small undertaking. Making a "prisoner snatch" is the most complex of military operations. From its very inception, it is one of the most carefully planned and aggressively executed military operations ever conducted.

This is not something that is negotiated. There are no parleys or peace talks over ransom terms. It is an all-out, no-holds-barred, total application of all your resources. It is not a walk in the woods or a routine patrol. It is an intensely focused, jaw-tightening, full-out concentration of energy and effort. It is planned long and in detail. It is rehearsed often and carefully. It is executed with extreme concentration. And when the moment of confrontation arrives, it is a shockingly quick, explosive, action-filled, almost out-of-body experience.

I have a couple of friends who were involved in such a prisoner snatch some years ago. In this case, however, they weren't taking a man captive; they were setting the captive free.

An American citizen had been taken prisoner by former dictator

Manuel Noriega's thugs in Panama. Kurt Muse, a businessman sympathetic to anti-Noriega elements, was languishing in the Carcel Modelo prison in Panama City.

Highly trained and well-rehearsed U.S. antiterrorist elements touched their choppers down on the roof. Four U.S. Army commandos dressed in black and wearing night vision goggles blasted a hole in the roof, blew the doors, and raced toward the second-floor cell where the American was held. Author Douglas Waller describes the very brief but aggressive scenario:

> For Muse, the next two minutes were a blur of smoke, flashes, and machine guns rattling. Then all was quiet. On the other side of his cell door, he heard a voice.
>
> "Moose, you okay?" a Delta commando whispered.
>
> "Yo!" Muse called back.
>
> "Lay down," the commando ordered. "We're blowing the door."
>
> Muse did as he was told. The door flew open in a cloud of smoke. The commando rushed in, slapped a Kevlar helmet and bulletproof vest on Muse, and calmly told him they would be heading for the roof. Just follow him.
>
> As they passed the end of the hall where Muse's guard had sat—the one with orders to execute him if there was a rescue attempt—Muse saw only a desk overturned and the rear wall covered with bullet holes.... But not [every enemy guard was] killed. One guard had cowered in a fetal position as the commandos stormed down the stairway. The assault team had handcuffed him to the railing. Muse marveled at the commandos' self-control as he passed the manacled and terrified guard.
>
> The commandos and Muse climbed aboard the helicopter on the roof. Muse was told to sit in the middle seat between the two operators. Three commandos jumped on each of the two pods outside the Little Bird [helicopter]. The chopper took off.[1]

In a matter of a few aggressive, carefully planned moments, the "tearing down of fortresses" had been accomplished, and a human being was delivered from the very real bondage of dark-force goons.

This is totally focused warfare. As Christian people, we are to be engaged in the same kind of aggressive, well-rehearsed operations that free the people around us from the bondage of the dark forces gripping them. We are to be at war with the commonly accepted perspectives of this age, both in our own lives and in our culture, that are contrary to God's intentions.

Just what are the fortresses in our culture? Where are we at war in our culture? There are many fronts, and we'll cover several of the major ones in the next chapter.

A critical step in spiritual warfare is identifying the enemy's guns so you will know where to engage. The enemy's shelling, however, is so constant, so persistently drumming that we begin to forget where and what they are. Like living beside the railroad tracks, we eventually no longer hear the trains. Our culture is so constantly bombarding our minds and hearts with the ordnance of hell that we have become deaf to it.

Our culture is so constantly bombarding our minds and hearts with the ordnance of hell that we have become deaf to it.

When it comes to taking thoughts captive, we usually think of our own thoughts, issues like personal purity, guarding our internal thoughts and attitudes (lust, jealousy, pride, bitterness, anger, et cetera). While that is an appropriate application of this passage's teaching, its emphasis actually concerns the concepts, philosophies, or perspectives of this world.

We are to be attacking the dangerous thought patterns in this world.

Those harmful thought patterns, of course, emanate ultimately from Satan's dark kingdom. Often they appear initially as good and healthy things. Satan presents himself capably as an "angel of light."

Today we must clear our ears, clear our minds, tune our hearts, and take a good long look at some of the devil's heavy artillery which is so destructive to our living out God's intentions. The charge to you and me as Christian soldiers is to close with and destroy—to be actively involved in the "destruction of fortresses."

These strongholds are dominating positions of strength, seemingly impregnable. They are patterns of thought, ways of thinking, that imprison people and are raised up against the knowledge and intentions of God. The Bible tells us that spiritual warfare involves offensively charging these strongholds and tearing them down—dismantling them piece by piece, brick by brick, until they collapse in a cloud of dust.

Think of how quickly the dreaded Berlin Wall disappeared when a million jubilant Germans poured into the no-man's-land and began chipping away at it with claw hammers! That great, hulking symbol of oppression that had stood for a full generation vanished almost overnight. In the same way, spiritual warfare involves aggressively dismantling the enemy's strongholds.

Let's take a closer look at some fortresses that have dominated the landscape of our culture for too many years. And please remember this: There are millions of captives within those fortresses. People are dying inside those walls! And you and I, like the elite force that rescued Kurt Muse from a dictator's prison, have the power we need in our Mighty Captain to set captives free.

C'mon, spirit warrior. Let's run to the guns!

Charge, men, and yell like furies!

STONEWALL JACKSON,
FIRST MANASSAS, JULY 1861

We commend ourselves in every way as true servants of God…
by speaking the word of truth, in the power of God,
with the weapons of righteousness for the right hand to attack
and for the left hand to defend.

2 CORINTHIANS 6:4, 7, AMP

Upon this rock I will build my church;
and all the powers of hell shall not prevail against it.

MATTHEW 16:18, TLB

CULTURE WAR

Old Stonewall Jackson had the right idea.

In contrast to the timid, blustering generals who controlled the fate of Union armies during the opening weeks of the Civil War, Jackson subscribed to a doctrine of aggressive, shocking, all-out attacks. "To move swiftly, strike vigorously, and secure the fruits of victory is the secret of a successful war," he declared.

We who are soldiers in Christ's kingdom have got to run straight at the adversary. It's an all-out, run-at-the-guns attack into the teeth of the enemy strongholds.

In spiritual warfare, however, we're not so much charging deadly bullets as we are advancing against lethal ideas. We're fighting patterns of toxic thinking that hold men and women captive, devastate the lives of children and teenagers, and shatter homes and families. Launched from enemy fortresses in our own nation, these poisonous philosophies blind and paralyze their victims, so that they are unable to experience the freedom of the knowledge of the true God.

Take Rita McClain, for example.

Through the last thirty years of her life, the enemy has had his way in her mind. For more than half a lifetime, she has wandered in dark, confusing thought patterns. Like so many of my generation—the children of the fifties and the young rebels of the sixties—Rita has flitted from one "lofty speculation" to another, each "raised up against the knowledge of God." As Paul put it to Timothy, she has been "always learning [but] never

able to come to the knowledge of the truth" (2 Timothy 3:7). Listen to her story
as recorded in *Newsweek* magazine:

> Rita McClain's spiritual journey began in Iowa, where
> she grew up in the fundamentalist world of the
> Pentecostal Church. What she remembers most about
> that time are tent meetings and an overwhelming sense
> of guilt. In her 20s she tried less doctrinaire
> Protestantism. That, too, proved unsatisfying. By the
> age of 27, McClain had rejected all organized religion.
> "I feel like a pretty wounded Christian," she says....
>
> Then, six years ago, in the aftermath of an emotion-
> ally draining divorce, McClain's spiritual life blos-
> somed.... She started with Unity, a metaphysical church
> near her Marin County, California, home. It was a reve-
> lation, light-years away from the "Old Testament kind of
> thing I knew very well from childhood." The next stop
> was Native American spiritual practices. Then it was
> Buddhism at Marin County's Spirit Rock Meditation
> Center, where she had attended a number of retreats,
> including one that required eight days of silence.
>
> These disparate rituals melded into a personal reli-
> gion, which McClain, a 50-year-old nurse, celebrates at
> an ever-changing altar in her home. Right now the altar
> consists of an angel statue, a small bottle of "sacred
> water" blessed at a women's vigil, a crystal ball, a pyra-
> mid, a small brass image of Buddha sitting on a brass
> leaf, a votive candle, a Hebrew prayer, a tiny Native
> American basket from the 1850s and a picture of her
> "most sacred place," a madrone tree near her home.[1]

Were you able to follow that? If it wasn't so tragic, it would almost be
comical. I remember how in the sixties and seventies many friends—and even
some relatives—wandered aimlessly from one fog bank to another. Following
first this voice then that one, they lurched from weekend seminars to com-
munal living, from quiet meditation to scream therapy, all in an attempt to
find themselves and true freedom.

Rita's spiritual pilgrimage managed to wander from the one true God as revealed in the Bible to the point where she deliberately bows on a daily basis to as many as nine gods at a time.

SAME WAR, DIFFERENT MILLENNIUM

Following Rita's story is not unlike reading the pages of the Old Testament. The pagan nations surrounding Israel all followed their own notions of spiritual diversity. God's instructions to His own people were quite clear—stay away from that kind of stuff! Further, when ·they did encounter the pagan centers of worship in the Promised Land, they were instructed to tear them down.

The pagan high places of today include such lofty speculations as higher consciousness, crystals, karma, reincarnation, and memory healing.

Whether it is destroying the pagan high places of the Old Testament, or tearing down the satanic lofty strongholds in the New Testament, it is basic to soldiering for the Lord.

The pagan high places of today are many and varied, but they are nothing new. They include such lofty speculations as higher consciousness, crystals, karma, reincarnation, and memory healing. They are espoused by a variety of gurus and spirit guides, and they promote strains of native mysticism, universal forces, and higher powers.

It is as though people know in their heart of hearts that something is missing from their lives. They decide to find it no matter what insane gyrations it requires. Eventually, all the gyrations end up back at the starting point: Satan's deception. The necessary and therefore inevitable dissatisfaction with our self-oriented material world has led us to a self-deceived infatuation with the dark-spirit world. And the only winner is Satan himself.

The Old Testament world which Rita misunderstood and rejected was, at the essential levels, identical to our own world today. And the great spiritual warfare passage of 2 Corinthians 10:3–5 is essentially the New Testament equivalent of some of the classic battle verses of the Old Testament.

Abraham's conflict with the false gods of his day was spiritual warfare, up close and in your face. His nephew Lot regularly fell in the ebb and flow of that cosmic tug of war. Moses' battle with the false gods of Egypt was nothing less than spiritual warfare on a nationwide scale. And who could forget Elijah, standing all alone on the desolate summit of Mount Carmel, eyeball to eyeball with four hundred prophets of the demon god, Baal. The inevitable refrain of all such battles is, "Who is the true and living God?"

Like Rita, people become confused, mesmerized. Attracted by the common thought patterns of the day, they are sucked into the strong points of the evil one's elaborate string of fortresses. The Lord's instruction to His own soldiers is to attack those deceptive thought patterns and destroy the lofty speculations that cloud reality and prevent people from coming to the knowledge of the true and living God.

That is precisely what Josiah was attempting to do in his day.

JOSIAH AND THE STRONGHOLDS

As a young king, Josiah discovered the reality of God's good Word—and caught fire! He read the Word of God like he'd never seen it before. Indeed, he hadn't seen significant portions of it. That exposure to pure truth began to change his perspective...then his heart...then his actions. He made a covenant that he would walk after the true God with all his heart and soul. Josiah was determined to give his people the opportunity to know the true God of heaven.

That's the story and the spiritual warfare recorded in 2 Kings 23: Get rid of the silly accoutrements of false worship and thinking and follow the true God. Here's a portion of the record of Josiah's tearing down the dark fortresses in his day:

> Then the king commanded Hilkiah the high priest...to bring out of the temple of the LORD all the vessels that were made for Baal, for Asherah, and for all the host of heaven [stars and astrological patterns]; and he burned them outside Jerusalem in the fields of the Kidron [Valley], and he carried their ashes to Bethel. He did away with the idolatrous priests...also those who burned incense to Baal, to the sun and to the moon and to the constellations.... He brought out the Asherah...and burned it at the brook Kidron, and ground it to dust, and threw its dust on the graves of the common people.

> He also broke down the houses of the male cult prosti-
> tutes which were in the house of the LORD…and he
> broke down the high places of the gates.
>
> 2 KINGS 23:4-8, BRACKETED COMMENTS MINE

Spiritual warfare is tearing down false spiritual fortresses, all of which ultimately belong to the dark prince, Satan.

Israel, or more properly *Judah,* was as self-deceived in the seventh century B.C. as Rita McClain—and countless others—are in our own day. Judah was deliberately and elaborately choosing to walk after Satan's ways. And there is a price to pay. Of course, the kingdom of Judah, like Rita McClain, was unwittingly experiencing the disorientation, pain, and scars of its ungodly choices. Judah, like many Christians, was adrift in its culture and mired in a false spiritual world of its own making.

But one fellow, a follower of the true God (in our terms, a Christian), decided not to lay down anymore. Josiah decided to run to the guns, to "destroy the speculations" of Satan's works in his day. He quite literally burned to the ground the strongholds that had a grip on the people. He ground them to dust and put them in the cemetery where they belonged.

In the midst of the dark world of spiritual warfare, where even well-intentioned people were walking the broad road to hell, a godly believer stepped up to the plate. Josiah loved the true God. He had grasped the fact that false thinking and pagan spirituality condemns its followers to an eternity apart from God. Josiah understood the necessity of engaging Satan's strongholds, of tearing down the satanic cultural fortresses of speculations and imaginations.

- He removed from God's house the idols of Baal and Asherah, exposing and expunging the trappings of false religion.
- He took on the false priests who were burning incense to the Baals, sun, moon, and constellations.
- He took on the booths used by perverted persons practicing ritual sodomy and prostitution.

It was spiritual warfare, plain and simple. And Josiah was a mighty spirit warrior. That's the spirit Paul so powerfully calls you to emulate in 2 Corinthians 10:3–5. Let's look at that landmark passage again—this time in a good paraphrase:

> The very weapons we use are not human but powerful
> in God's warfare for the destruction of the enemy's
> strongholds. Our battle is to break down every deceptive
> argument and every imposing defense that men erect
> against the true knowledge of God. We fight to capture
> every thought until it acknowledges the authority of
> Christ.
>
> PHILLIPS

And *you*, like Abraham, Elijah, Josiah, and every other believer of all time, are in a war. It's the same war and the same enemy. Only the era differs. It may be more subtle, in your case, than it was for Josiah in those days of Judah. But not that much different. Your adversary is just as eternally deadly today as he was in the misty dawn of Eden.

What does your enemy look like? Where is he attacking most viciously? What are the dark, ultimately satanic strongholds in our culture today? What fortresses must you dismantle? What are the guns toward which you must run?

Let's look at some of the fortresses you face. They are lofty patterns of thinking raised up against the knowledge of the true God. We'll look quickly at a handful of the readily identifiable. Even though we can only comment on a few—and briefly touch on a few more—my prayer is that your eyes will be opened to see the chain of dark strongholds Satan has erected within the borders of our nation.

DIVORCE

There is probably no greater satanic stronghold in our culture than the idea of disposable marriage. Divorce hurts individuals, destroys marriages, scatters families, tears churches apart, and at this moment is eating away at the very heart of our nation.

There is probably no greater satanic stronghold in our culture than the idea of disposable marriage.

We know from Scripture that marriage is at the center of God's plan to display His image. Destroying marriage, therefore, is at the center of Satan's strategy to blast mankind and mar the image of God.

Virtually everyone in our churches has been touched by divorce in some way. And like flying shrapnel, whoever divorce touches, it wounds. But we still do it! "I just couldn't take it anymore," we say. And so we roll over and die. As someone has said, "With every divorce, another small civilization dies." Hating it, we succumb to it.

In spite of professional counsel, prayer by friends, weeping by children and families, and sometimes even against the desire of one of the partners, Christians are still walking away from their sacred vows of marriage in record numbers.

But closing our eyes and wishing the subject would never come up will not make it go away. Sometimes being soldiers means having to do the hard thing.

Understand that I have no wish to create currents of guilt or to put anyone down. I do not want to "hammer" anyone. I do not want to reject anyone. I do not wish to heap guilt on anyone. But people, we've got to face this—in ourselves and in others. We cannot justify fighting other battles and running from this one. Martin Luther said it well:

> If I profess with the loudest and clearest exposition
> every portion of the truth of God except precisely
> that…point which the world and the devil are at that
> moment attacking, I am not confessing Christ. Where
> the battle rages, there the loyalty of the soldier is
> proved. And to be steady on all the battlefield [else-
> where] is mere flight and disgrace if he flinches at that
> point.

Lifelong marriage is near to the heart of everything God is concerned about. It is the centerpiece of civilization. The marriage covenant is the zenith of God's image glorifying Him. If that is so, then divorce is not just one more sin in a long list of human shortcomings. No, this one is somewhere near the magnum opus of human sin.

The staff of our church, and every biblically effective church, spends inordinate amounts of time being bombarded with the issues, questions, and pains surrounding marital breakup. Sometimes it feels like all we are doing is trying to clean up the battlefield after a terrible war. We have to cart off the victims in body bags and try to patch up the wounded long after the cannons have quieted. I do not exaggerate when I tell you we hear about it almost every day and deal with it in some way nearly every week.

When Jesus told us, "You shall know the truth, and the truth shall set you free," He wasn't just being poetic. Jesus was saying that the truth, no matter how difficult it may be to swallow, *will* set you free. The truth about divorce is a freeing reality. It will liberate your spirit, free your emotions, and strengthen your heart.

So let's look at some biblical truths regarding marriage and divorce.

PRINCIPLE #1: YOUR MARRIAGE DOES NOT BELONG TO YOU

Your marriage belongs to God. He invented it. He designed it. He brought you together. He delights in it. He holds the papers.

Breaking the marriage covenant is not a private matter. It is a spiritual matter, a church matter, and a public matter before the watching world and the angels in heaven.

Your marriage is a covenant of commitment you made before God. To walk away from your marriage is to trample on the very core of God's expectations of His children. Please hear me on this: Breaking the marriage covenant is not a private matter. It is a spiritual matter, a religious matter, a theological matter, a church matter, and a public matter before the watching world and the angels in heaven.

PRINCIPLE #2: GOD HATES DIVORCE

God's attitude toward divorce in the Scriptures is simple, direct, and impossible to misunderstand: "'I hate divorce,' says the LORD" (Malachi 2:16).

Which part of "hate" don't you understand? Hey, God said it, not me.

In our permissive, politically correct, I'm-my-own-god, no-fault society, we can believe anything we want about divorce, but, before God, it is an act of the gravest consequence.

PRINCIPLE #3: THERE ARE NO LEGITIMATE GROUNDS FOR DIVORCE IN THE OLD TESTAMENT

Deuteronomy 24:1 says a man may divorce his wife if "she finds no favor in his eyes." The Jews of Jesus' day used this as an excuse to divorce their wives at the drop of a hat. Wives must've lived in constant fear. But Jesus brought the Jews back to the heart of God:

> "Because of your hardness of heart Moses permitted you to divorce your wives; but from the beginning it has not

been this way. And I say to you, whoever divorces his
wife, except for immorality, and marries another woman
commits adultery."

MATTHEW 19:8-9

PRINCIPLE #4: JESUS OPPOSED DIVORCE

To the shock of His disciples, Jesus opposed divorce. They lived in a world
where divorce was commonplace, so they were stunned to discover Jesus
had no room for it (Matthew 19:1–12).

Our Lord's teaching on this issue is simple: "Everyone who divorces
his wife and marries another commits adultery, and he who marries one
who is divorced from a husband commits adultery" (Luke 16:18). What is
there to misunderstand?

A thorough search of the Bible will reveal that the only legitimate
grounds for terminating a marriage are: (1) adultery, (2) desertion on the
part of an unbeliever, or (3) death. And even in the case of adultery, I
believe God's heart is for the marriage to endure and be rebuilt by His
power (consider Hosea 1–3).

My prayer is that if you have been divorced for illegitimate reasons
you will not feel condemned. Yes, you disobeyed God. But that does not
mean you are defiled forever or beyond God's love. Confess your sin to
God *and to the others impacted by it.*

If you are in a second or third marriage and now realize you have violated God's standard and have never dealt with it, do so now. Confess it,
repent, and build bridges to the people you have wounded. Tell God you
sinned, either willfully or in ignorance. Tell Him you're sorry for it, that
you grieve for what you have done, and that you repent of it. Tell Him you
want Him to cleanse you of your unrighteousness. And He will! Jesus
came to save sinners, not to condemn them.

I've said it before: Eternity is too long and this life is too short to do
something foolish here. Your marriage is your greatest opportunity on
earth to reflect the glory of God, in whose image you were created. Don't
walk away from it.

NATIONAL MEMORY LOSS OR HISTORICAL REVISIONISM

After divorce, I think possibly the next most serious stronghold of our enemy
is our culture's tendency to rewrite history in the image of whatever agenda

is in vogue at the moment. Once again, Josiah's story sounds eerily familiar.

When God raised up Josiah to be a spirit warrior in his day, one of the greatest obstacles the young king had to overcome was forgetfulness. Fifteen times in the book of Deuteronomy, Moses warned the people entering the land to remember what the Lord had done for them and what He had commanded. Yet within a generation or two, they'd already forgotten.

So it was in Josiah's day. Under the rule of ungodly kings, the people had neglected God's Word for so long that significant portions of the Old Testament were not only unfamiliar, they were entirely forgotten. Over time they had passed out of circulation and, in fact, completely disappeared. If you had attempted in that day to order a copy of the Scriptures on amazon.com, you would have been told that it was out of print.

When Josiah was installed on the throne, it is likely that the prophet Zephaniah had a strong influence on the development of Judah's young monarch.

It is clear that Josiah determined to follow a godly course from the beginning. In 622 B.C. he ordered that major repairs be made to the temple. During the remodeling the high priest discovered in some long-lost archives what Scripture identifies as "a book of the law of the LORD given by Moses" (2 Kings 22:3–7). What the king read there regarding God's standards and judgments shocked him all the way down to his royal sandals.

It also brought a healthy fear to his young heart.

> "Great is the wrath of the LORD which is poured out on
> us because our fathers have not observed the word of the
> LORD, to do according to all that is written in this book."
>
> 2 CHRONICLES 34:21

It was like learning that you have an artery in your heart with 99 percent blockage. That next breath might kill you. Death and judgment hang in the air. Something has to be done very, very quickly.

Josiah hastily convened a national assembly and renewed the covenant which the book of the law had described. It was this recovered memory of Israel's spiritual history that sparked Josiah's spiritual warfare program and the purge of idolatry from the nation.

The loss of national spiritual memory is devastating to a people. Satan knew it well in the seventh century B.C. in Judah. It's still true today. The loss of national memory is one of Satan's strongholds in our own culture.

Loss of memory is a horrible experience. Some would contend that Alzheimer's disease is absolutely the worst way to die. The victim loses the mind, then the heart, and eventually the body follows. It is the same with national memory loss. Some have called it "cultural amnesia," or "the fracturing of history."

It is a deliberate devaluing of the past by simply forgetting it, or worse yet, by rewriting it. And its offspring is an overwhelming sense of rootlessness, followed closely by its first cousins, hopelessness and cynicism. The last thirty years are illustrative enough. We have wandered in a wilderness of forgetfulness. Our wanderings have led us straight from Woodstock in 1969 to Columbine in 1999.

We do not know who we are. We have lost ourselves, our roots, our values, our connection. We have hit a wall and jarred loose all memory of our identity. We are walking amnesiacs.

A recent Roper Poll of our current elite college seniors indicates that while virtually 100 percent of them can readily identify Beavis and Butthead, only about one-third of them know that the U.S. Constitution was the document that established the separation of powers in our government. Author Stephen Bertman reports that "Americans finished dead last" in a nine-nation survey dealing with basic geography. Fourteen percent of American adults surveyed could not even find the United States on an unmarked globe!

Syndicated columnist Georgie Geyer calls it "the intellectual fracturing within the history profession." She claims (I think rightly) that it is the result of the infiltration of our culture and universities by leftist academics. These people deliberately rewrite history for their own purposes. Radical feminists, for example, dismiss Western history as the silly myths of white males. Such revisionism causes us to lose sight of the ideals that formed this nation and make it worth preserving.

More than that, such revisionism ought to be of great concern to Christians, if for no other reason than the fact that Christianity as a spiritual faith and reality is firmly rooted in history—actual events in time and space.

Christian, how do you dismantle this stronghold of national memory loss? How do you tear down this fortress of forgetfulness? Read! Teach yourself history. Buy good books that don't subscribe to the revisionists' new "versions" of history. Buy almost any standard classroom text published before 1950. Americans think nothing of dropping a small fortune to attend a sporting event. Skip one now and then and use the money to buy a few good history books.

While you're at it, teach your kids. The revisionists may indeed control much of the public school curriculum, but they do not control your homes. Those precious children at your feet are utterly dependent upon the training you give them.

Fight the loss of history. Learn it yourself. Pass it on to those around you. Follow Josiah's example and do everything in your power to make U.S. history right.

EVOLUTION

Here's a huge stronghold—now deeply entrenched in our culture. If it weren't so pathetic it would be one of the most laughable things man has ever devised. When you think about it, it really belongs in a David Letterman monologue.

Let me illustrate. Recently in the "DriveTime" section of the *Oregonian,* they featured one of the "latest and greatest" luxury cars: the BMW M5, priced at seventy thousand dollars apiece. There were only a thousand of these babies made.

Now try to imagine the following scenario: A reporter approaches the engineers at BMW and asks, "Can you tell me how you came up with the M5?"

With straight faces, those white-coated Germans reply, "You know, it's truly amazing. We didn't come up with the M5! Here's what happened. We went into one of the company's enormous old warehouses, where no one had wandered for years. When one of the employees went in there—pushing his way through the cobwebs and debris of years—there in the back there were a thousand of these things—just sitting there. Bright, shining, ingenious, and fully functional. Beautiful interiors, wonderful engineering, powerful, all exactly alike. We don't know how they got there, but given our ignorance, we just decided to agree they simply evolved there…over inordinate amounts of time…out of, well, nothing."

Can you accept that? Of course not. Here's another one.

Let me tell you how the universe came into existence. The whole bit— men, women, animals, trees, stars, planets, everything—just evolved. Out of nothing. Over a long span of time. Given enough time, you see, everything developed out of absolutely nothing. Life and intelligence and conceptual immortality derived themselves from thin air.

Who could swallow such a tale? If you or I went on national television to tell how a thousand gleaming luxury cars evolved in a warehouse, we'd get laughed off the platform—or committed to an appropriate institution for evaluation. And yet that fanciful view of the BMW's origin is far more plausible than the theory of evolution. The BMW is *nothing* compared to the complexity of life from nothing.

The amount of blind faith that evolution demands is astounding. Anyone in his right mind knows that time plus chance produces *nothing*, let alone life itself. But here's the crux of the issue: The human heart knows that if we admit that there is an intelligence behind the obvious design, then the mighty and intelligent God surfaces. And then…well, then we find ourselves accountable to Him. And we humans insist we will be accountable to no one. Not even our Creator.

Aldus Huxley, author of *Brave New World* and a notorious skeptic, was honest enough to say, "I can't afford for there to be a God, because then I would be held accountable, and that would mean I could no longer sleep around. And since I want to continue to sleep around, I don't want there to be a God."

Christian, be aggressive in the face of the undeniable shortsightedness of evolution. Truth and the evidence are on your side. Run to the guns.

Where Evolution Leads Us

Evolution teaches us, fundamentally, that

life

is

meaningless.

Unfortunately we are beginning to believe that on a pretty large scale. Our self-centered thinking has begun to consume us. Not all that far removed in time from Darwin, a fellow by the name of Friedrich Nietzsche argued that the notions of good and evil were not rooted in reason or truth, but in power. Morality, he stated, is a shifting social construct created by the winds of culture and power. Nietzsche maintained that power determines morality: Might makes right. In Nietzsche's world, there are no absolute standards or values, only a kind of survival of the fittest.

That thinking appealed to some people. One was a German paperhanger by the name of Adolf Hitler. Hitler simply fleshed out Nietzsche's ideas, taking them to their logical conclusion. Admittedly, there was a certain consistency to Hitler's thinking. If all of life is an evolutionary stew…if there is no moral absolute…if morality evolves from power…and if it is only the fittest who will rule...then Hitler believed he was only doing humanity a favor by fostering a "super race" and culling out the less fit.

The Darwin-Nietzsche-Hitler triumvirate has much to do with our current state of affairs. The world paid horribly in blood for the logical extension of those freethinkers. We call it World War II. Its reverberations are still with us. Take, for example, certain recent events in our public schools.

A couple of swastika-wearing kids in a Colorado high school took ownership of that same life-is-zero, morality-is-relative, power-is-determinative philosophy. They applied it to their own circumstances and took action. In coldhearted, soul-dismantled calculation, they blew away a number of their classmates in the school library.

I guess you could say it takes a village to kill its children. It takes a whole culture thinking after Darwin, Nietzsche, Sagan, et al., to eventually consume itself. Here, in Randy Alcorn's words, is what our "village," carried along on the evolutionary train, teaches its children:

> You are the descendants of a tiny cell of primordial protoplasm that washed up on an ocean beach ten billion years ago. You are the blind and arbitrary product of time, chance, and natural forces.... You are a mere grab bag of atomic particles.... You are flying through lifeless space with no purpose, no direction, no control, and no destiny but final destruction.... In short, you came from nothing, you are going nowhere, and you will end your brief cosmic journey beneath six feet of dirt, where all that is you will become food for bacteria and rot with worms.[2]

Given these realities, the actions of Eric Harris and Dylan Klebold are logically consistent. The theory of evolution denies that we are creations of God Himself. It disallows man living in the image of God. It degrades our nobility and does not allow us to talk as if God might exist.

Life, therefore, is cheap. And ultimately meaningless. Nothing matters. As the kids say: "Whatever."

When Harris and Klebold asked themselves what mattered, they simply concluded that nothing much mattered, so they decided to go out with a bang. And, honestly, our culture does not have a lot it can say to rebuke their actions, much less rebut their thinking. It is simply a matter of power-derived morality determining who survives and who does not.

Welcome to the philosophy of hell.

POSTMODERNISM

Postmodernism flows directly from the fountainheads of Darwin, Neitzsche, et al. Unfortunately, it is the guiding perspective in American universities today. Simply stated, the core of postmodernism is its axiom that truth is a construct: Truth is whatever you want it to be—whatever serves your interests in the moment.

That is, you construct truth. You build it. You make it up for yourself. In the postmodern world, truth is the ultimate do-it-yourself project.

Another way of saying it is "everything is relative." There is no such thing as absolute truth. It's all a simple matter of perspective—how you see things. Therefore, to you there is only one perspective that ultimately matters—*your own!* What is true for you may not be true for others.

Of course, life doesn't work that way, does it? Without the exact sciences we make no progress. Two plus two represents some kind of standardization. If I jump off the roof, the law of gravity remains in effect whether I accept its reality or not.

But postmodern thought leads people to believe that it is not truth that matters, but only my truth that matters for me. My truth for me. Your truth for you. Now let's just get along: Live and let live. But, again, life doesn't work that way. When your truth runs up against mine and only the fittest survives, one or both of us will tend to resort to power. And we're back to Littleton. Or Auschwitz.

Michael Novak, winner of the Templeton Prize in 1994, described the foundational problem of our day. Without using the word *postmodernism* itself, Mr. Novak exposed its soft underbelly with these words:

> One principle that today's intellectuals most passionately
> disseminate is vulgar relativism, "nihilism with a happy
> face." For them it is certain that there is no truth, only
> opinion: my opinion, your opinion. They abandon the
> defense of the intellect.... Those who surrender the
> domain of the intellect make straight the road to fas-
> cism. Totalitarianism...is the will-to-power unchecked
> by any regard for truth. To surrender the claims of truth
> upon humans is to surrender Earth to thugs.... Vulgar
> relativism is an invisible gas, odorless, deadly, that is now
> polluting every free society on earth. It is a gas that
> attacks the central nervous system of moral striving....

"There is no such thing as truth," they teach even
the little ones. "Truth is bondage. Believe what seems
right to you. There are as many truths as there are individuals. Follow your feelings. Do as you please. Get in
touch with yourself...." Those who speak this way prepare the jails of the twenty-first century. They do the
work of tyrants."[3]

How tragically, destructively true.

Postmodernism is the inevitable and bottomless pit to which human self-
centernedness naturally descends. The Old Testament describes this formula
for chaos in the book of Judges, where we are told that "everyone did what
was right in his own eyes" (Judges 21:25).

Postmodernism is the ultimate form of cynicism—and the ultimate destination to which the train of human pride always leads. No one and nothing is to be trusted. No one and nothing is to be believed. Except, of course,
what the individual chooses—for himself. Postmodernism's mantra is clear:
"Value whatever you wish as truth, because everything is a lie." Marilyn
Manson (the stage name of one Brian Warner, taken from Marilyn Monroe
and Charles Manson) nailed postmodernism's bottom line: "Pick the lie you
like best."

Of course, like all heresy, postmodernism places the self at the core of the
universe: self-talk, self-esteem, self-improvement, self-renewal. Ultimately,
every one of these roads leads to hell. Sometimes they wind through
Auschwitz. Sometimes the curves are more subtle, and the landscape serene,
but the destination is the same. Fight it.

Examine yourself, soldier. Have you been drifting toward relative truth
in your thinking? Educate yourself. Dialogue with people. Engage in meaningful conversation. Get involved in local school committees and boards.
Read. Learn. Teach. Register to vote—and then do it.

POLITICAL CORRECTNESS

Political correctness is a very close first cousin to postmodernism. The politically correct (PC) movement may be one of the strongest of Satan's fortresses
today. It is nothing short of mind control. In a misguided attempt to offend
no one, the politically correct offend everyone. In a twisted, contorted
attempt to accept everyone, those who embrace the PC movement harass and

persecute those who disagree. In a perverted attempt to tolerate all truth, they end up tolerating no truth.

How ironic that the postmodern, truth-is-a-construct movement will not allow anyone to have their own truth. Only what is considered politically correct is true and right. In my opinion, the PC movement may be the most serious threat to our constitutional liberties in the history of this nation.

Ironically, it is the leaders of the free speech movement of the 1960s, now firmly entrenched in their tenured chairs in our universities, who would most vehemently deny free speech to those who disagree with them.

How does this PC stuff work itself out in our thinking process, in our educational system, for instance? At the University of Maine one course syllabus warns: "Any language that may be deemed sexist, racist, or homophobic, or may be found offensive by any minority group is prohibited. Use of such language can result in immediate failure of that paper and possible future action."

Here's a simple question: Who deems it? Who decides if I'm being racist or sexist? Who says so? The elite, of course. The politically correct, totalitarian elite. If it is not politically correct, you may not think it, let alone express it. You must learn to speak only in accepted speech codes.

On the campus of West Virginia University, the ominous-sounding Office of Social Justice drew up such a speech code, intended to define acceptable standards on campus. According to this document, the word *wife* is considered a "sexist" term. The student must use the term *friend* or *partner* instead. Sexual harassment is defined as "insults, humor, jokes, or anecdotes that belittle an individual's or group's sexuality or sex." Any breaches of the speech code result in a flood of "sensitivity seminars" or "diversity training" to make sure, ironically, that everyone's diversity conforms to the standards.

On many university campuses only the most ignorant of souls would venture to use such outdated and politically incorrect phrases as "man on the street" or "mixed race" or "ladies and gentlemen" or "man-made." Even the word *history* is in disrepute because, well, as any good postmodernist knows, there is no such thing as history—only impressions recorded by people writing their own opinions.

At Framingham State College in Massachusetts, popular English professor Eugene Narrett lost his job because he did not knuckle under to the demands of his senior college administrator to "stop your criticism of feminism." It appears that any carefully reasoned argument opposing what is considered the politically correct position is considered harassment. And any form of harassment is grounds for firing. This is nothing less than unvarnished totalitarianism.

There seems to be one unifying concept or value in PC thinking across our land.

It is consistently and virulently anti-Christian.

There seems always to be a PC bias against the Christian faith. The politically correct world is Christophobic. At Penn State in March 1997, a mocking exhibition "celebrating twenty-five years of virginity" consisted of a quilt formed from twenty-five pairs of women's panties with crosses sewn into the crotch. When Catholic students protested that this public demonstration created a hostile environment for Catholics at Penn State, the university president refused to deal with it. Why? Because he couldn't "imagine any circumstances under which the university would want to encourage censorship."

So censorship is unthinkable. Unless, of course, it's in the name of political correctness.

The current PC movement, being a form of mind control, is far more threatening to this republic and its democratic form of government than the missiles of the Soviet Union ever were. But the good news is that political correctness, like Communism, cannot stand the bright light of day. The speech codes, PC policies, sensitivity seminars, and diversity training are, by and large, merely attempts at mind control. It is a house of cards. Eventually these intolerant thought police will be seen for what they are—petty dictators. Such totalitarianism, however subtle, cannot ultimately handle the intense light of consistent, rational exposure. Thinking people will see through it all.

The key word is *thinking*. Do you think biblically? Do it, spirit warrior! Expose lies, challenge the hypocrisy—kindly, truthfully, and consistently.

But watch out! In the PC culture, the most politically incorrect person possible is a Bible-believing Christian standing up and saying that there is only one way to God. You can't get more politically incorrect than that.

THE ANIMAL RIGHTS MOVEMENT

It's hard to imagine a more direct attack on the image of God in man than this. The sulfuric smell of the dark forces permeates this movement. Traced to its headwaters, the animal rights movement, while apparently well-intentioned (the book of Proverbs certainly teaches the appropriate care of animals), is ultimately an attempt to obliterate the distinctions between humans and animals. In so doing, the animal rights movement is, in fact and deed, a direct attack upon the image of God in humans.

For example, the Great Ape Legal Project is focused on just such ludicrous thinking: to guarantee to animals the same kinds of rights guaranteed in our own Declaration of Independence—essentially, "the right to life, liberty, and the pursuit of happiness." (But, of course, such thinking does not apply to human babies in the womb. Nor, in the opinion of Princeton ethicist Pete Singer, does it apply to any living child whose parents do not want it. But I digress.) This reasoning is so convoluted it is hard to imagine its originating anywhere else but the deepest pit of hell.

Such Satanic thinking, as usual, completely reverses God's original intentions. Pete Singer urges us to treat animals as human beings and human beings as animals. That is, while animals are protected, even coddled, human beings may be bred, controlled, used, and even "put to sleep" if they are unwanted.

But not animals.

Singer's book *Animal Liberation* is the flagship of the animal rights movement. Singer arrogantly states, "It can no longer be maintained by anyone but a religious fanatic that man is the special darling of the universe."

Singer denounces what he calls our "speciesism"—that is, our valuing humans over animals. He contends speciesism is just as evil as racism or sexism. His audacity is calculated to advance his lie. He states bluntly, "It is speciesist to judge that the life of a normal adult member of our species is more valuable life than the life of a normal adult mouse."[4] The PETA people (People for the Ethical Treatment of Animals) who claim 700,000 members, 120 employees, and a 1999 fund-raising total of $16 million, say it equally clearly: "When it comes to feelings, a rat is a pig is a dog is a boy."

CASTLES ON EVERY HILLTOP

We're in trouble, soldier, if the world around us thinks like this, holding to these lofty speculations. The truth as revealed in the Bible is under siege, and it's never been a more dangerous time to speak out for Jesus Christ. So put on your armor, take up your sword, and run to the guns.

There are more enemy strongholds than I can cover here, but these are critical, in my opinion. Here is a list, with brief comments, of a few more enemy strongholds.

THE WAR ON GENDER

Doesn't it strike you as odd that this culture, which so prides itself on diversity, is trying to utterly destroy it in its most obvious and beautiful form? I speak, of course, about the differences between men and women.

We used to speak of the gender wars. But this is something different; this is a war on the very notion of gender. The movement toward androgyny, driven by radical feminist thinking, is a direct satanic assault on the image of God as male and female.

For all its healthy attributes, like most human activities, feminism knows no balance. It has swung the pendulum so far to the ridiculously radical that the enemy of God is having a heyday. The attempt to blur the divinely established male-female distinctions in marriage, family, church, and culture is a direct attack upon the image of God. The war on gender is foundational, spiritual, and theological before it is social, political, or ecomomic.

HOMOSEXUALITY

Isn't it amazing, how one to three percent of the population has the entire culture in anxious turmoil? The French philosopher John Paul Sartre (a blatant non-Christian) said it well: "Homosexuality is the ultimate expression of human defiance because logically it doesn't make sense." He's absolutely right—there is no support whatsoever in nature. If the test of the universality of truth is applied to homosexuality, it falls immediately. If homosexuality were universally applied, the human race would cease to exist. It is not hard to see that homosexuality is a satanic trump card in the destruction of the human race, the image of God.

The Bible clearly, overtly, unmistakably, and repeatedly condemns any act of sex outside of heterosexual marriage. Scripture calls homosexual acts "detestable" (Leviticus 18:22, NIV). But the public is seldom allowed to see the dark side of homosexual behavior and activity in our culture. The mainline media strains to present only a pretty, sanitized version. Thanks to such representations, the outside of the fortress looks warm and inviting. But inside, all is bondage and darkness.

ABORTION

Abortion is simply another logical extension of the Darwin-Nietzsche-Hitler thinking. Whether we kill humans selectively in Auschwitz, on the school grounds, or in the womb, there is a similar thread to the thinking. Born, unborn, or partially born, what's the difference? No matter how you choose your words (pro-choice), doctor your vocabulary (product of conception, fetal tissue, et cetera), or warp your thinking (just a medical procedure because it's in a hospital), abortion is still the murder of another human being. And the guilty will come to judgment before God for it.

PORNOGRAPHY

This stronghold is progressive, addictive, and corrosive. It is the drug of choice for an increasing number of childish adults who are unable to manage their appetites. Each and every night, four million American men visit pornographic Web sites. It slowly eats the heart, numbs the conscience, and destroys the soul.

Viewing pornography is—may I say it?—a form of narcissistic thumb sucking. How ironic that it is called "adult" activity. Using pornography changes the way we think of one another and it serves as the fountainhead of self-destruction. One government study showed that 87 percent of molesters of girls and 77 percent of molesters of boys admit to the regular, consistent use of pornography. This is not rocket science. Do the math. It's an obvious connection.

YES, THIS IS WAR

It's clear we've got a war on our hands. That's life on a sin-stained planet. This is a great day to be alive and to be engaged in that war. Can you hear the joy and anticipation in the apostle's words?

> The hour has come for you to wake up from your slumber, because our salvation is nearer now than when we first believed. The night is nearly over; the day is almost here. So let us put aside the deeds of darkness and put on the armor of light.
>
> ROMANS 13:11–12, NIV

I hope you are wonderfully excited about the opportunities you have in this world and this culture in this day! You ought to be! This is a magnificent time to be a Christian. The darker our culture grows, the brighter and more radiant our light becomes.

Don't be discouraged. Don't lose heart. Don't withdraw. Don't retreat. Run to the guns. Alexander the Great once said that the Persians would always be slaves because they did not know how to pronounce the word *no*.

Say it, spirit warrior. Stand up and say it. Take the words from one of Churchill's great speeches to heart: "Never give in. Never, never, never." Giving up is *never* a Christian attitude. Rolling over is *never* a biblical option. Despair is always a sin.

You and I have direct orders to stay in the fight. The Bible instructs us to occupy faithfully until He comes. Our Lord has given us a great commission—to make disciples of all peoples. And He has given us an equally potent cultural mandate, to "seek the welfare of the city where I have sent you...and pray to the LORD on its behalf, for in its welfare you will have welfare" (Jeremiah 29:7).

As Christians, we have the message the world so desperately needs. We hold in our Bibles the antidote to the deadly poison. The Christian message is the cure for what is killing us. And people are starting to wake up to it. Oh, we don't know what else to call it, but we know it has something to do with our roots, something to do with traditional values.

In early 2000, the state legislatures of Indiana, Kentucky, and South Dakota all officially approved the public display of the Ten Commandments. Indiana places the commandments in public display alongside such historic documents as the Magna Carta and our own Declaration of Independence.

Listen to the story, reported in the *Oregonian,* of one little silver-haired Christian soldier from Ohio hard at work in the battle:

> Dorothy Glasgow never intended to start a movement or pick a fight. She just thought young people needed some moral guidance.
>
> So three years ago, when Adams County built four new public high schools, Glasgow told her United Methodist Church pastor that it sure would be nice to post the Ten Commandments at those schools. The Rev. Ken Johnson took her idea to the local ministerial association, which purchased three-foot-tall granite tablets engraved with the commandments to stand outside each school.... Today, the school system in southern Ohio is embroiled in a federal lawsuit with the ACLU, which calls the tablets an unconstitutional effort to promote religion. Ministers are raising a defense fund for the cash-strapped school district.... Glasgow, who spent three years in a one-room Adams County schoolhouse,

where she memorized a Bible verse each week, explains
her efforts this way: "…we've lived too loosely, and we
have a sick society. Maybe this'll help."[5]

For better or worse, win or lose, that's what Dorothy Glasgow did. Quite
a little spirit warrior. In her own way, as best as she could think it through,
she ran to the guns in an attempt to influence the battle. Criticize her if you
will. Find the weaknesses in her strategy. But ask yourself, "What am I doing
to effect the battle's outcome?" The statement attributed to Dwight L.
Moody comes to mind. Criticized for his evangelistic methods and tactics,
Moody responded, "I like the way I do it better than the way that you don't."

So, fellow Christian, what will you do? How will you offer the message
to this battle-scarred world?

The battle is engaged and heating up. And there are many indicators that
it may very well be turning. But even if it doesn't, our orders are the same—
to actively seek the welfare of the nation where God has placed us. How? By
our intense commitment to biblical action. Be involved, soldier! Stand up
and engage! Run to the guns!

Another lady spirit warrior, Ethelwyn Wetherald, summed up our
responsibility this way in her poem "My Orders":

> My orders are to fight;
>   Then if I bleed, or fail,
> Or strongly win, what matters it?
>   God only doth prevail.
> The servant craveth naught
>   Except to serve with might.
> I was not told to win or lose,
>   My orders are to fight.[6]

PART 4

BEYOND *the* BATTLEFIELD

The war is over, so it is said, All men are home, or else they're dead.
Don't you know—I want to cry, That some of us have refused to die...
I wonder each and every night, How much longer I can fight.

EX-POW, CIRCA 1980

Look to the right and see; There is no one who regards me;
There is no escape for me; No one cares for my soul...
Hear my cry, For I am brought very low.

DAVID, CIRCA 1000 B.C.

We should like you, our brothers, to know something of the trouble we went
through in Asia. At that time we were completely overwhelmed, the burden was
more than we could bear, in fact we told ourselves that this was the end.

THE APOSTLE PAUL,
2 CORINTHIANS 1:8-9,
PHILLIPS

WHEN YOU FEEL LIKE A CASUALTY

They called it shell shock in World War I.

It was battle fatigue in World War II and Korea. And out of Vietnam it was called PTSD—post-traumatic stress disorder.

But whatever you call it, the debilitating effect is real. War is hellish and disorienting. Combat is stressful. And so is spiritual warfare! Life can become one long night of blackness, depression, and dysfunction. War wears out the soul. And even healthy spirit warriors are not exempt.

Even pastors and authors.

I resolved when I started this book that I would avoid using that hackneyed phrase: "Boy, I never experienced such spiritual warfare as when I was studying spiritual warfare." Well, I hate to admit it, but it's been true for me. This past year has been one of the most difficult seasons of my life.

I've had to face off with personal issues in my own life, Linda and I have had to do some hard work together on our marriage, and there have been professional issues related to the church ministry staff. Probably most painful and distressing of all has been the horrifying sight of seeing some of my battle buddies, good people and good friends, taking hits and going down in the battle. The wounds have been terrible—fractured relationships, shattered lives, bleeding souls, and the horrible, aching sense of lingering pain and loss.

Sometimes it has felt like the walls were closing in.

Discouragement has hung in the air like the acid clouds of smoke over the battlefield. At times the black shadows of depression, fear, and loss of hope have marked the night watches.

Discouragement has hung in the air like the acid clouds of smoke over the battlefield. At times the black shadows of depression, fear, and loss of hope have marked the night watches. It has weighed so heavily on me at times that I have wondered whether my lifetime of ministry has had any positive impact whatsoever.

I tell you what, though: When you stand in the battle with dear fellow soldiers beside you, men and women who love Christ with all their hearts, you can take the hill. And there's a light in the distance. It's the light of a new morning after a long night.

The worst of the battle is behind—I hope. But there will be another engagement tomorrow. That's the way it is in the life of a soldier during wartime. And that's why it's so critical that a good soldier know what to do when he feels like something of a casualty himself.

Imagine yourself in church Sunday morning. The choir has just finished singing a magnificent hymn to the sovereign, loving care of God. Its theme is clear: God is always in control. But it doesn't seem so to you. Reflecting on all that is happening in your life, you certainly don't feel the peace and rest of waiting on Him. In fact, you've been struggling with a number of issues for quite a while. And, frankly, it's got you down. It's been all gray skies and slush for a long time now.

I've been there. I know the truth for sure in my head, but I don't always feel it in my chest. If clouds of doubt and discouragement have begun to drift across your horizons, then this chapter is for you. Let's do a little battle work with discouragement. Hang in there, soldier.

THE SONG HE LOVED TO HATE

Let's go back to a season in the life of one of history's most celebrated warriors: David, son of Jesse. We'll step into the time in history when a certain hit tune was dominating the pop charts of ancient Israel. It was a ballad about the exploits of Saul, the king.

But Saul didn't like it one bit.

You see, the song also featured David. Young David didn't compose it, of course. The new military attaché to King Saul would never have sung it. And he most certainly would never have played a note of it on his harp in the presence of the king.

Be that as it may, folks were singing and dancing to the upbeat melody in the streets. It was a phenomenon—and took the country by storm. Every time King Saul went out he heard people singing the new hit. It would have been like trying to avoid the Beatles singing "I Want to Hold Your Hand," back in 1964—or Elvis's "Jail House Rock" in 1957. Like it or not, the song was everywhere. To the accompaniment of tambourines and lutes, the voices of joyful people filtered through palace windows long into the evening hours when Saul just wanted to shut it out and go to sleep.

Most of the lyrics have probably been lost to antiquity, but the chorus went like this: "Saul has slain his thousands, and David his tens of thousands."

The words really ticked Saul off. Most kings don't like to be number two in public esteem, and Saul was certainly no exception. He liked the "Saul has slain his thousands" part just fine. But the next phrase about David slaying his *tens* of thousands ruined the whole song.

Let's pick up the story in the Bible:

> Saul was very angry; this refrain galled him. "They have
> credited David with tens of thousands," he thought,
> "but me with only thousands. What more can he get
> but the kingdom?" And from that time on Saul kept a
> jealous eye on David.
>
> 1 SAMUEL 18:8–9, NIV

What had David done to deserve the king's anger? Nothing. From the moment he left the sheepfold and entered the king's service, he had acquitted himself with courage and honor. But no matter how much he tried to do right, things just kept getting worse. Look at the next verses:

> The next day an evil spirit from God came forcefully
> upon Saul. He was prophesying in his house, while
> David was playing the harp, as he usually did. Saul had a
> spear in his hand and he hurled it, saying to himself, "I'll
> pin David to the wall." But David eluded him twice.
>
> 1 SAMUEL 18:10–11, NIV

David had to flee the palace to save his life. All because of a song. Because Saul chose to listen to the music of the streets instead of the music of the harp. Because the devil would do anything to foil God's kingdom plans. Because Saul was not feeding his soul after God. And because one of Satan's demons took advantage of the situation and managed to use a popular, even innocent, song of the streets. It was the song—that dreadful song replaying again and again—that fueled Saul's imagination. Music has that kind of power, doesn't it?

The story gets even more complicated, because while David was on the run he and King Saul's daughter, Michal, somehow fell in love. For a brief period of time after the wedding, Saul seemed to soften a little. He evidently decided he should really try to get along with his son-in-law, and he invited him back to the palace. David resumed his duties as the king's assistant and resident musician.

But it didn't last long. Once again the tortured king fell victim to the darkness in his own soul and tried to kill David again with his spear. David had to run. He knew his career in King Saul's royal service was over, and there was no going back.

Being harpist for the king had suddenly become an extremely hazardous proposition. David would have felt safer fighting Philistines.

WHAT'S MY CRIME?

Those had to be incredibly difficult days for this high-strung young warrior. It's one thing to bear the consequences of your own mistakes, your own pride, your own sins. It's quite another—completely so—to be misunderstood, to have your motives questioned, to be selected arbitrarily as the target of another person's evil nature and jealous arrows.

Shrapnel is like that: It wounds innocent bystanders in every direction. Maybe you've been there. It's a rotten place. The dark kingdom will use any number of means to leave you wounded on the battlefield.

Shrapnel is like that: It wounds innocent bystanders in every direction.

A fugitive once again, David kept rehearsing the events in his head—over and over again. Pick it up as he conversed with his friend, Jonathan (who happened to be King Saul's son): "What have I done? What is my crime? How have I wronged your father, that he is trying to take my life?" (1 Samuel 20:1, NIV).

David was forced to hide in the wilderness. With only wild animals and the bright, indifferent stars for company, he crouched over small campfires, heating brackish water for a little tea to warm his bones. He had lots of questions—and precious few answers. Nothing to break the silence of his isolation. Have you ever noticed how you can hear the tiniest sounds when you're all alone? David became acquainted with the sigh of wind in the junipers...the dry rattle of stones slipping down a canyon wall...the furtive movements of small animals, deep in their burrows.

It was lonely. Agonizingly so.

Days stretched into weeks and months. Even years. Rather than forgetting his jealousy and anger, Saul became ever more obsessed with killing his former servant and son-in-law. David was running, dodging, hiding, not wanting to take the offensive—but not wanting to die, either. In desperation he even slipped across the border and headed into Philistine territory for a time, hoping to find a bit of rest in anonymity. But it wasn't to be.

It seems the hit song playing in the streets of Israel had wound its way to the streets of Gath, fifty miles over the mountains:

> Then David arose and fled that day from Saul, and
> went to Achish king of Gath. But the servants of Achish
> said to him, "Is this not David the king of the land?
> Did they not sing of this one as they danced, saying,
> 'Saul has slain his thousands,
> And David his ten thousands'?"
>
> 1 SAMUEL 21:10–11

These guys were no dummies. They knew that the slaying part in this very song referred to them, the *Philistines*. This wasn't a fella they wanted walking their streets at night. Who could blame them?

Once more, David had to take to his heels.

> So David departed from there and escaped to the cave
> of Adullam; and when his brothers and all his father's
> household heard of it, they went down there to him.
> Everyone who was in distress, and everyone who was in
> debt, and everyone who was discontented gathered to
> him; and he became captain over them.
>
> 1 SAMUEL 22:1–2

Sounds like a fun group, doesn't it? Talk about a bunch of disgruntled veterans! The symptoms of PTSD probably filled the camp. Slip your feet into David's sandals for a moment. As you duck to enter the cave, how do you feel? Your life feels just about like that cave smells: musty, dirty, full of animal waste, packed with a bunch of humans who feel wasted.

Do you think David had things pretty well sorted out? Do you think he understood what was going on? Did he have a good handle on what God was doing? Did he grasp how God would be teaching others through the millennia because of this situation?

Not exactly!

The good news is that we don't have to guess at what David was thinking at that moment: He wrote it down. Evidently the Holy Spirit wanted it recorded for future spiritual warriors like you and me—warriors who aren't feeling so great about their lot in life under God's control. David very likely inked the words of Psalm 142 while he was hunkered down in that very cave. Hiding out. Scared. Confused.

THE CRY FROM A CAVE

Read the psalm slowly. Stop at key words. Turn them over in your mind, expanding them. Try to feel with David. Picture an exhausted man barely mustering the strength to lift his arm, dip his quill in ink, and scratch these words on a piece of sheepskin.

> I cry aloud to the LORD;
> > I lift up my voice to the LORD for mercy.
> I pour out my complaint before him;
> > before him I tell my trouble.
> When my spirit grows faint within me,
> > it is you who know my way.
> In the path where I walk
> > men have hidden a snare for me.
> Look to my right and see;
> > no one is concerned for me.
> I have no refuge;
> > no one cares for my life.
> I cry out to You, O LORD;
> > I say, "You are my refuge,
> my portion in the land of the living."

Listen to my cry,
> for I am in desperate need
rescue me from those who pursue me,
> for they are too strong for me.
Set me free from my prison,
> that I may praise Your name.
Then the righteous will gather about me
> because of your goodness to me.

PSALM 142, NIV

If you look up Psalm 142 in your Bible, you'll see that it is called a *maskil.* That means it's a teaching psalm, intended to specifically model a spiritual lesson for us. It begins: "A *maskil* of David. When he was in the cave. A prayer." So let's learn a combat principle or two from this seasoned spirit warrior.

I cry aloud to the LORD. This is not a quiet whimper, but something like a yell. A shriek. I expect David's painful, frustrated scream reverberated off the back wall of the cave and spilled out into the valley.

I lift up my voice to the LORD for mercy. "I beg for pity." It's okay to beg God when your heart knows nothing else to do.

I pour out my complaint before him. The word translated "pour" is a very strong verb in Hebrew. We tend to think of polite activities such as pouring a cup of tea or pouring a bit of cream into our coffee. But the picture here is closer to vomiting! It's an involuntary, reflexive, regurgitating agony: "I've held this in as long as I can, but I can't hang onto it anymore."

Before him I tell my trouble. Here's a straightforward, wide-open declaration between two very authentic people: one human, one divine. David simply declares reality as he sees it: A taunting enemy, one who hates my guts, is tormenting me.

When my spirit grows faint within me. David was overwhelmed; there was no coping skill left in the man. "When I'm at the brink of exhaustion, when I think I can't take another step…" Those three little dots belong there, right in the biblical text. It's an ellipsis. David doesn't actually finish the thought. Just at the very point of going under, a thought comes to his mind. I believe it's just like the Holy Spirit to do that. Just that quickly the truth dawns on David's troubled heart. He hears someone speaking. It's his own voice saying, "I remember!"

Just when his soul can't bear it anymore, when he's about to go down for the third time, the truth of God's nature washes over him.

Just when his soul can't bear it anymore, when he's about to go down for the third time, the truth of God's nature washes over him. "But wait a minute! *You* know! It is You who knows my way. You know the path I've been traveling, Lord. It's been straight and narrow, the one You set me on. But, Lord, I gotta tell You something. This isn't making sense to me. Still, if I can just focus on You and Your character, I'll make it through this horrible mess! Okay, Lord, I'm changing my focus, my perspective, my attitude…everything. From this point forward, I'm just going to walk straight ahead, trusting You with my heart, my feelings, my soul, my future."

In the path where I walk men have hidden a snare for me. Don't miss this. There's a very important lesson here. David is on the right path, the very path God placed him on. He hasn't wandered off. And on *that very path* God allowed David's enemies to set a snare for him.

If that's not confusing—at least at first glance—I don't know what is.

My fellow pastor Barry Arnold grew up in Alaska. After college and preparation for the mission field, Barry and his bride returned to the interior of Alaska to plant a church among the Athabascan Indian people. While there they started their own family, successfully launched a new native church, and eventually returned to Oregon to join our pastoral staff.

On more than one trip to Alaska to visit them over the years—and later on a hunting trip or two with Barry—I fell in love with the Athabascan people and their way of life.

One cold January nearly twenty years ago, Barry walked me through twenty-degree-below-zero weather to check a line of snares. If you wanted to catch a snowshoe hare, you had to search that brush for the most beaten paths. Summer or winter, those rabbits would travel the same six-inch-wide freeways. A well-placed wire would always snare a rabbit—and there was fresh meat for dinner!

David says, "Lord, I've been walking the right path. The one You showed me. The beaten path. Why the trap? Why that loop of wire dangling in front of me? It feels as though You're against me, just as my enemies are against me. It feels like everyone and everything is against me."

This is about the time when alarm bells should have been sounding in David's soul. This is a dangerous, vulnerable moment for any spirit warrior. You've been there, too, I'm sure.

A MOST VULNERABLE MOMENT

You and I know that discouragement skews our perspective. When we're down we don't think clearly. One dear friend of mine calls it "stinkin' thinkin'." It's one of the sure signs of battle fatigue. And when those thoughts seize our mental gears, we are in severe danger of being victimized by our own feelings. We become highly vulnerable targets for deadeye enemy snipers. Why? Because in our self-pity we tend to turn toward selfishness and sinful indulgence.

I know one Christian brother who had carried a huge load for a long time—more than most of us could bear. He had a very difficult marriage. His teenage son deeply disappointed him behaviorally. Still he hung on. Work became exceptionally stressful for him—constant, high speed, unrelenting production. He was tired. Still he hung on.

Eventually, though, the weight became more than he could bear. He began to think, understandably, of himself. But his thoughts dropped below the wisdom line. He fell into self-pity and finally slipped outside all healthy boundaries.

Cunning foe that he is, Satan chose that moment to strike. He used that brief season of superdiscouragement to pull the trigger on my friend. A younger woman at work, with deep needs of her own, reached out to him. And my brother went down. Satan's .50-caliber sniper rifle—adultery—picked him off.

Many of us, his fellow soldiers, still ache over his loss. And our battle unit, our whole church, still limps from his wounding. Here was a strong, though wounded, spirit warrior who took a debilitating hit when the "stinkin' thinkin'" of self-pity disoriented him on the battlefield.

That kind of deep, lonely self-pity must've been something like what David felt.

So what will David do? Which way will this man after God's own heart turn? Dodging the snare entirely, David takes a flying leap into the arms of God. What a great life lesson! When the going gets tough, the tough run straight to God!

His heart in his hand, David talks openly and candidly with his Lord:

> Look to my right and see; no one is concerned for me. I
> have no refuge [no secure place]; no one cares for my life.
> I cry [same word as verse 1, "I shriek"] to you, O
> LORD; I say, "You are my refuge, my portion in the
> land of the living" [You're all I have].
> Listen to my cry, for I am in desperate need ["I'm
> as low as I can get." It's a word used to describe miners
> suspended by ropes over a pit. "This is really precarious,
> Lord. Are You really watching?"]; rescue me from those
> who pursue me, for they are too strong for me" [liter-
> ally, "They're bigger than I am, and I think I've had it"].
> PSALM 142:4–6, NIV, BRACKETED COMMENTS MINE

Some of us have never experienced that level of depression. Some of us have never felt the kinds of emotions David scrawled in his journal that day in the cave of Addulam. Others of us are all too familiar with both the feelings and the phrases.

We really shouldn't be taken aback. A friend of mine who was in a similar situation penned these words: "We shouldn't be surprised when we face anxiety, depression, doubt, and fear, because there is a spiritual war going on inside us, one that reflects the cosmological war on the outside."

Discouragement, depression, and the temptation to embrace self-pity are very much parts of spiritual warfare.

And here's the point of this whole chapter: Discouragement, depression, and the temptation to embrace self-pity are very much parts of spiritual warfare. We need to get a handle on them, recognize them, learn to deal with them, and refuse to go down to their blows. Yes, depression may strike us from a variety of sources, but some of those sources have everything to do with genetics and pure chemistry.

CHEMICAL DEPRESSION

Barry Arnold tells this very personal story:

> Three generations back on my mother's side, my great-
> grandfather Nichols had quite a reputation. Great-

grandpa was a dairy farmer like most everyone else in upstate New York. But everybody who dealt with Nichols knew that every once in a while Nichols would have what they called a "mad spell."

When Nichols got "the mads" everybody stayed away. Just left him alone because if you got near he was sharp, he was grumpy, he was unreasonable, he was morose." But just leave him be for a month or two and he'd come out of the mad spell and be all right.

Back in my great-grandpa's days the word *depression* related to the banking system, not to a person's emotions. What my great-granddad experienced was more than ordinary discouragement. Crop failures, animal diseases, and crooked people were part of every farmer's life. Great-Grandpa's "mads" were something much deeper.

You and I know that what Barry's great-grandpa was experiencing was deep and prolonged depression, probably chemically induced in the brain. Everyone experiences a disheartening chill now and then. Periodic letdowns are a normal part of life on a broken planet, where the spiritual battle always rages, and where reality often fails to meet expectations.

But hear me: *Deep, clinical depression can completely disrupt your life.*

There are many levels of depression, from mild to manic states, but it's not the purpose of this chapter to give you clinical definitions for a self-diagnosis. There are skilled professionals in the church and in the Christian community who are equipped to do that; if you think you may be up against real depression, get to one. We always say in our family, "Smart people get help. Dumb people don't."

"Smart people get help.

Dumb people don't."

DEPRESSION MYTHS

As we consider how discouragement and depression relate to spiritual warfare, let's try to dispel some common misconceptions. You might call them "myths surrounding depression."

MYTH #1: THE SIN OF UNBELIEF IS ALWAYS AT THE CORE OF ANXIETY

It's just not true. Sin can be at the root of depression, but it's not always so. With David, Job, and Elijah, it was not sin that led to their loss of perspective. Sometimes it's just the overwhelming pressure of life. The apostle Paul himself probably experienced it. He said at one point, "We were under great pressure, far beyond our ability to endure, so that *we despaired even of life*" (2 Corinthians 1:8, NIV, italics mine). Most Christians aren't ready to accuse Paul of the sin of unbelief.

MYTH #2: DISCOURAGED PEOPLE WOULD BE JUST FINE IF THEY WOULD ONLY HAVE ENOUGH FAITH, PRAY ENOUGH, AND READ THEIR BIBLE ENOUGH

Maybe not! It may be a whole lot larger than that. Such a statement sounds spiritual, but it ignores the fact that God allowed some of the greatest people of faith to remain in depression for years. Statements like that also reduce faith to a rather simplistic and insulting formula. "Just conjure up a little faith, and you'll be okay." No, it seldom, if ever, works so simply.

MYTH #3: IF YOU WERE TRULY WALKING WITH GOD YOU WOULDN'T BE DEPRESSED

In other words, "The best Christians are the ones with big grins on their faces." If you believe that, you've just smeared mud on giants of the faith like Charles Spurgeon, Martin Luther, David Brainard, and a host of others. It's quite possible to walk closely with God and yet still struggle with depression.

MYTH #4: DISCOURAGEMENT AND DEPRESSION ARE ALL IN YOUR HEAD

That one has a bit of truth to it. Modern research has shown us something of the brain chemistry that causes feelings of depression. We understand the brain enough to know that sad, sorrowful feelings coincide with reduced levels of certain chemicals in the brain. The shortage of these chemicals result in a decrease in brain stimulation, leading to a corresponding drop in good feelings.

Let me take a shot at explaining it in simple—perhaps simplistic—terms. Step inside your own head for a minute. Your head is full of billions of brain cells. Picture ten such cells (they happen to be nerve endings) all in a row. This first cell gets a good feeling, but in order for the good feeling to register with the person who owns these ten brain cells, that good feeling has got to travel through all ten cells. After it has traveled through all the cells, they vote on whether or not they feel good, and the majority rules.

So, cell number one releases good feeling, a chemical called serotonin, in the direction of cell number two. Cell number two is supposed to absorb the serotonin then pass it on to cell number three, and so on. But if the owner of that brain happens to be in a depressed state, cell number one decides to reabsorb some of the serotonin, instead of passing it on. That leaves less serotonin for cell number two to pass on. And if cell number two copycats cell number one, you can see what will happen on down the line. By the time it gets to cell number ten he votes "thumbs down." And the person says, "I think I feel terrible."

So in that sense, yes, depression really is all in your head. But there are many reasons for the reduced levels of serotonin in your brain.

ANALYZING DEPRESSION

The root causes of depression may be biological or genetic. Many studies have shown that it tends to run in families. If my friend Barry could say three words to his great-grandfather, they would probably be these: "Thanks a lot!" And then in the resultant conversation, it's likely that great-grandpa would have to thank some earlier ancestor. So let's not be so hard on the guy experiencing it. Let's take a good thorough look at the situation before coming to rash "spiritual" judgments. When a soldier is suffering on the battlefield, try not to shoot him again. Try instead to understand the full nature of the wound.

Depression can be the result of long-buried emotional pain. It can also be triggered by stresses on the job, financial pressures, grief, or some debilitating health condition.

On the other hand, depression can also be a common (and healthy) response to sin. One counselor said, "Some people who come in for counseling should feel depressed. They've made terrible choices." Sometimes feeling guilty is the result of actually being guilty. If you're sinning, you ought to feel bad about your sin! The plainspoken apostle James said it like this:

When a soldier is suffering on the battlefield, try not to shoot him again.

> Come near to God and he will come near to you. Wash
> your hands, you sinners, and purify your hearts, you
> double-minded. Grieve, mourn and wail. Change your
> laughter to mourning and your joy to gloom. Humble
> yourselves before the Lord, and he will lift you up.
>
> JAMES 4:8–10, NIV

Yes, authentic guilt is a God-given reality. The first steps in recovering from that kind of depression are repentance and confession.

Lingering discouragement, however, is often a result of simply not taking care of yourself. Listen, if you're living on the run, ignoring a balanced diet, sleeping weird hours, working too much, and not exercising, you're just asking for depression. It's like painting a big red bull's-eye on your back!

Dr. David Wenzel, a counselor and professor at Western Seminary and a member of Good Shepherd Church, estimates that if all the people coming to see him for depression were to start eating right, consistently get adequate sleep, and exercise regularly, about half of them (half!) would be able to deal with their problems through readily available resources like friendships and church groups.

Now then, with this background, let's take a careful look at medications.

"MEDIC!"

Medications can be incredibly valuable on a battlefield. Often, one of the earliest shouts you'll hear in the midst of a firefight is "Medic!" or "I'm hit!" Sometimes your wounds are beyond your own ability to fix. You may be able to stop the bleeding for a while, but eventually it's a good idea to get some skilled help. If you're hit hard, you need some extra attention, particularly from a trained source. That's what competent professionals are there for.

However, there are times when prayer, food, sleep, exercise, friendships, Bible reading, and talking are not adequate. The depression spiral may have become too tight, and you may need more help to get back in the battle. The wound may go too deep. In those cases, it is often beneficial to turn to certain medications.

One of the earliest shouts you'll hear in the midst of a firefight is "Medic!"

Medications can be very useful tools to give a person the ability to re-engage in relationships and objectively evaluate the factors that may be contributing to depression. Medications that increase the levels of serotonin in the brain (by preventing cell number one from reabsorbing what it's supposed to pass on) are wonderful tools.

Those who say Christians should never use antidepressant medications need to be careful of a double standard. If they're going to reject, in the name of consistency, the use of drugs developed to stimulate brain nerve cells, they should probably also refuse nerve-deadening drugs like Novocain. To use Novocain under professional care and then to criticize another for using an antidepressant under professional care may be the height of hypocrisy.

When most people get a good toothache, they welcome the dentist's Novocain. But then, if you're "above" nerve-deadening drugs and your tooth hurts, perhaps you should go on over to any car repair garage. They've got pliers. If you've got a headache, you'd better just pray harder. And if you get diabetes, forget the insulin. Just beat it. Or die.

You get the point. Don't be too quick to cut people down for using medication under professional care. Medications administered by careful, competent physicians can be extremely helpful in dealing with depression.

Having said that, let's balance it with a warning. Any medication can be abused. Frankly, it's scary to think of all the people who get prescriptions for antidepressants after a ten-minute conversation with a family doctor. There's got to be more to it than that. More talking. More process. More evaluation. Especially for Christians. We've got to seek the full picture. We've got to ask, "Is there a spiritual battle going on here? Are there spiritual factors relating to this discouragement that need to be addressed first?" Don't just camouflage your symptoms with drugs. Get to the root. And spiritual cure may be the only real cure.

A Few Words from the Front Line

Satan wants to use discouragement and depression to win spiritual battles by convincing you that you're defeated and have no hope.

God has blessed Good Shepherd Church by allowing us the opportunity to support many missionaries. We love them and regard them as our own. We don't even call them missionaries; we refer to them as the "Associate Staff." They are ours and we are theirs. They just serve Christ and our body in another location.

David and Karen DeGraaf are among the best and brightest of these warriors. As missionaries from our church who work as Bible translators, their work is long, hard, and sometimes very lonely. Dave and Karen are heroes—and they're winning battles. The following are Dave DeGraaf's wise words, taken from a personal letter:

> The most important factor for Christians dealing with depression is the response of other Christians. As the severity of depression increases, the depressed person's ability to think clearly, to remember what's true, to take in Scripture, to pray, and to hear the Spirit's voice can be severely impeded. This is especially true at the onset of depression.
>
> One's initial experience with depression can be a real shock. An unsuspecting person can be totally blind-sided, and the ensuing disorientation can leave gaps in one's armor that Satan will target with precision and violence.
>
> Using a warrior metaphor, depression can be like getting a head wound in battle. When that happens, the response of the rest of the soldier's platoon is critical not only to the survival of the wounded guy, but to the survival of the unit.
>
> What if, when the guy went down, his buddies called to him and said, "You didn't have your helmet on! Everything would be fine if you'd keep your helmet on. Now just put it back on and start fighting!"
>
> It might be that the guy wasn't protecting himself like he should have been, but this kind of advice at this time isn't appropriate. The soldier may not even be able to hear. And, if this is all the support he gets, he may not live to put it into practice the next time.
>
> With a head wound there's a lot of blood and confusion. Most in the unit (certainly the wounded man himself) are in no position to assess the damage. The best thing his buddies can do is to cover him and drag him to where a medic can assess the wound and administer first aid. It might be just a skin laceration that the medic can suture.
>
> It's also possible that he needs to be evacuated. The grunts aren't equipped to patch their buddy up or even

decide if he needs a chopper, but their response is crucial. If they don't cover him, if they don't drag him to a medic, if they're not yelling encouragement—"Hang on Joe, you're going to make it!"—nothing's going to work right.

By coming together to support their wounded comrade, they reaffirm their commitment to each other in a powerful and tangible way. And when their wounded buddy rejoins the unit, he'll be a better soldier. Not only will he remember to keep his helmet on but he'll never forget what his friends did for him.

And every time his buddies see him they'll remember to keep their helmets on too!

Now there's some solid advice from a frontline, combat-seasoned spiritual warfare veteran. He's been in the battle. And he's still standing firm! He's fighting the good fight, and he's winning!

You can, too. After all, my friend, you're a Christian soldier.

For we must all appear before the judgment seat of Christ,
that each one may be recompensed for his deeds in the body, according to what he
has done. I have fought the good fight…in the future there is laid up for me the
crown of righteousness, which the Lord…will award to me on that day.

PAUL, CIRCA A.D. 67,
2 CORINTHIANS 5:10;
2 TIMOTHY 4:7-8

At great risk of his life…[and] by his outstanding leadership,…expert planning…
and dauntless devotion to duty, he…undoubtedly saved the lives of many…
who otherwise would have perished. He gallantly gave his life.

MEDAL OF HONOR CITATION
FOR DOUG MUNRO,
GUADALCANAL,
SEPTEMBER 27, 1942

For the Son of Man is going to come in the glory of His Father with His angels,
and will then repay every man according to his deeds.

JESUS, CIRCA A.D. 30,
MATTHEW 16:27

BATTLEFIELD DECORATIONS

On February 24, 1981, retired Green Beret Master Sergeant Roy Benavidez stood before the president of the United States in the White House. Ronald Reagan placed the beautiful sky-blue, white star-crested ribbon bearing the nation's highest battlefield award, the Congressional Medal of Honor, around the sergeant's neck.

It was a great moment for the old soldier and long in coming.

The first Medal of Honor was awarded in 1863 to a Union Army private, Jacob Parrott. Since the Civil War, 3,411 American heroes have been recognized with the nation's highest award for valor—155 of them are alive today. The Medal is bestowed on those who have performed acts of such "conspicuous gallantry" that they have risen far "above and beyond the call of duty."

Listed among the heroes are generals and privates, sailors and soldiers, airmen and marines—men of every color and creed, from every corner of this great nation. As a symbol of authentic heroism, the Medal of Honor has no equal in American life.

"WE DON'T HAVE PERMISSION TO DIE!"

Roy Benavidez was a Green Beret serving in the most secret and elite special operations unit of the Vietnam war. The existence of the Military Assistance Command Studies and Observation Group

(MACSOG) was carefully concealed—and totally denied—by the U.S. government. SOG was the somewhat innocuous, coded acronym for this magnificent unit that lived beyond the edge, across the borders, behind the enemy's lines, usually with fewer than ten men in a patrol.

The secret unit reported directly to the joint chiefs of staff in the Pentagon. Only a few inside Vietnam—General William Westmoreland and a select handful of his senior officers—were ever briefed on SOG operations. SOG always got the most dangerous assignments, patrolling deep inside Cambodia, Laos, across the DMZ (demilitarized zone), and all along the Ho Chi Minh Trail. The elite unit usually operated without any artillery support—and was often even without air support.

SOG identified targets for B-52 strikes, rescued downed American pilots, and wreaked all kinds of havoc on Vietcong (VC) and North Vietnamese Army (NVA) operations. The enemy was so desperate to eliminate SOG patrols that they devoted a minimum of forty thousand soldiers in Laos and Cambodia to the effort.

At one point, a single SOG patrol fought what is probably the most lopsided battle in U.S. military history—one fourteen-man team fought off a mass attack by two thousand enemy troops. SOG soldiers, though few in number, were awarded hundreds of Purple Hearts for combat wounds—and no fewer than ten Medals of Honor.

One of those medals now belongs to Roy Benavidez.

A sergeant first class at the time, Benavidez won his medal not long after the Tet offensive in early 1968, the "bloody year." On May 2, 1968, a SOG patrol was inserted by chopper forty-eight kilometers inside Cambodia's "fishhook," about seventy-five miles northwest of Saigon. Though hit almost immediately by NVA regulars, the patrol fought its way through a whole enemy platoon before calling for extraction. But so many NVA surrounded them—pouring heavy gunfire into the little unit—that landing was impossible. The choppers were forced away, losing one gunship to ground fire in the process.

The SOG patrol leader was dead, and every other member of the patrol was either dead or seriously wounded. They were about to be over-run and there was no one to help. The situation was desperate.

Back at the special forces base camp at Loc Ninh, Sergeant Roy Benavidez was monitoring the radio and heard gunfire that sounded like "a popcorn machine." He grabbed a medic bag and, to the surprise of the pilot, piled in to an available helicopter and demanded to be flown to the battle site.

Arriving at the landing zone he made the sign of the cross, tossed out the medic bag, and jumped ten feet to the ground, sprinting seventy-five yards through withering gunfire. On the way he was hit in the leg by an AK-47. He convinced himself it was a thorn vine that had grabbed him and kept running.

He dove through the brush to join the hurting team on the ground. Four were already dead, the other eight badly wounded. Benavidez bound their wounds, injected morphine, and gathered ammunition off the ground. Ignoring the NVA bullets and grenades, he armed himself with an AK-47 and rallied the surviving soldiers. Grabbing a radio, Benavidez called for air strikes on the enemy positions. In the process, he took a second bullet in his leg, and then injected himself with morphine.

Another Huey helicopter landed and Benavidez started hauling one of the wounded team members to the chopper. He took a third bullet, this one in the back and through a lung. He almost passed out but managed to get back on his feet, only to see the Huey on its side, with the pilot and door gunner dead. Coughing blood, Benavidez freed the rest of the crew members before the chopper exploded, and with the remaining team members formed a defensive perimeter.

Mortar shells exploded everywhere. Benavidez called the Air Force F-4 Phantoms in "danger-close"—meaning on top of himself. He was shot again, but ignored it. A few minutes later he took another slug. By now he was bleeding heavily from bullet wounds all over his body. The blood from a head wound made it difficult to see. Another gunship went down. One wounded man whose leg was missing pleaded with Benavidez to kill him. The sergeant barked back, "We don't have permission to die!" By now Benavidez and the team had been on the ground almost eight hours.

Then, under heavy supporting fire, another Huey made it to the landing zone in one final extraction attempt. The onboard medic helped Benavidez drag and carry wounded men to the chopper. As the badly wounded sergeant staggered under the load, an NVA soldier clubbed him with an AK-47 and thrust his bayonet toward Benavidez's midsection. The American grabbed the bayonet blade, cutting his own hand in the process, pulled the enemy soldier to him, and stabbed him with his knife.

While loading the wounded, Benavidez picked up a rifle and, as best as he could see through the blood dripping over his eyes, killed two enemy soldiers charging the helicopter. Then strong arms pulled Benavidez himself aboard the chopper. When he collapsed on the wounded bodies, he was holding his own intestines in his hands. As the Huey lifted from the landing zone, blood trickled out its side doors.

The helicopter made it back to Loc Ninh with seventeen men on board, some alive and some dead. The doctors thought Benavidez was dead and ordered a body bag, but the tough old sergeant managed to signal with his last ounce of strength.

Everyone at Loc Ninh assumed he would die at the hospital in Saigon, but Benavidez recovered gradually and in 1976—eight years after the battle—he was finally discharged from the hospital, though with an 80 percent disability. When his old commander discovered he had actually lived, he asked the Army to award the Medal of Honor. It took five more years, but finally two witnesses were found, a special act of Congress approved the late award, and President Reagan draped the coveted medal around Roy Benavidez's neck.

Roy Benavidez had to wait thirteen years for his Medal of Honor. The web of regulations and the machinery governing such high awards can sometimes grind slowly. Witnesses are required, but in this case most of them were dead. Finally, though, years after his heroic efforts, all the necessary elements came together, and he received his reward.

When you stop to think about it, the time frame in these deliberations usually isn't all that critical. Every battlefield decoration is awarded after the battle. When the bullets have stopped flying, when the nerves have settled, when the after-action battlefield reports are reviewed, the soldiers are decorated.

Every battlefield decoration is awarded after the battle. When the after-action battlefield reports are reviewed, the soldiers are decorated.

A DAY OF FINAL RECKONING

That's the way it will be for you, Christian soldier. When the battle is over, when life is done, when the fight is finished, you will stand before your Lord, the Commander in Chief. It will be in His house, not the White House. There will be men and women there from every tribe and tongue all across the globe. Awards will be given to every stripe of person—high and low, short and tall, black and white, male and female, yellow and red, great and small.

And you will receive your reward. There will be no more waiting. There will be no need of witnesses.

The only true God, who judges in righteousness and knows all the details, will Himself make the presentations at the judgment seat of Christ. Paul anticipated just that moment when he said such words as these:

> For we must all appear before the judgment seat of
> Christ, so that each one may be recompensed for his
> deeds in the body, according to what he has done,
> whether good or bad.
>
> 2 CORINTHIANS 5:10

> I have fought the good fight, I have finished the course,
> I have kept the faith; in the future there is laid up for me
> the crown of righteousness, which the Lord, the righ-
> teous Judge, will award to me on that day; and not only
> to me, but also to all who have loved His appearing.
>
> 2 TIMOTHY 4:7-8

Do you ever wonder what motivates a soldier like Roy Benavidez? Ever try to imagine just what makes a guy do those things? There are probably several motivations. One is certainly the sense of soldierly camaraderie, even love that soldiers—the band of brothers—have for each other. Another motivator is the sheer fear that is always present on a battlefield.

Roy said it this way: "When you're shot, you feel a burning pain, like you've been touched with hot metal. But the fear that you experience is worse—and that's what keeps you going."

So, love and fear. One more major motivator is hope, the hope of surviving, the hope of going on.

Yes, even the hope of reward.

How does it work? How are eternal rewards determined for battles well fought in this life? Let's look at this intriguing subject of biblical battlefield decorations for Christian soldiers.

Some day beyond all days...sometime beyond all time...every redeemed believer will stand at the *bema* (judgment seat) of Christ Himself.

THE BEMA SEAT

The word *bema* is the English transliteration of a Greek word that appears twenty-two times in the New Testament. It's in Romans 14:10 where Paul is addressing Christians: "You, then, why do you judge your brother? Or why do you look down on your brother? For we will all stand before God's judgment seat [bema]" (NIV).

Bema has different meanings depending on the usage. It can represent kind of a courtroom reality. For example, when Jesus stood before Pilate, Pilate sat on the bema to judge. Herod's throne is called a bema in Acts 12. In Acts 25, Paul stood before a bema upon which the Roman governor Festus presided.

The word also refers to the elevated rewards platform common at sporting events. It is similar to the three-tiered victory stand at modern Olympic games. Athletes went to the bema to receive commendation and approval.

In Scripture, the judgment seat of Christ is a subject that, unfortunately, lends itself to intense speculation and imagination on the part of theologians. Preachers and writers, feeling the need to fill in where the Bible leaves off, risk error in wanting to present a neat package with a pretty bow tied on top.

We're going to try to avoid those errors by reading a lot of Scripture—and admitting that this is one of those subjects where God's Word is perhaps somewhat vague—or at least not as explicit as we might like it to be.

For infinitely wise and completely unfathomable reasons, many of the photographs God provides us of future events are out of focus. Read Ezekiel, Daniel, and Revelation. Each of these books contains images we can't positively identify, descriptions that leave our heads spinning, and time lines that weave their way through mazes of interrelated yet enigmatic events.

These blurry but nonetheless real images, as retouched by theologians, depict widely differing interpretations of what will happen in the last days. That's why there are differences (even on our own church staff) as to how to interpret various future events. But what is clear is that Christ will one day evaluate our individual lives for the purpose of passing out His rewards.

Many men and women much smarter than I have spent lifetimes drafting theological road maps, or systems of theology. The problem with these comes when the theologian does not resist the temptation to allow the system to supercede the theology. This often happens in places where the scriptural picture is less than perfectly clear—such as the final Bema Judgment of Christ.

Interpreters often begin by piecing together a frame, the outside boundary of the biblical puzzle. Then they attempt to find places within that frame for all the individual pieces. The overwhelming temptation, once they've established the outer edge, is to force pieces of Scripture into spots where they just may not belong. It drives us nuts when truths don't fit into our neatly completed frame.

But God doesn't fit in our frames, boxes, or lock-tight systems, does He?

His plans, purposes, and priorities resist our attempts to reduce them to an orderly outline. That really bothers us Western thinkers, who need to see everything line up in a logical fashion. Much as we might like to have our information delivered in that manner, however, it just isn't always the case in Scripture. The Bible wasn't written for Western thinkers alone.

Many people don't have a problem with this lack of conceptual tidiness. The truths of God's Word don't seem to be nearly so difficult for so-called spherical or circular thinkers—folks who can live quite comfortably with what appear to be contradictions or paradoxes. This spherical thinking group, by the way, includes the vast majority of people on our planet.

TREADING CAREFULLY

In addition to these complications, I have to confess to a certain fear as we consider the final Bema Judgment of Christ. If it were possible, I would write two different messages on the bema for two groups of readers: those who lean too far toward legalism and those who lean too far toward license. It may be that you should not even hear the other message because it might actually hurt you more than help.

SOME NEED TO BE COMFORTED

If this is you, my fear is that you will leave this chapter with foreboding guilt and unnecessary fears. Because of your past and your makeup, you lean toward rules and appearances. I'm concerned that you may find yourself carrying anxieties you shouldn't carry, because your ear will be so sensitive to the harsh words, the judgment words—when you should be hearing words of grace, love, forgiveness, reward, and intense pleasure in the presence of Christ instead.

I hope that you would find great comfort in the bema—like an artesian well of sweet, cold water in a gray and desolate land. You should anticipate it gladly because your sins are covered by the blood of Christ and you are attempting to follow Him. For you, the bema will be a joyful payday, a hilarious celebration in which you'll lose yourself in worship and adoration of the King.

I also hope that your anticipation of that day will not be dampened by a misunderstanding of the message of this chapter. Does Titus 2 describe you?

> For the grace of God that brings salvation has appeared
> to all men. It teaches us to say "No" to ungodliness and
> worldly passions, and to live self-controlled, upright and
> godly lives in this present age, while we wait for the
> blessed hope—the glorious appearing of our great God
> and Savior, Jesus Christ, who gave himself for us to
> redeem us from all wickedness and to purify for himself
> a people that are his very own, eager to do what is good.
>
> TITUS 2:11–14, NIV

In other words, you need to hear a message of rejoicing and grace, anticipation and longing.

SOME NEED TO BE SHAKEN

I also fear for another kind of reader. Some people seem to have a deficiency of interest in rules and lean instead toward dangerous liberty. If this is you, I fear that you might hear only a message of grace and forgiveness—when you need to hear words of accountability and judgment. People like this are not motivated by grace. In fact, they tend to see the grace of God as license.

If you are living disobediently, if you are persisting in secret and willful sin, the message you need to hear is about the terrible holiness of God—and the fact that you'll stand aghast and dumfounded at the bema. The last thing you need is a message of comfort and consolation. Instead, you need to wake up and see Christ, the One who judges actions, thoughts, and even motives. You need to see how the choices you're making right now will affect your time at the bema—and your eternity thereafter. You should be gripped and convicted, not comforted, by what you hear.

So ask God right now, in your own private prayer, to give you what you need to know on this important subject. Pray that you will not miss what He wants you to have.

WE MUST ALL APPEAR

Now then, because God speaks through His Word, let's hear from the Bible:

> For we must all appear before the judgment seat [bema]
> of Christ, so that each one may be recompensed for his
> deeds in the body, according to what he has done,
> whether good or bad.
>
> 2 CORINTHIANS 5:10, BRACKETED COMMENT MINE

The exact time of the final Bema Judgment is difficult to lock down. Some people believe it comes immediately after one's death; others place it after Christ comes to take all believers home; and still others believe it will happen simultaneously with the great white throne judgment (Revelation 20). The timing may not be certain to us, but one thing we know for sure: It will happen after this life. What is absolutely clear is that at some point every believer will stand before Christ to give account.

I believe that every human being who has ever lived will appear, after death, at one of two judgments: either the Great White Throne Judgment or the final Bema Judgment.

The great white throne is the most dreadful, frightening place in the universe. It is for unbelievers only, and results in eternal punishment in the lake of fire. It is a judgment unto condemnation, and there is no second chance. If ever you needed extra motivation to reach out to non-Christian friends, just imagine them standing all alone in that place of shame and nameless terror.

Only believers are at Christ's bema. Scripture is very clear that there is no chance you could be eternally condemned after appearing before Christ's bema. Salvation is not an issue here. It is not a judgment unto condemnation, but it is a judgment of evaluation.

In John 5:24, Jesus said, "I tell you the truth, whoever hears My word and believes Him who sent Me has eternal life and will not be condemned; he has crossed over from death to life."

In Romans 8:1, Paul wrote: "Therefore, there is now no condemnation for those who are in Christ Jesus."

The purpose of the bema, then, is for evaluating believers' works and bestowing various degrees of rewards on them. We see it again in the book of Revelation:

The time has come for judging the dead, and for reward-
ing your servants the prophets and your saints and those
who reverence your name, both small and great.

REVELATION 11:18, NIV

And again, in the book of Matthew:

For the Son of Man is going to come in His Father's
glory with His angels, and then he will reward each person according to what He has done.

MATTHEW 16:27, NIV

WHAT REWARDS?

You will receive rewards, the Bible says, "for the things done while in the
body." Like what? What things? I'd like us to look at just a few rewards—
out of perhaps many others—that will be given at Christ's Bema
Judgment.

The purpose of the bema, then, is for evaluating believers' works and bestowing various degrees of rewards on them. You will receive rewards, the Bible says, "for the things done while in the body."

YOU WILL RECEIVE REWARDS FOR SHOWING HOSPITALITY AND MEETING NEEDS IN THE NAME OF CHRIST (HEBREWS 6:10; MATTHEW 10:41)

I have very little idea what such rewards might
look like. Are they all the same or are they different? Luke 19 talks about faithful people being put
in charge of cities. Is that a temporary mayoral
position—or permanent? Are the bema rewards
the crowns that believers will cast at Jesus' feet? Are
there other rewards? Different kinds? Are the
rewards material or immaterial? Some have suggested that they may involve varying capacities to
perceive and enjoy the glories of God and the wonders of heaven.

Scripture isn't specific. We only know that the
rewards will be much more desirable and much
more satisfying than any of us could begin to
imagine.

You may have heard strong sermons asking, "Will you be left empty-
handed at the bema when everyone else is holding rewards?" That makes

for a motivating sermon, perhaps, but it's probably more imagery than literal truth.

Honestly, few people should be left completely empty-handed. Some rewards come fairly easily. It is likely that every man will have praise of God who appears at the bema. Jesus even told us exactly how to get the hospitality reward: "If anyone gives even a cup of cold water to one of these little ones because he is my disciple, I tell you the truth, he will certainly not lose his reward" (Matthew 10:42, NIV).

Every year folks in our church send hundreds of thousands of dollars to Christian relief agencies. That's because our people are giving cups of cold water—to brothers and sisters in Sudan, earthquake victims in Turkey, and persecuted Christians in Nigeria and around the globe. Rewards will be given for helping others in the body of Christ.

YOU WILL RECEIVE REWARDS FOR SUFFERING FOR CHRIST

The Lord of the church will not overlook those who have suffered for the sake of His name. His eye today is on the Sudan, India, Pakistan, China, North Korea—and a thousand other places around this world where His blood-bought people are being harassed, kidnapped, beaten, raped, deprived, and even sold into slavery. He sees everything; He misses nothing.

> "Blessed are you when people insult you, persecute you and falsely say all kinds of evil against you because of me. Rejoice and be glad, because great is your reward in heaven, for in the same way they persecuted the prophets who were before you."
>
> MATTHEW 5:11–12, NIV

Those who endure in God's name and by His sustaining power will be honored with recognition beyond the power of words to describe.

You will be rewarded for how you run the race God has prescribed for you.

God's plan for your life is a personalized plan.

His plan for you isn't the same as His plan for me.

God's plan for one of our church members, Churchill Jackson, included a wheelchair. I don't know why a man who loved bicycling so much should be in a wheelchair as a result of a simple flu shot. I don't know why I'm not in a wheelchair instead of "Church." I may join him someday, but, until then, it's not part of God's plan for me.

God's plan for your life may include a profitable business. Others have lost all they had in businesses that failed through no fault of their own. God entrusts great wealth to some while others live out their lives on earth with very little. Wealth isn't God's plan for everyone any more than martyrdom is God's plan for everyone.

Not everyone goes to China.

Not everyone battles cancer.

Not everyone endures marital heartache.

Not everyone loses a child.

Why do Linda and I have three healthy children when others don't? Why were we born in America, the land of plenty, instead of Sudan, a land of persecution and hardship? These are unanswerable questions.

All we know is that God has a race for you to run. Remember how Paul describes his?

> Do you not know that those who run in a race all run,
> but only one receives the prize? Run in such a way that
> you may win. Everyone who competes in the games
> exercises self-control in all things. They then do it to
> receive a perishable wreath, but we an imperishable.
>
> 1 CORINTHIANS 9:24–25

Several years later, he wrote these words: "I press on toward the goal to win the prize for which God has called me heavenward in Christ Jesus" (Philippians 3:14, NIV).

You cannot and should not compare your race with others'. Instead, focus on running your personal race to the glory of God, and you will be rewarded at the bema for the way you steward your time, energies, and resources.

YOU WILL BE REWARDED FOR HOLINESS

Peter tells us:

> As obedient children, do not be conformed to the for-
> mer lusts which were yours in your ignorance, but like
> the Holy One who called you, be holy yourselves also in
> all your behavior; because it is written, "YOU SHALL
> BE HOLY, FOR I AM HOLY." If you address as Father
> the One who impartially judges according to each one's

work, conduct yourselves in fear during the time of
your stay on earth.

1 PETER 1:14–17

So the bema will be a place of rewards and words of affirmation from
Christ. Perhaps you desperately need to hear that God is pleased with you. You
can anticipate the bema and revel in the fact that it will be an encouraging,
joyful time with Christ because you are living well. With Paul, you can say:

I have fought the good fight, I have finished the course,
I have kept the faith; in the future there is laid up for me
the crown of righteousness, which the Lord, the righteous Judge, will award to me on that day; and not only
to me, but also to all who have loved His appearing.

2 TIMOTHY 4:7–8

A SOLEMN WORD OF WARNING

I need to add a final word if you belong to that other group—those who
need to see Christ the Judge on His throne, not Christ the gracious
encourager wrapping His arms around you.

Did you notice the last four words of 2 Corinthians 5:10? Here's the
verse again: "For we must all appear before the judgment seat of Christ,
that each one may receive what is due him for the things done while in the
body, *whether good or bad*" (NIV, italics mine).

Even though the bema will be dominated by joy, not remorse,
Scripture is clear that you will be aware of and accountable for all your
works, all your actions, all your decisions, and even your motives. It says
"whether good or bad."

The Greek word behind *bad* is usually translated "evil" or "sick."
Somehow, both good works and evil deeds will be represented at the bema,
and those works will be the basis for greater or lesser rewards. The writer
of Ecclesiastes understood it:

The conclusion, when all has been heard, is: fear God
and keep His commandments, because this applies to
every person. For God will bring every act to judgment,
everything which is hidden, whether it is good or evil.

ECCLESIASTES 12:13–14

Every Christian's life will be made evident by Christ's evaluation. Some Christians' works, done in the wrong way or for the wrong reasons, will be consumed by the fire of God's judgment, though the Christians themselves will be saved "as through fire" (see 1 Corinthians 3:11–15). I take this to mean that they will survive the judgment but will be left "rewardless," much as one who escapes his burning house with only the clothes on his back. His life's work is nothing but ashes. Who can imagine how devastating such a judgment would be?

UP IN SMOKE

When I think of ashes and work gone up in smoke, I can't help but remember what happened to my friend and me when we were young college students in the summer of 1965.

It was the Fourth of July, and the Boise Cascade Lumber Mill in our town had closed its doors for the holiday. Only two college guys would be dumb enough to volunteer to clean the mill's huge boilers during that three-day shutdown. Looking back, I can't believe that we would do it. But we did. My buddy Russ and I volunteered to spend our Fourth of July in the sweat, dirt, and ashes.

Now admittedly, there was a healthy reward: double-time pay. The mill's three-day shutdown supposedly allowed time for the boiler to cool off so it could be cleaned out. It had two days to cool before we had to attack it. But anyone in his right mind should've known that a boiler of that size could never really cool down in a day or two!

Picture two idiot college boys with picks and shovels in the terrible confines of a massive boiler. Our mission? To break up the waste "clunkers" from the burning sawdust that refused to be consumed. Those things were hard as rocks. Hot as fire. And in the sealed compartment of that boiler, ventilation was only a dream.

We're talking sweat, heat, dust, and no means of cooling.

At one point, we two rocket scientists, desperate to cool down even a degree or two, dragged a huge industrial fan in there and turned it on. Swoosh! In an instant what little air there was became a swirling mass of dust and ash. We couldn't see our hands in front of our faces. And we almost couldn't breathe. I think my lungs are still affected today.

But hey, we finished! It took all day and well into the night. When the last shovelful hit the conveyer at 1:30 A.M., we crawled—unspeakably exhausted—through the tiny boiler door, stacked the picks and shovels, and headed for the only two cars in the lot. With weary waves and grins, we pulled out and headed home.

Wow. Double time. That was serious money! Each of us had visions of a big payday dancing in our heads.

But it all fell apart when we got to the stoplight at the end of the street.

Stopped side by side in the lanes waiting for the light to change, the temptation was too much to bear. And like any two goofy, competitive college kids in cars at a light, we forgot our exhaustion and challenged each other to what we used to call a "drag." The light turned green, we tromped on the accelerators, and the tires squealed!

We got less than a hundred yards before the flashing red and blue lights sprang out of the night, to the accompaniment of screaming sirens. Several squad cars surrounded us. They wrote us up, drove us to the station, and we had to pay the fine on the spot.

Every single penny of that hard-earned boiler money!

Now, multiply that one day of lost wages—that one experience of disappointment, futility, and loss—by a thousand. Or ten thousand. Or a million. Imagine a life's work going up in an instant of white-hot, holy fire. What devastation! Unspeakable.

The bottom line is pretty clear: The bema will result in the bestowal of greater or lesser rewards—depending on how you stewarded your life.

OPPORTUNITIES SEIZED...OR LOST FOREVER

So, just what will the bema be? I don't think it will be what one of my fellow pastors pictured as a youngster. He remembers, as a teenager, hearing messages about the bema and picturing this place where he was standing in front of Christ, billions of people watching him—and Jesus being angry because he had not measured up. Behind His throne, on this huge screen, all the ugly stuff the boy had ever done, all the mouthy things he'd ever said, all the hidden things he was ashamed of were up there for everyone to see in Technicolor and Dolby sound. There he stood: a naked, despicable disciple.

How he dreaded that day! There's no way he wanted to go there. There's no way he could look forward to seeing Christ. He couldn't even imagine longing for His appearing. In fact, honestly, he'd rather never see Jesus than face such horror.

That's probably not the bema represented in Scripture. The bema appears to be a place of greater and lesser rewards. It is not represented as a vindictive, punitive examination.

We are all tempted, at times, to impose our own sense of justice, our own feelings of indignation, on the bema—because there are so many who are sinning and getting away with it. Murderers get off scot-free. Rapists repeat. People who claim to know Christ live like pagans. They take advantage of Christ's forbearance. They thumb their noses at His laws. And they get away with it. It consoles us to imagine them suffering at the bema. But I expect that is pressing the bema beyond scriptural intent.

I believe that believers will not have to answer for all their sins at the bema, certainly not their confessed sins. When 1 John 1:9 says, "If we confess our sins, He is faithful and righteous to forgive us our sins and to cleanse us from all unrighteousness," we take that as the truth. Those sins are forgiven. They won't be brought up at the bema.

The psalmist celebrates this truth: "As far as the east is from the west, / So far has He removed our transgressions from us" (Psalm 103:12). And in Isaiah, God declares: "I am He who blots out your transgressions...and remembers your sins no more" (Isaiah 43:25, NIV).

There's no asterisk after such verses. There's no fine print that reads, "Temporary and conditional forgiveness only. You'll meet all your sins again at the bema."

I know, I know: There is grave danger in emphasizing God's grace, in not interpreting the bema as a place of punishment and deep remorsefulness. And yes, our society has certainly lost its fear of God. Our churches invite permissiveness and promote mediocrity. There is a danger that some might misinterpret the covering of grace as permission to sin.

Believe me, it's a lot easier to teach guilt than grace. It's easy to motivate through "judgment is coming" kinds of words. But I don't believe that is the point of the bema. What I believe we do find at the bema is a grave recognition of missed opportunities and a deep acknowledgment of lost rewards. Still, it is all covered by an overwhelming sense of God's incredible grace that forgives and accepts us in spite of our unworthiness. Those kinds of thoughts ought to be powerfully motivating to us to make some major changes in our lives.

- You may be in the middle of an adulterous relationship right now. Maybe it's gone on for years. No one knows.
- You may be a church leader, a pastor, a missionary, a Sunday school teacher, or a growth group leader—and you're secretly watching pornographic videos or the Playboy channel. Maybe your affair is with disappearing images on a computer screen.
- Church attendance may, for you, be a mask of spirituality covering addictions to which you turn for real consolation.
- You may be cheating the government by dealing in cash.
- You may be robbing God week after week by not tithing, or you may be throwing a few bucks into the offering box just to appease your conscience now and then. And no one knows.

Listen. Those are serious matters in God's eyes. And even though you will not be punished at the bema, you will—perhaps for the first, awful time—realize what you've traded for your sin. And it won't be worth it.

There will be strong accountability at the feet of Christ. There will be a realization of how much more you could have done—had you made different choices in life. The Bible says so.

> Now if any man builds on the foundation with gold, silver, precious stones, wood, hay, straw, each man's work will become evident; for the day will show it because it is to be revealed with fire, and the fire itself will test the quality of each man's work. If any man's work which he has built on it remains, he will receive a reward. If any man's work is burned up, he will suffer loss; but he himself will be saved, yet so as through fire.
>
> 1 CORINTHIANS 3:12-15

When you and I enter the presence of the living God, a lot of things are going to change. Instantly. Our perspectives, for one. And our value systems.

All the accomplishments you've been so proud of, all the awards you've received, all the accolades,

When you and I enter the presence of the living God, a lot of things are going to change. Instantly. Our perspectives, for one. And our value systems.

the newspaper clippings, the trophies you've won—and, yes, even those highly prized medals—will be instantly vaporized in the presence of God if they were not done for the glory of God the consuming fire.

Isaiah asked, "Who of us can dwell with the consuming fire?" (Isaiah 33:14). Paul reminds us that God dwells in unapproachable light (1 Timothy 6:16). We know what laser light can do. God's light is millions of times more intense, more revealing, more consuming. And the rewards at the bema will be distributed on the basis of what survives that kind of light.

Your motives—those things you've always kept hidden—will be fully and completely revealed. Read carefully the Word of God:

> Therefore judge nothing before the appointed time;
> wait till the Lord comes. He will bring to light what is
> hidden in darkness and will expose the motives of men's
> hearts. [All in the light. Exposed. But look at the next
> sentence; all of the exposure is for the purpose of reward
> giving or reward withholding, not punishment.] At that
> time each will receive his praise from God.
>
> 1 CORINTHIANS 4:5, NIV, BRACKETED COMMENTS MINE

That's the bema. The judgment seat of Christ. Why does God tell us about the Bema? Five reasons.

1. To give us every advantage in preparing for that day. Knowing what is coming we should "Fix our eyes not on what is seen, but on what is unseen. For what is seen is temporary, but what is unseen is eternal" (2 Corinthians 4:18, NIV).

2. To cause us to help and encourage one another toward increased rewards. "And let us consider how we may spur one another on toward love and good deeds. Let us not give up meeting together, as some are in the habit of doing, but let us encourage one another—and all the more as you see the Day approaching" (Hebrews 10:24–25, NIV).

3. To increase our longing for His coming. We should be living holy lives "while we wait for the blessed hope—the glorious appearing of our great God and Savior, Jesus Christ" (Titus 2:13, NIV).

4. To motivate us to redouble our efforts in the building of His church. "Let us also lay aside every encumbrance and the sin which so easily entangles us, and let us run with endurance the race that is set before us" (Hebrews 12:1).

5. To motivate us to be holy as He is holy. "But like the Holy One who called you, be holy yourselves also in all your behavior" (1 Peter 1:15).

Say what you will, but the hope of reward is a powerful motivator for us humans. And it really doesn't matter whether we're eight, eighteen, or eighty!

When I was in college ROTC, our professor, Major Goetzman, announced that he had secured seventeen seats on an Air Force plane to take seventeen students to visit the battlefield at Gettysburg for three full days. He said he would take the top seventeen scores on the military history final exam. Was it motivational? You bet! The whole class worked like history majors anticipating that exam!

And, yes, I made the grade. Sixteen ecstatic classmates and I stayed at the Army War College at Carlisle Barracks in Pennsylvania. For three days we walked in the footsteps of some real heroes. The major had motivated us to study by offering a very tangible hope of reward—with the warning that those who didn't apply themselves would miss a wonderful opportunity.

The hope of eternal reward shines in the distance like a reachable star.

The Bible does that too. From one end of the Book to the other, it portrays the hope of reward and warns about what we could lose.

Think of it! The hope of heaven awaits us! The hope of eternal reward shines in the distance like a reachable star. And every one of us is only a single heartbeat away from standing in the presence of our Redeemer and Lord.

Let's be ready, soldier.

Let's make this day count for that one.

Ain't gonna study war no more, no more…ain't gonna study war no more.

NEGRO SPIRITUAL,
NINETEENTH CENTURY

*Thus says the Lord God, behold, my servants shall rejoice…[and] shout joyfully
with a glad heart…the former things shall not be remembered…
there will no longer be heard the voice of weeping.*

ISAIAH,
EIGHTH CENTURY B.C.

This world is not my home. I'm just a-passin' through…

CHRISTIAN HYMN

*And I saw a new heaven and a new earth; for the first…had passed away…
and I heard a voice from the throne saying, "Behold, the tabernacle of God is
among men…they shall be His people…and He shall wipe away every tear from
their eyes….Behold, I am coming quickly."*

THE REVELATION OF
JESUS CHRIST

COMIN' HOME

Dreams are wonderful. Have you ever had one? I don't mean the fleeting mental images that dance in your head when you lay your weary head on the pillow; I mean a real dream. A longing so deep you could taste it. A vision that grips you and holds you through the years.

One of my childhood dreams was to own a Jeep, an old Willys military Jeep. I can recall being six or seven years old, lying on my back on my bed upstairs, one leg crossed over the other at the knee. And focused! So deep into a comic book drama that my bedroom and my little hometown in central Washington faded from reality. I had a small collection of comic books portraying the Korean War, filled with images of grim-faced, unshaven GIs, of Heartbreak Ridge, the Chosin Frozen, and Hamburger Hill. The panels brimmed with courage, sacrifice, and heroism—a faraway world that became very real to me.

And those pages were also filled with something else: images of army guys tearing around the landscape in quarter-ton Jeeps. What wild mustangs were to America's cowboys, Willys Jeeps were to America's GI heroes on the Korean peninsula. At the back of every comic book, of course, were advertisements. Among the inevitable promotions for goofy novelties and Charles Atlas body-building courses, there was one particular ad that had me dreaming of great adventure.

It was an ad for a real, army surplus, quarter-ton Jeep. A beautiful little Willys you could actually buy—still in the box! And it seemed to me like they were practically giving them away!

Oh, my mind began to dream. What I could do with one of those Willys! Our principal form of family entertainment in those days was a drive on the dirt roads and logging trails of the hills around our home. I visualized myself behind the wheel of one of those Willys, roaring up and down the hills, cockpit open, laughing into the wind. Now that was a dream! A little taste of heaven.

I nursed that dream, off and on, for a lifetime. The little boy dream became a big boy dream. Then just a while ago, almost a half-century later, I came across one—a real Willys Jeep—in cherry condition. I confess, it was like a vision, a revelation. There it sat beckoning to me. Not in a box, but completely assembled and ready to rumble.

And this time I could afford it.

It's sitting in my garage now. Just a few minutes ago I piled out of the seat after an exhilarating summer evening drive with the wind in my hair. My wife, Linda, indulges me. Actually she loves those drives, too—mostly for what they do for me. She loves the transformation. That little '52 Willys (with a small block Chevy V8) truly takes me into another world—a world of lightheartedness and wonder. Crazy, huh? But I love it!

Multiply that remembered joy and longing by infinity, and you have a God-sized dream.

You had childhood hopes and dreams. Push the recall button and pull one of them up on the screen of your memory right now. Got it? Turn it over in your mind. Remember it? Kind of makes you smile a bit, doesn't it?

Now, multiply that remembered joy and longing by infinity, and you have a God-sized dream.

GOD HAS A DREAM

If you were God and had a dream, what would you do? You would make it happen, wouldn't you?

And that is precisely what is happening in time and space. It is a dream that explains so much of human history. It is a dream that includes man being created in His image—a dream that reverberates with fellowship, joy, worship, and rest. God's dream, quite literally, is heaven. Heaven on earth...and beyond...forever.

Here are two portions of God's dream:

> In the beginning God created the heavens and the earth.... Then God said, "Let Us make man in Our image, according to Our likeness."... [I]n the image of God He created him; male and female He created them. God blessed them.
>
> GENESIS 1:1, 26–28

> "Behold the tabernacle of God is among men, and He will dwell among them, and they shall be His people...and He will wipe away every tear.... And He who sits on the throne said, 'Behold, I am making all things new.... I am...the beginning and the end.... He who overcomes will inherit these things, and I will be his God and he will be My son.'"
>
> REVELATION 21:3, 4–7

From Genesis to Revelation, beginning to end, God has dreamed of a forever family—people living together like He does in perfect transparency and oneness. God and man in deep, authentic, interpersonal intimacy, walking together in the cool of the day. Imagine the fellowship. Imagine the joy and adventure. Imagine the rest, security, and worship.

Such magnificent intimacy can only rise out of a willful, determined decision to love and trust. It is a choice. For this reason, God created man with a capacity to choose love and trust. For this reason, a single tree in the Garden of Eden became a focal point to demonstrate that choice. Man, created with a capacity to choose love and trust, chose instead to disobey, to reject love and trust.

And the whole world fell apart! Sin destroyed everything. Human love became a dim shadow of God's intention. The trust disintegrated. The fellowship was broken. The joy dissolved. The adventure became terror. And life died. Death ruled on the planet.

But God, being God, intends to redeem. You've read His plan in the Bible. God has redeemed His people. He will reclaim the planet. He will restore the joy, fellowship, adventure, worship, rest, and more. That is the

message of the Bible from cover to cover, from Genesis to Revelation—
God will redeem, reclaim, restore. God will see His dream realized.

And that is heaven.

He will bring the spiritual war to a successful conclusion, and then He will bring His warriors home. From every tribe and tongue, from every cemetery plot and isolated grave, He will raise His warriors from the dead. And they will come home!

God's dream centers upon His forever family being home in His house, His eternal dwelling place. God's dream, which is ultimately the foundation of every human dream, has everything to do with being at home. He will bring the spiritual war to a successful conclusion, and then He will bring His warriors home. Every one of them! There will be no killed-in-action memorials. There will be no missing-in-action bracelets. From around the world, from every tribe and tongue, from every cemetery plot and isolated grave, He will raise His warriors from the dead. And they will come home!

God Himself will lead the parade of victorious warriors, and it will make the returning legions of Rome and the fanfare of emperors look like a small town pet parade. "But thanks be to God, who always leads us in his triumph in Christ" (2 Corinthians 2:14). And then it will be home! At last. In heaven!

The apostle Paul described his own impending death in terms used by soldiers at the conclusion of a long campaign. He talked about fighting to the finish (2 Timothy 4:7–8). He expressed very openly his anticipation of a good soldier's reward, a crown of righteousness. And Paul called his death a "departure" (4:6).

The word he used for *departure* is actually a military term. It refers to soldiers pulling up tent stakes to march back home. For the average soldier, a departure was a matter of striking camp. That's the imagery Paul uses to refer to his own warrior's death. He's striking his temporary dwelling because he's heading home to his permanent abode. Heaven!

It is important for us to think long and hard—not to mention accurately—about heaven. Doing so will change our lives now. It will make us better soldiers. We'll fight more effectively when we visualize what life will be like after the end of the war. We've all heard the old adage "Old soldiers never die." That's actually true for the Christian solider. The "retirement" home of the spirit warrior is larger than life in more ways than our limited, very finite, minds can possibly imagine.

A. W. Tozer said it well: "Let no one apologize for the powerful emphasis Christianity lays upon the doctrine of the world to come. Right there lies its immense superiority to everything else within the whole sphere of human thought or experience.... We do well to think of the long tomorrow."[1] C. S. Lewis said, "It is since Christians have largely ceased to think of the other world that they have become so ineffective in this one."[2] The apostle Paul summarized it this way: "We look not at the things which are seen, but at the things which are not seen; for the things which are seen are temporal, but the things which are not seen are eternal" (2 Corinthians 4:18).

A FEW BACKGROUND DETAILS

The Bible gives us just enough information about heaven to blow our parameters and expand our minds. We can understand some things about heaven, but our minds will never fully comprehend, let alone exhaust, its magnificence. We know enough that we can hardly wait to get there. Heaven is beyond anyone's wildest dreams!

Here are a few more things Scripture teaches us about heaven.

HEAVEN IS REAL, HEAVEN IS LITERAL, HEAVEN IS A PLACE, AND HEAVEN IS UP.

Jesus Himself taught it. And He should know!

> "Truly I say to you, unless you are converted and
> become like children, you will not enter the kingdom of
> heaven.... See that you do not despise one of these little
> ones, for I say to you that their angels in heaven con-
> tinually see the face of My Father who is in heaven."
> MATTHEW 18:3, 10

This literal heaven is *up* from anywhere on the globe. The Bible says that when Jesus came to earth, He "descended" (Ephesians 4:8–10) and when He left earth, He "ascended"(Acts 1:11). When Jesus comes again, the Bible says He will come "down" (1 Thessalonians 4:16) and the church will go "up" (1 Thessalonians 4:17). When the apostle John was to be given a tour of heaven, he was invited to "come up" (Revelation 4:1). Yes, heaven is literal and up! Every child knows it.

I'll never forget years ago when our sons were young. After a family devotion about heaven, our middle boy, Blake, had a question. With the wonderful, trusting, and very practical faith of a child, he wanted to know exactly how we were going to get there. His voice was filled with genuine excitement and there was a visible sparkle in his eye. He asked with obvious and sincere glee, "Are we going to have to wear seat belts, or does God have r-e-a-l-l-y long arms?"

HEAVEN IS EVIDENTLY HUGE, AND HEAVEN IS A PLACE

The vocabulary of heaven involves several key words, concepts, and phases:

- Heaven is the dwelling place of God (Deuteronomy 26:15; Matthew 6:9).
- Heaven is the dwelling place of God's angels (Luke 2:15; Matthew 28:2; Hebrews 12:22).
- Heaven is the dwelling place of God's people (Revelation 4–5; Luke 16:22, 25; Hebrews 12:23).

Jesus Himself said, "I go to prepare a *place* for you" (John 14:2, emphasis mine). He wasn't kidding. My friend Randy Alcorn says it as only he can: "Jesus didn't say 'I go to an indescribable realm devoid of physical properties, where your disembodied spirit will float around, and which is nothing at all like what you've thought of as home.'"[3]

Jesus is preparing a place, and does He ever know how to build! Over the course of this last year our first two grandchildren were born. And you should have seen our sons and daughters (in-law) prepare a place for the little ones' arrival home. The preparation of the nurseries had their full focus for a long time. One son even completely remodeled the room— new Sheetrock, new wiring, new paint, new everything.

And then there was the necessary "equipment." The room, the bed, the stroller, the car seat, the wallpaper, the dresser, the changing table, the window coverings, and the wall hangings. Not to mention the teddy bears and toys. You see the point: Everything that child could ever need, and more, went into the preparation of the place.

Now here's the obvious question: If young and inexperienced human parents go to such great lengths and take this kind of loving, excited care to prepare a place, what must our place look like since the infinite Father-

Provider-Carpenter has been working at it now for a couple thousand years?

"In my Father's house are many dwelling places; if it were not so, I would have told you; for I go to prepare a place for you...that where I am, there you may be also" (John 14:2–3). If heaven were a state of mind—or anything less than a very real and literal place—Jesus would have told us so.

Heaven is a place on the map of God. It is local and real. It is not air. It is not ethereal or vague. In contrast to this earth, which was marred by the Fall, heaven is stable, secure, and eternal (Hebrews 11:8–10).

Heaven is huge. It is not a planet, though it may include multiple planets as we conceive of them (Revelation 21:16). Heaven is described as a city (Hebrews 11:16; 12:22; 13:14; Revelation 21:12). It has trees, water, fruit, and animals. According to Scripture, the city has its own lighting system, which requires no power source. The city's water and food sources are virtually unlimited (Revelation 22:1–2). It is complete with walls, gates, streets, rivers, and buildings. But it differs from earthly cities in that it experiences no malfunctions. It is splendorous and brilliant, like jewels (Revelation 21:11).

The holy city itself is described as being 1500 miles wide and 1500 miles long—giving it a base of 2,250,000 square miles. Additionally, it is 780,000 stories high. That is more than enough room to accommodate (even by our miserable human standards) far more people than have ever lived (Revelation 21:16)!

And socially and psychologically, the environment is spectacular. No sin, no pain, no cemeteries, no regrets, no sorrow, and no taxes—it's all been paid in full, far in advance.

WHAT DOES HEAVEN HOLD FOR US?

Many things! But here are seven very specific features which heaven holds. There is one verse indicated for each here, but there are many other specific and supportive verses as well.

SHEER JOY

Heaven holds amazing joy for those who will enter.

> You will make known to me the path of life;
> In Your presence is fullness of joy;
> In Your right hand there are pleasures forever.
>
> PSALM 16:11

Sheer, unmitigated, deep, down-in-the-soul joy! It's almost impossible to describe, but you'll know it when you see it.

I once heard sheer joy on our phone's answering machine. It was our son calling. His wife and daughter had gotten home from the hospital and settled in their home. The new mother and her parents had gone out for a brief walk in the beautiful Central Oregon evening. Blake had stayed in the house with the newborn. He took the moment to give us a call.

Since we were away, he left his message. His voice on the answering machine was animated. You should have heard the tone of voice: "Dad! Mom! Jami Lyn and her parents are out for a walk. I'm here alone with little Rylee..." Pause. "She's in my arms..." Long pause. "I'm just looking at her...and feeling...and reflecting. I think this may be the best week of my life."

That says it all. A child has come home. Multiply that father's sheer joy by the infinity of our heavenly Father and you have at least a small taste of His infinite love for us.

There is probably no writer in America more accurately immersed in the wonders of heaven than Good Shepherd's Randy Alcorn. We claim Randy as our own because he grew up here in Gresham and was one of our original pastors before starting his present Eternal Perspective Ministries. He and Nancy and the girls are still a very active part of our fellowship. Randy has studied, pondered, reflected, and written more carefully on heaven than possibly anyone else in this country today. He is biblically alert and imaginatively sacred in his portrayals of heaven.

In his book *Edge of Eternity*, Randy recorded an imaginary conversation and some follow-up comments. *Charis* (taken from the Greek word for *grace*) is here the name of heaven. Listen in:

> Charis has a song for every star. It is a country of explosion, expanding with every song, becoming ever larger.
>
> Marcus stretched out his hand, and the air's fabric ripped open, so I could...peer into the City of Light as if it were but a few feet away. People laughed, greeted each other, embraced, conversed with animated expressions. I kept hearing the word "Yes!" It struck me as strange, as I'd always believed if there was a heaven it was a place of naysayers.
>
> In Charis I saw citizens busily working, learning,

and exploring, overflowing with the joy of discovery. They seemed immersed in delight....

This joy and fulfillment in heaven—in the "country of explosion"—will erupt not only from positive experiences, but also from what is not there. No arthritis, no handicaps, no cancer, no mosquitoes, no taxes, no bills, no computer crashes, no weeds, no bombs, no drunkenness, no traffic jams and accidents, no septic tank backups, no door locks, no phone calls selling storm windows at dinnertime. No mental illness. No pretense, no wearing masks. Close friendships but no cliques, laughter but no putdowns. Intimacy, but no temptation to immorality."[4]

Folks, heaven is filled with unmitigated joy. Listen to the experience of Randy's character Dani:

The wild rush of Joy, the rapture of discovery overwhelmed her as if she'd just gotten in on the greatest inside joke in the history of the universe. Now she saw and felt it with stunning clarity. Her unswerving patriotism had been reserved for another country. Every joy on earth, such as the joy of reunion, had been but an inkling, a whisper of greater Joy. Every place on earth had been a rented room, a place to spend the night on a journey.[5]

PERFECT KNOWLEDGE

Yes, heaven is sheer joy. It is also a place of perfect knowledge.

John wrote: "Beloved, now we are children of God, and it has not appeared as yet what we will be. We know that when He appears, *we will be like Him,* because we will see Him just as He is" (1 John 3:2, emphasis mine).

Paul told us: "For now we see in a mirror dimly, but then face to face; now I know in part, but then I will know fully just as I also have been fully known" (1 Corinthians 13:12).

Other than the presence of our Savior, this may be my favorite thing about heaven. Perfect knowing is total familiarity. It is a family term. It is complete, honest transparency. What you see is what you get. It's how you are with your closest family and friends. No need to be other than you are. No airs, no posturing, no guarded words. Just together. Honestly.

Ah, the sheer pleasure of being at home with Christ and with each other! The point is this—heaven will be familiar to us! It will be like coming home after a long time away.

Have you ever been away from home for a long time? I recall the Christmas of my freshman year in college. The four months of that semester had been my first extended time away from home. I got off the train after three days crossing the country. I smelled the sagebrush even in the dead of winter. I heard the whistle of the ancient lumber mill. We jumped into the old Ford, crossed the bumpy railroad tracks, and drove past my childhood haunts on Summitview Avenue. I could hardly wait to get to 3309 Jefferson, to my room, to flop on the bed and just look around—to see the familiar sights, my place, where I belonged.

Home!

The snow was whiter than it had ever been before, I think. The air fresher. The bed softer. The people cheerier.

Some years later, after my tour of duty in Vietnam, I experienced those coming home emotions in an even more poignant way. I had left a very foreign and hostile environment to come home to my wife and son, the old familiar valley, the sights and sounds so well known to me. Honestly, it was something of a shock at first. To return to my hometown, to my wife, to my son, to my old jeans, to my old comfortable civilian shoes. It was almost too good to be true. It was…home! At last.

I know a seasoned missionary from that same old familiar Yakima Valley. Clarence Church served for several decades out of our country with Wycliffe Bible Translators. I asked him if he'd ever been homesick for the valley. He responded immediately and strongly.

He told me that a friend from back home had once written him a letter.

"I have come home at last! This is the land I have been looking for all my life."

As welcome as the letter was, it wasn't the news from home that moved him to tears. When he cut open the envelope, he found that his friend had cut a sprig of sagebrush and dropped it in before he sealed it. That pungent, familiar fragrance washed through Clarence's senses. He wept—missing his home.

In C. S. Lewis's beautiful Chronicles of Narnia series, one of Aslan's creatures enters heaven with

these words: "I have come home at last! This is the land I have been looking for all my life, though I never knew it till now. The reason we loved the
old Narnia is that it sometimes looked a little like this."[6]

That's precisely the spirit of Hebrews chapter 11. We are actually
strangers here on earth, but very much at home in heaven. Listen to the
sense of heaven being home at last as portrayed by the Holy Spirit:

> All these died in faith, without receiving the promises,
> but having seen them and having welcomed them from
> a distance, and having confessed that they were
> strangers and exiles on the earth. For those who say
> such things make it clear that they are seeking a country
> of their own. And indeed if they had been thinking of
> that country from which they went out, they would
> have had opportunity to return. But as it is, they desire
> a better country, that is, a heavenly one. Therefore God
> is not ashamed to be called their God; for He has pre-
> pared a city for them.
>
> HEBREWS 11:13–16

RICH FELLOWSHIP

Heaven is not only sheer joy and perfect knowing, it is also a place of wonderful fellowship.

> Then we who are alive and remain will be caught up
> together with them in the clouds to meet the Lord in
> the air, and so we shall always be with the Lord.
>
> 1 THESSALONIANS 4:17

We will enjoy deep and rich fellowship—with our Lord, with our
believing family members, and with our believing friends. And we will
meet new and wonderful believing friends there, perhaps even among the
angels. The fellowship will quickly go deep.

Some time back I spent an evening at Fort Bragg, North Carolina. I was
in the home of a dear friend, a true spirit warrior: Major General Jerry Boykin.
Jerry was the commanding general of the U.S. Army Special Forces Command
at the time. He was responsible for all the Green Berets. In his home that
evening, we enjoyed a very special dinner with about twenty people.

I had previously met only three or four of them. But before the evening was over, I felt I had known many of them for a long, long time. Our spirits were united in a matter of moments. We saw our connections to each other more clearly than perhaps a room full of strangers normally would.

The General said that he and his wife held many gatherings in their home—most of them professional. On this occasion, however, the attendees were all believing Christians, every one of whom, by the General's description, had had significant impact on his life. He then went around the room one by one telling each of us how we had touched his life deeply. It was very moving. Beyond words.

Can you imagine doing that in heaven? Your faithfulness has impacted others in ways you have no way of knowing now. There, on the other side, they may be recounted firsthand.

It is the fellowship of spirit warriors. Christian soldiers who fought the good fight, finished the course, and came home victorious.

At the General's house the other night, there were tears. And joy. And depth! I found myself praying, "Thank You, Lord, for this little taste of heaven, a heavenly hors d'oeuvre." (Oh, man, can you imagine the wonderful campfires in heaven! Toasting chunks of fresh manna over the golden flames!)

There will be a fellowship of the redeemed in heaven that cannot be equaled by any other fellowship in human history. It is the fellowship of spirit warriors. Christian soldiers who fought the good fight, finished the course, and came home victorious.

There is a fellowship among fellow soldiers that goes deeper, stays longer, and is far richer than normal human relationships. After all, soldiers face ultimates together. Soldiers face the enemy together. Soldiers carry one another. Soldiers live and die together.

John McCain, a Navy pilot and a prisoner of war in Hanoi for more than five years, writes of his relationship with a fellow soldier, Bob Craner, this way: "He was my dear friend, and for two years I was closer to him than I had ever been to another human being." Some time after they were released, Craner described how completely these two warrior-partners relied on each other:

> McCain and I leaned on each other a great deal. We were separated by [a thick wall of] about eighteen inches of brick, and I never saw the guy for the longest time. I

used to have dreams…we all did, of course, and they
were sometimes nightmares…and my world had shrunk
to a point where the figures in my dreams were myself,
the guards, and a voice…and that was McCain. I didn't
know what he looked like, so I could not visualize him in
my dreams, because he became the guy—the only guy—I
turned to, for a period of two years. We got to know each
other more intimately, I'm sure, than I will ever know my
wife. We opened up and talked about… everything
besides our immediate problems—past life, and all the
family things we never have talked to anybody about. We
derived a great deal of strength from this.

McCain felt just as strongly:

A great deal of strength indeed…Bob Craner kept me
alive. Without his strength, his wisdom, his humor, and
his unselfish consideration, I doubt I would have survived…. Whenever I was plagued with doubts about
my own situation or my own conduct, I turned to the
voice on the other side of the wall.[7]

Now if the fellowship of a couple of earthly soldiers in a questionable
war can go so deep, how much deeper might it go for spirit warriors in
spiritual warfare? Much deeper! Heaven's new friends and old relationships will be the richest of fellowships.

RELAXING REST

In heaven, we will finally understand what true rest is all about.

I heard a voice from heaven, saying, "Write, 'Blessed are
the dead who die in the Lord from now on!'" "Yes,"
says the Spirit, "so that they may rest from their labors,
for their deeds follow with them."

REVELATION 14:13

Heaven is not about lazy people lying around wasting time. Not by a
long shot. Forget halos and harps. And forget boredom. There is no such
thing as boredom there. But there is rest. Plain, refreshing, restoring,

renewing rest. All that is right with rest on earth is but a foretaste of the quality of true God-honoring heavenly rest.

Joe Bayly, in his little book entitled simply *Heaven,* captures the spirit of heavenly rest in this brief exchange:

> I'll say, "Hello, Lord. I'm tired."
> And he'll say, "Rest, because I have work for you to do."
> "Rest?"
> "Yes, remember I myself rested on the seventh day of creation. So rest is not incompatible with heaven's perfection."[8]

In fact, heaven's rest has something to do with the very nature of God Himself. Perhaps our rest will, like the Sabbath rest, be devoted to constant worship.

GENUINE WORSHIP

Heaven is a place of worship like you've never known it before.

> Then I looked, and I heard the voice of many angels around the throne and the living creatures and the elders; and the number of them was myriads of myriads, and thousands of thousands, saying with a loud voice,
> "Worthy is the Lamb that was slain to receive power and riches and wisdom and might and honor and glory and blessing."
> And every created thing which is in heaven and on the earth and under the earth and on the sea, and all things in them, I heard saying,
> "To Him who sits on the throne, and to the Lamb, be blessing and honor and glory and dominion forever and ever."
>
> REVELATION 5:11–13

Can you imagine the sheer joy
   and ecstasy
      of worship
         in heaven itself?

We will all be full participants. No one will have to hold back for lack of voice or musical ear. No one will feel incapacitated because of sin or hypocrisy. All will fully participate in the glory of heavenly worship in spirit and in truth. Listen to a description of such in Randy Alcorn's book:

> We rejoined our comrades in the great camp of Charis [heaven], embracing and shedding tears and slapping each other on the back. Then warriors around me turned toward the masses of untold millions gathered in Charis. The army began to sing, perhaps hundreds of thousands, perhaps a million.
>
> I added my voice to theirs and sang the unchained praises of the King. Only for a moment did I hear my own voice, amazed to detect the increased intensity of the whole. One voice, even mine, made a measurable difference. But from then on I was lost in the choir, hardly hearing my voice and not needing to....
>
> Then suddenly the multitudes before us sang back to us, and our voices were drowned by theirs. We who a moment earlier seemed the largest choir ever assembled now proved to be only the small worship ensemble that led the full choir of untold millions, now lost to themselves. We sang together in full voice, "To Him who made the galaxies, who became the Lamb, who stretched out on the tree, who crossed the chasm, who returned the Lion! Forever!"
>
> I looked at the Great Throne, and upon it sat the King...the Audience of One.
>
> The smile of His approval swept through the choir like fire across dry wheat fields...And in the moment I knew with unwavering clarity, that the King's approval was all that mattered—and ever would. [9]

"To Him who made the galaxies, who became the Lamb, who stretched out on the tree, who crossed the chasm, who returned the Lion! Forever!"

FULFILLING SERVICE

Heaven will be a place of sheer joy, perfect knowing, rich fellowship, relaxing rest, genuine worship, and satisfying service.

> For this reason, they are before the throne of God; and
> they serve Him day and night in His temple; and He who
> sits on the throne will spread His tabernacle over them.
>
> REVELATION 7:15

Joe Bayly captures the spirit of heavenly work in this brief exchange between himself and his Lord in heaven:

> "[I will] work [here]?"
> "Of course. Did you think heaven would be an
> eternal Sunday afternoon nap? My people serve Me in
> heaven. I have work for you to do."
> "Like what? Keeping all the gold polished?"
> "[No.] Ruling angels. Managing the universe for
> Me, being responsible for whole cities."[10]

HEALTHY RESPONSIBILITY

In addition to fulfilling work, heaven will include a measure of healthy responsibility for each of us.

> And there will no longer be any night; and they will not
> have need of the light of a lamp nor the light of the
> sun, because the Lord God will illumine them; and they
> will reign forever and ever.
>
> REVELATION 22:5

Heaven will be filled with people—all living for God's glory. There will be activity and organization. The universe will reflect His glory, and we will have a responsible role in it.

Heaven is more magnificent than your wildest dreams! Sheer joy, perfect knowing, rich fellowship, relaxing rest, genuine worship, fulfilling service, and healthy responsibility.

Heaven is our home. Because heaven is God's home. Heaven is nothing less than the Father's dream come true. Heaven is our Savior's home.

And there He will gather His forever family around him. Heaven is full of old soldiers who've fought the good fight.

Hang in there, soldier. This war will be over one day. And we'll go home. And the future will be out of this world!

In heaven we will enjoy the victory with our Lord and Commander, our Savior and Friend:

> And I heard a loud voice from the throne, saying,
> "Behold, the tabernacle of God is among men, and He
> will dwell among them, and they shall be His people,
> and God Himself will be among them,"...[and] they
> will see His face.
>
> REVELATION 21:3; 22:4

For conference or speaking information
contact Stu Weber at:
Stu Weber
2229 N. E. Burnside, #212
Gresham, Oregon 97030

NOTES

CHAPTER ONE

1. Gregory Bond, *God at War* (Downers Grove: InterVarsity Press, 1997), 19, 55.

CHAPTER TWO

1. Donald Grey Barnhouse, *The Invisible War* (Grand Rapids: Zondervan, 1965), 51.

CHAPTER THREE

1. Bruce Wilkinson, "Walk Thru Eternal Rewards," (Atlanta, GA: Walk Thru Bible Ministries), TN 6–7. Taken from Bruce Wilkinson's "Walk Thru Eternal Rewards" Seminar Notebook.

2. Ibid., TN 7.

3. I'd recommend you read Randy Alcorn's book *Money, Possessions, and Eternity* for some healthy, careful thinking and planning in this area.

4. Charles R. Swindoll, *The Quest for Character* (Portland, OR: Multnomah Press, 1987), 26. Original poem by Ralph Waldo Emerson.

5. Randy Alcorn, *Money, Possession, and Eternity* (Wheaton, IL: Tyndale, 1989), 140.

6. Dan Wooding, "Trojan Horse of Success," *Wireless Age* (May 1999): 8.

7. Bruce Wilkinson, "Walk Thru Eternal Rewards" seminar, (Walk Thru the Bible: Atlanta, GA), 62.

8. Randy Alcorn, *Money, Possession, and Eternity* (Wheaton, IL: Tyndale, 1989), 150.

CHAPTER FOUR

1. A private printing for broadest distribution published by Mrs. George B. Tullidge in August 1944 in Staunton, Virginia, in booklet form. "A Paratrooper's Faith." Not copyrighted.

2. Stephen Pressfield, *Gates of Fire* (New York, NY: Bantam Books, 1999), 41.

3. Ibid., 241.

CHAPTER FIVE

1. Ranger Training Brigade, *Ranger Handbook SH21-76* (Fort Benning, GA: United States Army Infantry Center, June 1998), introduction.

2. Ibid., preface.

3. Dr. Wayne Grudem, *Systematic Theology* (Grand Rapids, MI: Zondervan, 1994), 127, 130–132. I urge you to purchase a copy for your personal study. Dr. Grudem is one of the more highly respected systematic theologians in evangelicalism today.

CHAPTER SIX

1. C. S. Lewis, *The Best of C. S. Lewis* (Washington, D.C.: Canon Press, 1974), 13.

2. I strongly urge you to get a copy of Randy's work in this area of spiritual warfare. The book is entitled *Lord Foulgrin's Letters*. Randy, always an excellent writer, has outdone himself on this one. Picking up where C. S. Lewis left off in *The Screwtape Letters*, *Lord Foulgrin's Letters* represents an eavesdropping on the secret correspondence of a senior demon and his ugly counsel to subordinate demons. Between the letters, Randy creates an earthy setting, unfolds a thoughtful story line, and develops characters (referred to by Foulgrin as human "vermin") to make the book intensely personal and gripping. It is spiritually encouraging. It is personally convicting. Get it. You'll be a better spirit warrior for it.

3. Bob and Gretchen Passantino, "The Bondage Maker," *Christian Research Journal* 21, no. 4. Article can be accessed on-line at www.equip.org.

4. Used by Permission, *Christianity Today,* May 27, 1970.

5. Michael Martin, "Spiritual Warfare," *Answers in Action Journal,* Spring 1996, 6. Taken from the article "The Bondage Maker," found at www.equip.org.

CHAPTER SEVEN

1. David Jeremiah, *Invasion of Other Gods* (Nashville, TN: Word Publishing, 1995), 149.

2. Larry Libby, *Somewhere Angels* (Sisters, OR: Multnomah Publishers, 1994), 1.

3. If you do wish to get just one current, biblically careful, easy to read book on the subject of angels, I would recommend David Jeremiah's *What the Bible Says About Angels,* by Multnomah Publishers, 1996.

4. Billy Graham, *Angels* (New York: Pocketbooks, 1975), 32–3.

5. Fred Dickason, *Angels, Elect and Evil* (Chicago: Moody, 1975), 13.

6. Billy Graham, *Angels* (New York: Pocketbooks, 1975), 7.

7. Dr. Wayne Grudem, *Systematic Theology* (Grand Rapids, MI: Zondervan, 1994), 397.

CHAPTER EIGHT

1. Randy Alcorn, *Lord Foulgrin's Letters* (Sisters, OR: Multnomah Publishers, 2000), afterword.

2. Demons often work effectively within ungodly families who have a wicked influence on their offspring, but there is no scriptural warrant for so-called "ancestral" or "generational bondage," i.e. inheriting personal demons from ancestors apart from personal involvement by the child. Passages such as Exodus 20:4-5 speak of the consequences of sin being visited to the third and fourth generations, but never of inheriting demons. The consequences of sin may be the natural result of a sinful lifestyle, such as babies born with AIDS. They may be the judgment of God falling on relatively innocent persons such as the babies who starved in the siege of Jerusalem. Children raised in an occultic environment will normally come into contact with the demonic and may be influenced toward personal demonic involvement as a result of their environment. However, the believer is delivered from all demonic authority by the triumph of Christ. The protecting and empowering work of the Spirit is sufficient for all believers no matter what their family background.

CHAPTER NINE

1. "If I Were the Devil" by Paul Harvey can be found on numerous Web sites on the Internet, including www.buchanan.org/pray-p-devil.html.

CHAPTER TEN

1. *The Works of Josephus,* translated by William Winston (Hartford, Conn.: The S.S. Scanton Co., 1900), 19.

2. John Piper, *A Godward Life, Vol. II* (Sisters, OR: Multnomah Publishers, 1999), 122–3.

CHAPTER ELEVEN

1. Douglas C. Waller, *The Commandos* (New York: Dell Publishing, 1994), 246–7.

CHAPTER TWELVE

1. David Jeremiah, *Invasion of Other Gods* (Nashville, TN: Word Publishing, 1995), 3.

2. Randy Alcorn, "Two Sources of Self Esteem: Secular & Christian" from www.epm.org (article can be found on this site).

3. John Piper, *A Godward Life, Vol. II* (Sisters, OR: Multnomah Publishers, 1999), 110.

4. Randy Alcorn, *ProLife Answers to ProChoice Arguments* (Sisters, OR: Multnomah Publishers, 2000), 78.

5. Joe Frolin, "Two Tablets Are Causing Headaches," *The Oregonian,* June 10, 2000, p. C6.

6. John William Garvin, ed., *Canadian Poets* (Toronto, Canada: McClelland, Goodchild & Stewart, 1916), 170.

CHAPTER FIFTEEN

1. Randy Alcorn, *In Light of Eternity* (Colorado Springs: WaterBrook Press, 1999), 12.

2. Ibid., 144.

3. Ibid., 12.

4. Ibid., 53–4.

5. Ibid., 56.

6. C. S. Lewis, *The Chronicles of Narnia: The Last Battle* (New York, NY: MacMillan Publishers, 1970 edition), 171.

7. John McCain, *Faith of My Fathers* (New York, NY: Random House, 1999), 230–1.

8. Joe Bayly, *Heaven* (Elgin, IL: David C. Cook, 1977), 12, 14.

9. Randy Alcorn, *In Light of Eternity* (Colorado Springs: WaterBrook Press, 1999), 62.

10. Joe Bayly, *Heaven* (Elgin, IL: David C. Cook, 1977), 16.

Lock Arms in the Battle of Life

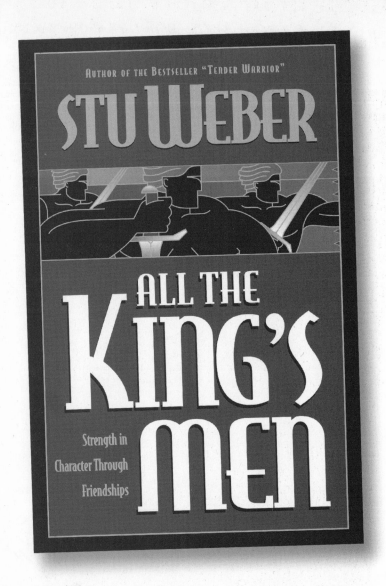

AUTHOR OF THE BESTSELLER "TENDER WARRIOR"

STU WEBER

ALL THE KING'S MEN

Strength in
Character Through
Friendships

Stu Weber shatters the myth that strong men stand alone, affirming that
to achieve your full potential as a husband and father, you must seek the
company of men who share your Christian standards.

ISBN 1-57673-342-4

"Strength in Godly Balance"

—*Leader—Protector—Friend—Lover*—

EVERY MAN'S PURPOSE,

EVERY WOMAN'S DREAM,

EVERY CHILD'S HOPE . . .

TENDER WARRIOR

God's Intention For A Man

STU WEBER

Leader. Protector. Friend. Lover. Men are expected to fill a wide variety of roles. It can be difficult to achieve a healthy balance. But God has provided a powerful blueprint for balanced manhood, and Stu Weber takes an in-depth, life-changing look at this plan.

ISBN 1-57673-306-8

Men, Explore Your Role as
—*King—Warrior—Mentor—Friend*—

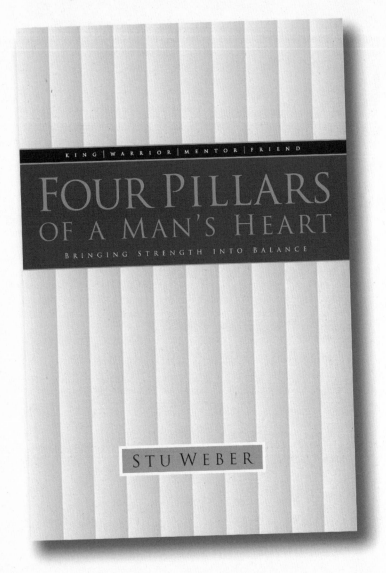

Building upon the "Four Pillars of Manhood" model set forth in his bestseller *Tender Warrior,* Stu Weber leads you on an expanded, in-depth biblical exploration of men's roles as King, Warrior, Mentor, and Friend.

ISBN 157673-450-1